BOOKS BY

VIRGILIA PETERSON

A MATTER OF LIFE AND DEATH *1961*

BEYOND THIS SHORE *1942*

POLISH PROFILE *1940*

A MATTER
OF LIFE
AND DEATH

A MATTER OF LIFE AND DEATH

VIRGILIA PETERSON

ATHENEUM

NEW YORK

1961

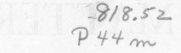

FOR

GOUVERNEUR PAULDING

WITH GRATITUDE AND LOVE

As the generation of leaves, so is that of men.

HOMER, *The Iliad*

FOREWORD

For a long time, I wanted to write about my life. When at last I sat down to it, I was driven by an irrepressible need, a high wind of compulsion, to do so in the form of a letter to my mother.

While the work was in process, I often wakened at night to wonder why it should be of such overwhelming moment to me to expose and explain myself. I do not know. I can only say that it was. But I dare to hope that, at least here and there in the course of the narrative, I have so managed to transcend my own particularity that, for better or worse, it becomes an American story.

CONTENTS

I

THE FACTS OF LIFE

THIS NARRATIVE, IF I HAVE THE BREATH TO SUSTAIN and complete it, will be, of all the stories you enjoyed, the only one ever written for you and yet, were you still here to read it, the one least likely to be read. I have only to glance back across the years at any of those reckless moments when, swept up and throttled by an irresistible need to explain, I launched into the kind of self-justification and self-extenuation that even a friend can scarcely endure, to see your eyes, so large behind the thick lenses, light up with the indignation I most commonly enkindled in them. You might have begun my narrative, since the printed word had the same power over you as drink over the alcoholic. But you would not have finished it. Indeed, by the time you had turned this first page, you would have been sweeping the rest of it off the bed or the table and on to the floor with the impatient gesture of a Lady Macbeth. I can hear you say, in a voice which, low as you kept it, would still manage to sound the note of triumph: "I always knew she was insane."

A note of triumph flowers inevitably in the voice that pronounces someone else insane, since to this verdict the answer is never definitive. What does it mean to be insane? What, for that matter, does it mean to be sane?

Is it not largely, except of course where the knife replaces the tongue, a relative, a subjective matter? I disagree with someone, I shock someone, I appear to someone—within his or her very special context—irrational: *ergo,* I must be insane. For, since I stand at the extreme pole from that someone in viewpoint, should I prove to be right, that someone might have to question his or her unquestionable sanity.

But insanity has long been a charged word, a key word in our family, as you well knew when you chose to use it—not because we have had anyone among our relatives put behind bars (though there have been examples of behavior that might have justified it), but simply because of my father's being an alienist, as his profession was called at the turn of the century when doctors in that field still considered themselves pioneers in the imponderable rather than pollsters of ponderability. Having an alienist in the family, living under his ample, stalwart wing, we had what is probably an unusual and certainly a mixed feeling about insanity. We were more familiar with it, more unafraid of it than are most people, more aware of its high incidence, the freakish turns it takes, and the fact that it does not necessarily represent the whole, but sometimes merely an almost imperceptible fraction, of personality. At the same time, however, because of my father's marked reluctance ever to apply the word insane; because of his insistence that his patients—no matter how they might appear to us—were not lunatics but ailing friends; because of his tenderness toward them and his reluctance to laugh at them, which, even as a child, I recognized as a kind of consideration he did not feel called upon to show to me; above all, because he was continually pointing out that between sanity and insanity lay the most delicate, the most shrouded, the most poignant of fulcrums, we knew better than other people that insanity was more tragic than any other tragedy that could befall. And so, on those critical occasions when, having tried and failed to vanquish me by any other means, you resorted to calling me insane to my face or behind my back to friends who made haste to repeat it to me, you and I both knew what you were doing. It was the last, the most lethal of your weapons, your ultimate strategy at once of attack and defense. You were giving me the kiss of death.

But in that sense I have refused and continue to refuse to die. This narrative is my *sursum corda*, my attempt to rise up out of my own limitations and those the fear of you imposed on me, and look for some meaning beyond the experience of being both your daughter and myself. If, despite my attempt to lift it above the stale zone of argument, it remains no more than a rebuttal, it will have failed. There is no rebuttal to the dead. Like a missile dispatched into outer space, it will simply spin on till spent.

HOW, I KEEP WONDERING, DID THE MISUNDERSTANDING, IF so mild and conciliatory a word can be used for the thorny, corrosive thing between us, first begin? For you, who did not easily concede me an idea, an opinion, or —if you will—an obsession, would surely concede that this misunderstanding did exist. You yourself so often said that I started out as the right kind of child, pliable, obedient, not in any way remarkable of course—for I did not write lyrics about Japanese fishermen or Siamese dancers or Greek gods as did my sister, nor could I draw a jonquil and make it look like a jonquil despite the efforts of the teacher who came twice a week for a whole winter to show me how, whereas my sister drew historical paper dolls and stained-glass windows without any lessons at all—but there had been little to complain of about me, as you later kept pointing out, until at about ten I began to suffer the sea change that turned me into the insoluble problem you claimed I had become, that turned me, I think, against you and hence against myself.

We lived, in that halycon day before either you or I had suspicions of each other and when my sister was still my ideal and my friend, just west of Fifth Avenue in one of those four-story brownstone houses with a stoop, the whole singularly intimate, almost cozy block of which has since been engulfed by the unintimate and uncozy buildings of Radio City. Looking backward down the tunnel of memory into that distant house, I remember the inhabitants better than the house itself. The cook and the kitchen maids I scarcely knew, as they worked in the basement where I was seldom allowed to go. A white-haired, white-faced housekeeper flitted from floor to floor whispering her orders and once, as I passed her on the stairs with a kitten under my arm, whispered: "Cats suck your breath." There was also, I am sure, a parlormaid, for I remember a lace-aproned figure going at dusk to draw the velvet portières of the drawing room, a room which I only entered on invitation, either to curtsy nicely to one of your callers, or, once a month, to have my lesson in speech from a professor who hid as I approached and, sounding his consonants and vowels with unctuous precision, said: "Bzz, bzz, I am a little bee," a phrase I had to repeat after him, and one which, echoing down the years in my unconscious, perhaps accounts for the fact that today the last lady in the last row of the lecture hall often comes up to the platform after my speeches to tell me that she has not missed a word I said. Upstairs, up the long, dark, thickly carpeted stairs that frightened my sister in the orthodox way that long, dark stairways are supposed to frighten children there was your room where I once (at least, all I can remember is once) saw you breakfasting in bed beside my father, wearing a mignonette-sprigged wrapper, and smiling the natural, open kind of smile I do not remember having seen you smile again. Still further upstairs, there was my room, of which I have no recollection whatever, except that over it presided a Scotch woman whom I loved, and whom I saw again nearly twenty years later when she came for tea to the two-room apartment into which I had moved as a bride and remarked, with a gathering of her brows and with much the same intonation as my father had used on the eve of the wedding, "I'd never ha' thought ye'd be marrying a poor mon." About the only other memory I have of the brownstone house is stepping out of it on Sunday mornings in what you called my Rembrandt hat with the brown velvet coat to match and my white kid gloves tied together with a string to keep them from losing each other, to walk up Fifth Avenue beside my father in his striped trousers, black coat, and silk hat. We were not, however, on our way to a religious service. In our house, only the servants went to church. I think it was you who once explained to me that they needed church, poor things, since they had so little else in life.

While the house was one of thousands exactly alike in the New York of that day and would be gleefully boxed by modern sociological box-makers as "upper-middle"—the class we undoubtedly belonged to, though it was years before I realized that despite silks and vel-

vets, shelves of poetry, servants, large limousines, and
the distinguished way we spoke, we were not "upper
upper"—it must have seemed, at least to my father, a
rather noteworthy acquisition. For my father, like nearly
all the best American men I have known, was what is
called, with pride by some, by others with reservation,
self-made. You were properly proud of my father's
achievements in his profession and even enhanced them
by the interposition of a telling, but not quite accurate,
adjective here and there when referring to them, and still
prouder of the remarkably pure, carved lyrics he so often
placed at your feet, as the discreet penguin places a stone
before the bird he courts. But of his origins you were
not exactly proud. It was not because you belittled them
but on the contrary because you puffed them up that I
understood, as I grew older, that you would have preferred him to have been born to impressive folk.

My father's father and mother were Swedes, she of a
more educated milieu than he, and they crossed the seas
in a sailing vessel in 1859 and settled in Minnesota where,
promptly, my father was born. This much you told me.
His mother, my grandmother, a plump, emphatic, mysterious personage, had come to live with us by the time
I remember my family. On one of the rare occasions
when she confided in me (she confided far more in my
sister, not only because my sister was older but because
she was, my grandmother felt, more like my father
whom she openly adored, while I, she decided, was more
like you whom she openly detested), she told with pride
of sitting up all night in her Minnesota cabin with my
father in her arms and a rifle across her knees in case
of Indians. I remember trying to visualize the scene as
she described it, and forgetting entirely that at that
time she had been only eighteen years old, I wondered

why so obviously frightening-looking an old lady should fear a mere Indian when it was clear that it would have been the Indian, had he presented himself, who would be afraid. When I knew my grandmother, she was quite a sight. Clothed by you, her extravagant daughter-in-law whose closets had always been and always would be crowded with the purchases no one ever asked you to refrain from making, she wore black dresses to the ground with boned collars to the chin, a heavy belt from which hung a beaded reticule, and black bonnets, identical in shape, but varying as to the material they were made of, the lavender or white or black tucks and frills they were lined with, and the shiny ribbons with which they were tied. How many of these bonnets my grandmother possessed at any one time depended more upon your conscience, apparently, than her need, for you said to me years afterwards in the midst of a homily on the conduct of human relations: "Whenever I was angry with your grandmother, I went out and bought her a bonnet. I always felt better after that," and to this principle my own girlhood closet often bore witness when, after one of your scoldings, I would find in it your present of an expensive new dress.

That my grandmother, whose Viking outlines could not be altogether concealed by her Victorian costume, had been in her middle years not only the first piano teacher in Buffalo but a considerable pianist herself, you also told me, and that she had supported my father through his medical training was part of our accepted family lore. What you did not tell me, however, but what I nevertheless heard, no doubt from my sister who could never repress such secrets, was that my father's mother had an affair with a traveling actor when my father was still a baby, that he was kidnaped by his father, taken to Sioux City, Iowa, where his father re-married and begat a new family, and that my father was eighteen before he saw his mother again. Since neither you nor my father himself ever talked about his father, he would not have become a reality in my mind at all, had I not met in Sioux City, long after my father's death, a venerable little woman who came up to the lecture platform and laid her hand on my arm. "I went to school with your Dad," she said. "He was always bright. But his father was a big, dumb Swede. We were all glad when your father got away." I knew that my grand-mother herself had married again, since her last name was not the same as ours, but whether or not he was the traveling actor was not and now never will be disclosed.

Even without the bald light cast by Freud upon this later era in which no nook or cranny is left dark enough for the shamefaced emotion to hide in, the explanation for my grandmother's fevered possessiveness, her arro-gant adoration of my father, is not hard to find. Freud-ian hypothesis, on the other hand, does little to explain the unfailingly tempered patience and gentle neutrality with which my father bore it. If the shadow of Oedipus fell athwart him, it was too tenuous for the lay eye to recognize, and anyway, detesting Freudian theory as he made it only too clear that he did, it would be both unfilial and impious to suggest, now that he has so long been dead, either that he loved his mother too little or too well. It seems to me clear enough, without benefit of the amateur analytic speculation that so often darkens more than it illuminates, that in return for her support of him throughout his years of special training both in America and abroad, as also in return perhaps for his very existence, he brooked his mother, if not with joy, then with lifelong courtesy. For what crowned all other traits in my father was his benign, unflaunted sense of duty. Would that I could have said as much of me.

WHETHER YOU TOOK AS MUCH PRIDE AS MY FATHER IN that brownstone house into which you moved soon after your marriage, with your mother-in-law and your first baby, and in which, eight years later, I was born, is doubtful. Though your father too, like mine, was self-made in the sense that he wrested from sweat and toil his education, his livelihood, and his position of consequence in the small town in Texas where he eventually settled, you, the eldest of his many children and perhaps, as you believe, his favorite, were by no means self-made. You spent your girlhood in a house not so different either in size or comfort, and no less well staffed, after all, from the house over which you came to rule in New York. That Texas house on a wide street of the town, dark brown too, both outside and in, with its bay windows and inserts of stained glass, its large fireplaces and impressive stairway, was as much my grandfather's achievement as the New York house was my father's. My grandfather, after having fought for five years in the Confederate Army, had ridden empty-handed from his native Tennessee into Texas, fallen in love with the girl he hired to help him teach the school in which he got his first job, and married her. He had eventually become president of the town's main bank, as you enjoyed pointing out, though without ever telling me by what laborious steps in a wholesale grocery business. When my father (of whom your father, like all fathers, had been so doubtful when first you announced your intention of marrying him) traveled across the country to fetch you, the local newspaper devoted three columns to your New York trousseau and the solid munificence of your wedding presents. It must have been hard even then to remember that you had been born in a two-room house with a lean-to for kitchen and had slept through your early childhood in a trundle bed. Your Rome, like so many Romes in America, had indeed been built in a day.

From a much enlarged daguerreotype, in which your hair, then black, is impeccably neat, as indeed it was even in death, in which your beruffled dresses are too imaginative and too perfectly fitted to your small, slight figure to have been designed by the local hands of that day, and in which your eyes, not yet enlarged by the pince-nez you wore in my early childhood (and which to my horror and yours I once knocked off and broke) do not yet foreshadow the reproachful look which was to become fixed in them long before I grew up, I see how pretty, how fashionable you must have been. I see too, *mirabile dictu*, that you once had the potentiality of being gay.

Though as you told me with some satisfaction, you had never, until you were more than seventy years old, made a bed (and you deliberated over your bed as though you were preparing an altar), the only silver spoon you were born with was that of your father's character. You were no julep-drinking colonel's daughter bred in a white-columned house on a plantation. Your flirtations, while they qualified—I was told—numerically, did not take place under snowy magnolias or family portraits but in a buggy on a dusty road with a watermelon for shared refreshment. Nevertheless, you had your colored mammy to coddle you; when you drove downtown to shop, you sat in the family carriage

and ordered a bolt of cloth to be brought out for your
inspection; and the balls you attended were often in New
Orleans, Charleston, or Richmond as well as at home.
You grew up to be willful, arch, imperious, elaborately
charming and devious in the so-called tradition of the
South, and if in a mathematics examination you fainted,
that was only to be expected from a lady by definition
made up of fragility and flame. The fact that you mem-
orized Shakespeare and Browning, that your awe for
scholarship was genuine, and that your rather remarkably awakened social conscience, though it still did not
extend at that time beyond paternalistic kindness,
brought you often and generously to the doors of the
poor, may have set you apart from your contemporaries
in the society into which you were born. All the same,
you were so good an imitation as to be almost a replica
of what we northerners call a southern belle.

Indeed, I know more about your early years than you
ever thought I did, more than you wanted me to know,
though let us acknowledge that to know is by no means
necessarily to understand. For from the known to the
fully apprehended is as much a leap in the dark as faith
itself.

I know, for instance, that your mother, that devout
Presbyterian who taught you about predestination, damnation, and sanctification, who never touched playing
cards except with the tongs to lay them on the fire, and
who was to become a founder of women's clubs and a
pillar of her state, had suffered so much in her child-
bearing season that the doctor had given her morphine,
and that she had fallen victim to the habit. And I know
that you, her daughter, rather than being proud that
she succeeded (where so few succeed) in recovering,
could never quite forgive her either for the responsi-

bility for her household and younger children that her long illness placed on your shoulders or for what you considered the disgrace. Was it then, I wonder, at the very threshold of your womanhood, that you made the decision, consciously or unconsciously, never again to assume responsibility for work but only for directing it; never to lift a tray, measure a temperature, cook a meal, wrap a parcel, press a dress, drive a car, fetch or carry for yourself or for anyone else, but always to delegate these endlessly repeated tasks upon which the dormitory of daily existence is built? Brilliantly accurate as was your memory when it came to capturing the cadences of verse, you could never remember where you put down the letter that had just left your hands, let alone remember what I had asked or told you a moment before. "I never heard of such a thing," was your characteristic answer, whether I asked for permission to lunch with a friend or, when I was grown, permission to marry. Hating responsibility, you still demanded authority. You ruled, not so much by judgment, but by your mastery of the weapons of ill health, disappointment, exacerbated (though admirable) perfectionism, and superior articulacy. You had discovered by instinct how to build, divide, manipulate, and maintain that small empire that was your home.

But there was one thing, above all, about your origin that you would have given anything you possessed to keep secret; one thing that must have appeared to you, since you hid it so carefully, too terrible to reveal; one thing that evidently ate into your bowels and galled your soul; one thing that weighed so heavily on your private scales that neither your parents' position in the town where you grew up, nor all your acquisitions, nor all your interests, nor the mounting reputation of

my father who was by the time you married him well
through the doorway to success, nor the comforts he
gave you, nor the journeys to far lands on which he took
you with all the fresh food for the inner self that they
provided, nor the more than obvious promise of my once
so poetic sister, nor, of course, my own supposedly
planned and welcomed existence could counterbalance.
It must have been that to which my father referred
when, on the single occasion on which he conceded that
you were not always just, he added: "But remember,
you must make allowances for your mother. She was
warped in youth."

What was this warp, this mould, this parasite against
which no abundance of what even the most wildly in-
satiable nature must have recognized as blessings could
avail? Was it really only the fact that your father never
knew his father, that he did not, properly speaking, have
a father at all? Was it because of this that one evening
when, as a married woman, I casually referred to some
king's bastard, you fell back upon the couch with a
moan and had to have the smelling salts, which were
never far from your hand, administered and be helped
upstairs to your room? Is it possible that this, only this,
was at the root of your anxiety, your self-consciousness,
your excessive preoccupation with appearances which
rose up around us and swamped the air we breathed?
Could it have been no more than this that so imprisoned
you within yourself that I could almost count the occasions when some spectacle or book or idea liberated
you from your secret oppression and so enkindled your
imagination that you set us momentarily and deliciously
free to share it? As I remember your father, and he did
not die till after I was grown, he wore no visible scar,
and if he had once been wounded by his so-called lack of

identity, the wound had long since healed. Did you, who prided yourself on your liberation from old superstitions, actually believe that the sin of the father's father (if to conceive a child can be a sin) is visited upon the children and children's children? Not being myself a Victorian as you were Victorian, at least in the social sense, I cannot conceive of suffering from such a cause. How much more romantic, for instance, keeping it on the level of mere sentiment, to have a father whose mother faced the consequences of passion and brought up her son, than to have, like my father, a mother who ran away! And on an entirely different level, does not each one of us stand or fall alone? I would be no more ashamed that my father's mother was unwed than if he had sprung full-blown from the head of Jove. Your father's life bore witness for him.

But I am forgetting what should never, all modern psychological theory to the contrary, be forgotten. There is no plummet to sound another's soul. It goes without saying that we cannot foresee in the tiny perfection of the embryo curled in its warm encasement the shape of the man to come. Now, today, as I study the faces of my grown son and daughter and see again in my mind's eye his orange-splotched choleric infant's grimace and the pear-shaped head and filmy eyes she had when I first looked at her, I cannot say that I could have foreseen even the external shape they have at present, any more than anthropologists, for all their conjectures, can reconstruct from the jawbone that unrecorded time has so grudgingly yielded them, the quality, texture, and manner of primeval man. And oppositely, it should also go without saying, I insist, that no matter how earnestly the analyst behind the classic couch and the patient lying on it put their heads together

to reconstruct that patient from infancy, to gauge
each caress and sting of experience, they cannot conclude
with finality what the patient is and why. Not only are
there as many conflicting truths as there are people to
claim them; there are equally multitudinous and conflicting truths within the individual. Just as we can
never be sure of the history of a nation, or of an era in
the life of that nation, or of a single day in an era of the
life of that nation, so we can never be sure of the whole
or of a part of the whole history of any person. There
was your view of yourself, and my view of you, and the
view of all those who ever touched or hinged upon you,
and then there was the you (as with each of us) beyond
and outside (or inside?) all those yous, the one complete and authorized version of you which, if it existed,
could exist only in God. That I did not understand you
is small wonder. And this brings me to concede, though
concession is as hard for me as it was for you, that
logically, historically, indeed inevitably, you could not
have understood me. I can only blame you that you did
not try.

THE FRUIT OF DISCORD HAS A FLESH AS FIRM, A BLUSH AS
wholesome as any other. It is only by looking back to
the time before and the time immediately after the first
bite of it that one realizes that within that hearty-ap-
pearing fruit lay coiled the power to destroy innocence
for good.

Late one night when, after listening for a while to
the unmistakable stress of altercation that came to me
through the bathroom that adjoined my sister's room to
mine in our new Park Avenue apartment, I had finally
fallen asleep, I woke up to find her leaning over me.

"It's me, Frog," she whispered. "Wake up and listen. You know that evening dress I bought? She tried to tear it off me. She wanted to burn it. Father actually came in and took her away."

"So now you're in wrong?" I asked.

"So now," she sighed, "I'm in wrong again. And do you know what?" she added, fiercely. "I hate her."

It was not the first time that my sister, who by day ignored me airily now that she was almost a woman, had come by night to complain of you. Nor, for that matter, were hers the only complaints of you I had heard. There was the red-faced Irish waitress whom I had found sobbing in the pantry over one of your arrows of irritation that had made its mark. There was your own personal maid, a withered, frail creature whom I had seen running from your room, gasping: "A little air! A little air!" There were the several trained nurses, returning with you from the hospital after your various operations, who rubbed your back and feet and guarded your door (from me and other intruders) for a few days and then departed, stiff-mouthed, one succeeding the other, with the hope on my father's part, I daresay, that enough of them could be found to tide you over. And there were the not infrequent mornings when, on my required visit to your bedside before school, you frowningly sent for Mademoiselle, who made me change my dress while muttering loud enough for me to hear: "Such a fuss over nothing!" And sometimes in those half hours after supper when I had to go down to my grandmother's apartment just underneath ours to play Bach preludes on her piano while, with her swollen fingers that no longer fitted the keys, she drummed impatiently on the windowpane, she would invite me to a game of double solitaire and then, leaning

across the card table, would look into my eyes and heave
a sigh and say: "Your poor father! My poor son!"

It was not that I was not aware, before that particular
nocturnal visit from my sister, of the discord that, like
the ghost in an ancient castle, made its sudden, untimely
appearances and left, when it vanished, a catch of fear
for the hour, the inexorable hour, when it would come
again. It was simply that on that occasion, blurted out
so unexpectedly, the word "hate" burst into my consciousness, echoed down my nerves, grafted itself upon
my shocked but unresisting mind. One could hate one's
mother.

Doubtless not that same night, and more likely over
a longish sequence of nights, but surely in the nighttime
when darkness blacks out the day's distractions and self
lies fully exposed to vulnerable self, I began to put together the little sharp-edged pieces of my experience and
make a picture for myself of an unloved and unloving
child, perhaps a waif abandoned by a real mother for
some unimaginable but undoubtedly insurmountable reason and now adopted by this alien family with which I
dwelled. How weak, how tenuous is loyalty, unless moment by moment and year by year the example of loyalty is set, unless each impulse of loyalty given is matched
by a loyalty received. And how strong, on the other
hand, and how swift at its task of undermining, is dis-
loyalty, serving, as it does so well, to justify and excuse the self that forever hungers for justification and
excuse.

Where the apple reddens, said the poet, never pry. But
pry I must into the reddening of that apple my sister
tendered me and whereof I ate, in order to discover how
and when and why there first opened the fissure which I
have called our misunderstanding and which was so to

widen between us down the years that even a scream for help from one of us could not and did not penetrate the other's inner ear.

YET THERE WERE SONGS ON SUMMER EVENINGS IN THE fine houses you and my father rented on Long Island, in New Hampshire, or in Maine, in those days before you bought and embellished, on a hill overlooking a confluence of rivers, the place of your own in Connecticut which, because of my father's brief experiments with sheep and pigs, you called the Farm, despite its professionally landscaped garden, the professionally designed wing on its main house, the bamboo shoots and other exotic plants from the Department of Agriculture in Washington that surrounded its guest house, its playhouse, its garage, its raked lawns and driveway, and its tailored stone fences. Sitting on those earlier rented terraces and porches, you in your fluffy dresses and my father in his white flannels, we filled the dusk with our cultured but not musical voices, singing familiar rounds. You were especially fond, I remember, of the one that ends: "Merrily, merrily, merrily, merrily, Life is but a dream." And in its moments of peace that life, anyway to me who was so unaware of its cost and of those menaces to living that are penury, disease, and death, was indeed a dream rounded out almost every night with a dreamless sleep.

It was in one of those rented houses poised like a great water bird on the edge of a lake that I saw in your face one evening a look I do not remember having seen again. I had been sitting with you and my father, watching the sky pale, and had then trotted out alone along the pier and lowered myself into the rowboat moored to it.

Untying the rope, I leaned too far over while pushing
off the boat and fell in. I could not swim. My father
waded in after me up to his chest. As he set me, wet
and dazed, on the shore, he laughed. Because he laughed,
I laughed too. Dripping as I was, you put your arms
around me and took me upstairs. "You can get warm in
my bed," you said. I stretched out in a dry nightgown
with a hot-water bottle at my feet. You sat down beside
me. "I was stupid," I said. "But you laughed," you answered with a smile. Hearing and seeing your approval,
I slept; nor did I know till the next morning that I had
been transported and tucked into my own bed during the
night.

After that, when I skinned my knee or pinched my
finger, I made a point of laughing. But, quick as you
were to be alarmed and prompt as you were to send for
cotton and iodine, you no longer noticed my bravado.
And later, when it was not my knee or my finger but
my heart that I skinned and pinched, I forgot to laugh
or to remember to say "how stupid," and I forgot, too,
the warmth and the rue of the maternal smile.

But in those summers there was also, for excitement,
my sister. I can see her now as she was when I used to
peer at her from behind the door. Long-throated, her
dark hair rolled up, her full lips smiling, and her eyes—
those yellow danger signals in her delicately structured
face—bright with satisfaction, she was dipping and bend-
ing and gliding and turning, sometimes alone and sometimes with some tall youth, while out of the great horn
of her victrola came a masculine voice, singing: "You
are like the figure on the Mecca cigarette, You have got
a figure that I never will forget," or, with a pin re-
placing the needle on the record to keep the forbidden
words from being overheard: "If you talk in your

sleep, my God! don't mention my name!" That she seldom invited handsome girls, that if there happened to
be one in the neighborhood she would find a reason to
hate that particular one and would even, if the name
came up at table, bang down her knife and fork, rush
upstairs and lock herself in her room, seemed to my
parents, and still then to me too, merely part of her fas-
cinating temperament. Neither you nor my father then
suspected how inflamed was her young blood. But by
the time she was eighteen and I ten, I knew full well
from her nocturnal confidences that boys crushed sweet
blossoms into her teeth and told her she was their only
consolation.

In winter, countervailing the routine of mornings at
school where in my English and language lessons I was
always volunteering to recite what I was so sure I knew
and in my mathematics and geography lessons was making myself as inconspicuous as possible so as not to be
called upon to recite; counterbalancing the routine of
afternoons spent roller-skating in the park or trying to
get myself chosen by one side or the other for a game of
prisoners' base; offsetting the mortification on rainy
days of being called for in a hired coupé by my grandmother, who despised horseless carriages as much as she
despised Debussy and Wagner; countering the winter
dusks that settled so early over the city and found me
alone in my own room, longing for something or someone, unspecified in my imagination, to set me alight; in
counterpoint to this life of mine which, had I not had
my sister's to compare it to, might have seemed less
flat, less hollow, less bereft of peaks—there unfolded the
drama of the world above me, the adult world of home.

The table in the Della Robbia dining room, where
the portrait of you and my sister, painted to make you

both look like wolfhounds, hung between majolica
plates, was often being set by nervous maids for one of
those dinners to which it went without saying I was not
invited but at which, from behind the screen at the pantry door, if I happened to be in right with the waitress
(in wrong and in right were the two poles between
which my childhood swung), I could assist unseen. Into
the drawing room, however, there was no way of looking secretly. Yet it was in there, not when you had
callers, for what they looked like and did and said I was
sure I already knew, but when callers came for my sister,
that I most desired to see. This room, long enough to
hold not only the Steinway grand but also the red and
green painted clavichord (that emitted, when I dug into
its little black keys, only a decorous twang), and high
and wide enough to encompass easily the copy of Tintoretto's Bacchus rising out of the sea and tending a
wedding ring to an absent Ariadne eliminated in discreet
censorship of the master's mind, achieved, if not quite the
look of grandeur you had perhaps anticipated, at least
an impression of culture that no one could miss. But because this room opened on the front hall with no doors
to close on it, my sister, who by then felt a need for the
privacy that would free her to investigate the intentions
of her callers, had christened it the Forest of Haunted
Deer. But it was not you who did the haunting. Often,
when she had callers, you remained in your room on
the floor above, with a small, lace-bordered handkerchief, dipped in eau de cologne, laid across your eyes.
The possible consequences of leaving her alone with a
caller were not always sufficient to outweigh your me-
grims and bring you downstairs. Also, because she was
poetic, and, more simply, because you loved her (you
did love her and, despite all that happened later, you

loved her to the end), you trusted her and wanted her pleasure. Nor was it my father who interrupted her trysts, if only because he was too busy with what went on in other people's families to look carefully into what went on in his own. Yet he was not unaware of my sister's propensities. Like most second-generation Americans, he was very American and viewed with ill-concealed scepticism the Europeans among her beaux. "Well," he would say to me when I ventured into his room where at the end of the office day he sought refuge with the evening paper, "I suppose your sister is entertaining another waiter from the Plaza." And then he and I would exchange one of those winks which, coming from my preoccupied and habitually silent father, seemed to me the accolade.

It was I who haunted my sister, stalking her on tiptoe out to those marbleized back stairs of the building where she escaped with a caller, even stalking her downstairs into that last resort which was my grandmother's apartment and where once, while my grandmother lay back in her chair feigning sleep but watching, I suspected, from beneath imperceptibly raised lids, I saw my sister being kissed. "Why do you close your eyes? Why do you close your eyes?" I chanted afterwards, and though she pretended not to understand me, she knew to what I had referred. What would you have said and done, I wonder, if you had realized what she, what I, was up to; where she, where I, was bound?

Not a few of those who came to that apartment for one reason or another were or would be important people. But the visitor who lent himself the most importance —a real visitor, this one, since he stayed with us for several weeks—was the Indian poet Tagore, the first man I have observed you to revere and at the same time almost your only acquaintance about whom my father permitted himself to smile when I was alone with him. Like the servants, though for other reasons, I hated "The Poet," as we were told to call him. He was said to love children. Every afternoon, therefore, he was treated to a brief colloquy with me. "Do you see those buildings across the avenue?" he asked in his musical English, pointing at the far side of Park Avenue. "They are there, are they not?" I nodded. "But if you cease to think of them, my child, if they are no longer in your inner vision," he explained, "they do not exist." To me, however, then and now still today, they existed and exist regardless of my vision, as do the nebulae in the heavens, as does the plankton in the sea, as—if He exists at all—does God. For reality, whatever The Poet thought, is neither what I fancy I see nor yet what I see, but what is.

What was it you sought in offering our roof for so prolonged and undoubtedly costly a visit from The Poet? It was not, I am certain, only to win out over other New York hostesses. Perhaps, after all, in his criss-crossing of real and unreal, in his disengagement from daily fret, in his quest for large meanings, he answered some unrealized need in you.

BUT, LEST I SEEM TO HAVE FORGOTTEN OR TO BE NEGLECT-ing the more simply familial aspects of life at that time, lest I seem not to have valued or to value them, let me hasten to say that our Christmas, for instance, was as warm and festive as any child could want. It was not precisely Christ's birthday that we celebrated, for though we sang—and you particularly enjoyed our singing—the many carols in His honor, my sister and I were taught little more of Him than we were taught about Thor and Frigga, the Walkyrie, Cupid and Psyche, and the other Olympians. But we knew, of course, how He had been born, since the carols had given us the salient facts about Mary's journey, the manger, the birth, and the star-guided visitors. Moreover, we knew that, like Confucius, like Gautama, like Mohammed, He had been a man of parts. But if I had then found out that other people knew He was the Son of God, it had not come to me from my Swedish grandmother nor from my Texas grandmother (a Presbyterian whom I saw rarely and who, in not speaking to me of God when she might have, exercised what I now realize to have been considerable restraint), nor from my father, nor from you with whom he fully agreed about the Incarnation, but rather it must have come to me from a maid or a nurse. This was not, however, because you and my father were anti-God. You were both too well educated, too well aware of the unsolved mysteries of those universes beyond universes which had begun to unfold under the eye of science, to suppose that there was no Plan. But my father had been brought up without religion, and you, in part no doubt out of rebellion against your mother and in part out of your entirely praiseworthy desire to join the intellectual mainstream of your time, had turned your back on the God of your childhood. Inevitably, you had both been swept into the Darwinian embrace. You were both convinced that it had been proved with finality that it was not in the image of God, but in the endlessly perfecting and eventually perfectible image of the ape that we were made.

But if at Christmas we did not celebrate precisely the mystery of the Son of God, we had, on the material yet affectionate level of exchanging presents, a mystery of our own which seemed to me meaningful enough until, so many years later, I participated in another kind of Christmas. It was in Poland, where for Christmas Eve we fasted on herring and cold potatoes served on a table strewn with symbolic hay; where we attended midnight Mass in the frosty chapel and heard from the throats of cold, ill-clad, and hungry peasants the tidings of peace and joy that have for two thousand years irradiated those who believed in them; where, on Christmas itself, we broke the blessed wafer with every member of the household and exchanged with each the antiphonal of praise for that occasion that, in fine, I experienced for the first time a Christian Christmas. Only then did I perceive that for many people, for many poor people to whom the receiving of a bolt of cloth or a pair of shoes or a bag of candies meant an added chance for survival, the Present that moved them most did not come wrapped in fringed tissue with ribbons red and green. Only when I saw my small children at the foot of a fir specially hewn out of those alien forests and saw them gaze with such a shine on their faces as they have never had again at the angel atop that tree, did I realize what an imitation my own childhood Christmas had been. Only when my three-year-old daughter explained to me one Christmas morning with the light of discovery in her eyes that "God is like the buck in the bushes: you never see Him, but you know He's there," did the emptiness of Christmas without Him send a shaft of pain through my heart.

But that was many years and many shafts of pain later, and meanwhile let me not forget those Christmases in the Park Avenue apartment when my father, dressed in a great red Santa Claus suit, handed each of us a gay and tender poem he had written himself; when my grandmother gave each of us something she had painstakingly stitched and disguised in a froth of artfully manipulated paper; when you gave us each some luxury you had been at obvious pains to choose; when we were all at pains to cheer that kindest of women, my father's life-long secretary, and the two or three other guests whom we always invited because they had nowhere else to go; and when we set out to enliven even those of the servants who a few hours before had been grumbling about the "Madam" and hinting that they did not like "the place." Internecine feuds and hostility between maid and mistress were shelved for that occasion. Over the flutter-ing candles in the darkened room there hung, though perhaps only the maids would have so defined it, the peace the occasion enjoined.

I remember one Christmas Eve when the front door-bell rang in the midst of the family celebration and my father, who went to open the door himself, came back into the room with a pale, tense-looking man without an overcoat. "I want you to meet an old friend of mine," he said, keeping his hand on the man's arm. "This is my family," he said to the man with a smile. "Won't you sit down and let us give you some hot coffee?" For a moment there was silence and then, after a quick glance at my father, you rose to the situation with your unfailing social tact and breached the awkward moment by handing one of us another present. Despite the pres-ence of a stranger, the celebration went on. After a while my father stood up. "And now," he said, quietly, "I will just take my friend home." He did not return till long after I had been sent to bed. He had taken his "friend" all the way back in a cab to that home beyond the city which was an asylum. Even if we had known (as you undoubtedly suspected) what was wrong with

my father's "friend," we would not have behaved otherwise. This was perhaps the closest we came to the meaning of Christmas.

WHERE IN THE BRAIN, I WONDER, IS MEMORY SEATED?
Does anyone understand why it sleeps and why it
wakes? We are told that its sleep is often consciously or
unconsciously induced, when the thing remembered
becomes so painful that the only way consciousness can
live with it is to tuck it into some corner of the unconscious where, even if it can be heard from time to time
turning and twisting in that Procrustean bed, it is at
least out of sight. No doubt some such writhings go on
in everyone, but how widely people differ, all the same,
in their ability to consign memory to this artificial
sleep! There are those who, even if they would prefer
forgetting, cannot achieve it, and others again who prefer, by poking their finger into the bruise of memory,
to keep it sentient. But some appear to have mastered the
technique of forgetting, and I say "appear to have mastered" advisedly, for a thing can seem to have been lost
yet in fact it can only be mislaid, there being no real
limbo for memory. Of these, I have seen no one in all
my life as proficient as you in the art of appearing to
have forgotten what it suited you to forget. But to what
you disapproved, to your grievances, to the long list of
injustices which you felt that I, especially, but also my
sister, and even my father, not to speak of former
friends, acquaintances, and the countless people whom
at one time or another and in one capacity or another
you paid to help you, had perpetrated against you, your
memory was more than faithful. And if I have neither inherited nor acquired your most admired characteristics,

I am more than kin to you in the persistence with which I too have collected and still collect injustices. I can only add that I have been more exposed than you ever were to the proverbial slings and arrows, not just because of what would now be classified, humiliatingly classified I always feel, as sibling experience, but because of all that came afterwards and perhaps as a result of it —my entanglements with men which for you would have been unthinkable; my impractical exposing of myself to another and totally alien society in Europe in which I so vainly attempted both to take and not to take root; my loss through war of the last chance to effect this grafting of myself upon a foreign family; and still more my return home to you and to a hand-to-mouth existence which came upon me so unexpectedly, found me so ill-prepared at an age when professional capacity in any field should have long since been proved, and drove me, like the pestilence-stricken leaf, into that world over the gates of which is written: Here Dog Eats Dog. I am aware, of course, that in listing the reasons I have had and you never had for collecting injustices, I am being specious, since the word reason has no place in this process and since no matter how long a list I concocted, it would be but a footnote compared to the opportunities for collecting injustice that thousands of non-collectors have had. I am back, of course, at my favorite—my inexcusably favorite— pastime of self-excuse. And if I go on to point out that it was you who first forced upon me my apparently fixed and unchangeable stance of self-defense, I will only be losing myself further still in the labyrinth of my justifications. Yet it is true. Or at least I believe it to be true that, for the early set of this mould of mine, you were to blame.

"I have never," you often said, "lifted a hand against my children." As a matter of fact, in my case, I seem only to remember now two occasions—and these some thirty years apart—when you did, and both might long since have been buried under your tongue lashings, had they not been dealt me for reasons I could not understand.

I must have been very small that first time when, Mademoiselle having come to help me dry myself after a bath and having abruptly and with an oddly hostile expression dropped the towel, sped from the room, and returned with you in her wake, you picked up my hairbrush and stuck my backside with it, saying in a tone so low that it gave the effect of a shout: "Never, never let me catch you doing such a thing again!" The trouble was that I did not know what I had done, did not know indeed till many years later when moral attitudes had changed and when you yourself might even have suspected that that spanking was a mistake. What you stirred in me then was a sense, not yet of outrage, but of guilt. Yet I can imagine all too well how I must have looked at you, for I have not forgotten the expression on my small son's face when, because he was playfully resisting my attempts one night to get him to bed and out of that adult irascibility so incomprehensible to the young, I slapped his face. His eyes darkened, and the light that had been in them before was never quite so clear again. In my turn I had given him his first injustice.

"How sharper than a serpent's tooth it is To have a thankless child!" Of the Shakespeare you quoted me, this was the verse you most often spoke, for, as you had taught me and as I was to see reiterated in the papers you left upon your death, you were convinced that King Lear, and King Lear alone, had suffered as you suffered from your children.

The second time you struck me, so very long after the first, came at a moment when, though you could not have known it, I had just made for you a sacrifice of so private a nature that I could not have borne to have spoken of it and which proved a turning point in the whole trend of my life.

Late one night as I came in with my Polish husband from the first outing we had had together on what was to have been both his holiday and my attempt to re-instate myself as the good companion he needed and I had been steadily failing for many months to be, the concierge of a Paris hotel handed me the telegram that precipitated one of the gravest of the misunderstandings accumulated by then between you and me. The telegram said that my father was dead. I can still hear the intake of my husband's breath as he read the words over my shoulder and feel the grip of his hand on my arm, swift as the grip of the news on my heart. I knew at once that I must go to you. And I knew, too, that I was afraid to go. It must have been hours later, near the end of the night, that my husband came in to me from his ad-joining room, sat down on the edge of my bed, and said, in a voice I had not heard him use since before the birth of my children, indeed since before we had married: "Don't go. Stay here with me."

And yet I went. I let him return alone to Poland, I left the bridge between us, already fallen into disre-pair, still sagging. I came, laden with two losses, the one no heavier than the other, to do what I could for you. On a hot evening at the Farm, every flowering bush, every young tree, and every live chirp and rustle and murmur of which reincarnated my father in our memories, I found the courage to ask you if he had left any word for me. "I cannot remember," you answered me, after a pause, "that he mentioned you at all." I said nothing. You turned then and looked up at me. "Why did you come?" you asked. We were standing side by side on the terrace. The mist was rising from the rivers at the bottom of the hill and drifting across the ghostly garden. Stung, alike by your answer as by your ensuing question, I said: "Because I thought Father would have wanted me to come." Even the fading light could not conceal your look. "You!" came your voice then, vibrant and sudden. "You! I don't like your face!" And with that, you struck me, for what may have been only the second but was certainly the last time.

Yet I know that before another day had passed you had succeeded in forgetting it, or in making yourself believe that you had forgotten it, which is very nearly —though not quite—the same thing. Had I reproached you with it, you would have denied it.

But I am unable to solve to my own satisfaction what it is that makes memory, or at least my particular memory, keep and lose what it seems always to be keeping and losing. Why does it so almost automatically lose what pleased and keep what gave pain? I can understand that memory must be selective, else it would choke on the glut of experience. What I cannot understand is why it selects what it does. For it seems, loath as I am to admit it, to make its selections in spite of me. I try to keep house in my memory, to decide, since presumably I am its only housekeeper, what should be folded away on its shelves and what thrown out as untidy, useless, or potentially harmful, but my memory has a will of its own and goes on, in defiance of command, rejecting the moments of warmth and beauty which I know should be preserved against those of ugliness and cold, and placing in evidence where I cannot fail to note them the rusted needles and fishhooks, the nettles and harpoons which no one in his or her right mind would feel it wise to preserve.

Am I then, as you openly said upon a few critical occasions, not in my right mind? For my mind tells me, always tells me, that pleasure is less pleasure than lack of pain, that beauty is less beauty than lack of ugliness, that warmth is less warmth than lack of cold, that joy is less joy than lack of grief, as night is less night than lack of day. Perhaps therefore you put your finger on it after all when you insisted on assuring me that either because I was too thin and did not drink enough milk or because I was incapable of appreciation or gratitude, I was not in my right, but indeed in my wrong, mind.

MY EYE AND EAR BEGAN EARLY TO CHOOSE WHAT THEY wanted to record on the plastic of memory, and their choice, whether or not it was tied to emotion, fell more often on the dark side than on the bright. There was, for instance, to show the bend in the twig that was my eleven-year-old self, the journey of several months in the Far East on which you and my father took my sister and me. My father had been in Japan once before as the doctor-companion of some not quite normal rich young man and had wanted long since to return to see China, not only for its art and natural beauties, but because he had become convinced that in Confucius was embodied more wisdom than in any other man who ever lived.

You and he had been in Europe often enough, establishing my sister and her Mademoiselle, together with my grandmother, my father's secretary, my nurse and

me, in this or that health-inducing climate of France or
Switzerland and from there had traveled to wherever
there was a mountain or monument. Moreover, by the
time this journey to the Far East was decided, Europe
had already been rocking for two years in the blast
of the first World War and there was actually no other
direction for American tourists to travel than eastward,
by way of San Francisco and Honolulu, to Yokohama,
Nagasaki, Shanghai, and that citadel of my father's imagination, Peking.

Few Americans of my age, except for the much-
lugged-about children of diplomats, were taken to an
Orient where, ironical as it seems today, the most serious
dangers were the lack of milk and the chance of spoiled
fruit, and I therefore have never had an opportunity to
compare the impressions of other youthful travelers in
Japan and China with mine. But what I remembered best
immediately after the journey and still remember best all
these decades later is not the towering golden Buddha of
Kamakura, but the first blind, noseless, scabby beg-
gar I saw on the street; not the tier upon blue-roofed
tier of the Chinese emperor's summer palace, nor the
great blocks of primeval stone outside Nanking, nor any
of man's handiwork at all in fact, but the swarms of
mangy boys, naked as I had never seen a boy before,
thrusting their hands into my face and whining for
alms. What I still remember about the grown-up, splendid dinner party in Shanghai to which I was brought is
not what we ate or drank, nor the porcelain and painted
screens and lacquered table, but the mute, drooping face
of a Chinese bride who, placed between me who could
not and her new husband who would not speak to her,
did not receive from anyone so much as a glance. What
I remember best about the tea ceremony in Japan, by

which it was hoped I would be influenced to grace, is not the ritual of sipping and passing the black, rank brew from hand to hand, nor yet the face of the old Tea Master, nor in fact any of the symbolic gestures which you memorialized in a long poem that was later printed in an American magazine, but simply the grotesque, indeed the hilarious sight of first my father, then you, and then my sister crawling on your knees through the kennel-like ceremonial door, folding yourselves with decorum around the table, and wearing a mask of serenity on your faces which my father alone among us knew how to wear. What I remember best about the sacred island of Miajima, apart from the astonishing sweetness of the young, tame, spotted deer, is the anguish of my father when, after you had swum the only three strokes that you were capable of, you sank with a faint gasp and he had to pull you out; and about Nikko, apart from its arched red bridge, I remember only being handed by the temple priest a stick that he had shaken out of a box with a slit in it and around which was furled, on thin fragrant paper, what our guide said was my fortune. "Seven little devils," he read out to me, "will chase you all life." The only way to rid myself of them, he said, would be to come back to the temple another year and try my fortune again. Ever since, I have looked over my shoulder to see if all seven of them were still there.

To be sure, I remember the rain-light on Japanese umbrellas, the soft giggles of Japanese maids, the insucked hiss of complex courtesy with which the most casual remarks were prefaced or greeted, and to be sure I remember the brook-wetted, hushed gardens which even the blind could not forget. But more clearly, far more clearly, I remember the sweating backs of the coolies who pushed and pulled my father's rickshaw, the febrile cries of the porters on the Shanghai Bund, the stumpy feet of the amah who was supposed to take me for walks, the smell of the curried rice she kept in my bureau drawer, and the man I saw being kicked by a policeman. And perhaps because I had read *Les Misérables* on the boat going out and had learned, not from you who evaded my question but from my sister who never evaded a question of that kind, what it was that poor Fantine had to do after she had sold her hair in order to support her daughter, what I remember best about the geishas I saw in Kyoto who were, though four or five years older, the same size as me, is nowhere near so much the swish of their beautiful painted clothing, the fall of their thick, soft sashes, the sound of the biwas that some were plucking or the grace of the hands of those who danced, but the fact that, if they had not already done so, they were to sell themselves to men.

I know well with what a stricken air you would have judged this residue of the unusual opportunity you and my father gave me and how you would have sighed and protested against the waste. But as I look back on it now, while I too regret the limitations of my sensibility, I see that I was after all in pursuit of something, something I have been hotly pursuing ever since, something I would probably at the time have called and would even still call today by that absurdly abused, but biologically impeccable pseudonym—the Facts of Life.

THE VERY PHRASE, THE FACTS OF LIFE, WAS ENOUGH TO make you clear your throat. Yet if this phrase has sluttish connotations, it has had sluttishness thrust upon it, not so much by sluts as by those who find it easier (and they are the great majority) to guffaw at the clumsiness of our genesis than to face its tragic implications. For when to beget can be made funny, to die may not be so hard. To you, however, and rightly enough, begetting was not funny. What was wrong, I think, was that you shied away from even a breath of that furnace, out of your fear, not of death, but of life itself. And unable as I was at that age to grasp your fear, I was torn as though pulled by horses driven in opposite directions between the suspicion, aroused by your silence about these Facts and by my sister's *sotto voce* enlightenments, that they were shameful and the insistent prompting of my instinct that they were the all-in-all.

It would be hard to convey, for instance, my excitement—tight throat, hot hands, and fast pulse—when I first saw and heard, alone with my sister, a performance of *Madame Butterfly*. As, with rapt eyes and throbbing voices, the little diva in her rather bad kimono and the tenor swelling out of his fake white uniform sang the duet which was in exaltation, my sister whispered, of a night of love, I was sure that nothing could match this excitement, and when at the end the little lady disemboweled herself so discreetly behind a screen, I felt certain that hara-kiri was a small price to pay for what she had had. I could not know then how subservient are nights of love to the participating mind, or how captiously the mind participates. Nor can I know now if mine alone was captious.

Moreover, I could not help being aware that the Facts of Life, which are not plural at all, by the way, but entirely singular and single, were as shameful and as exciting to others as they were to me. Even if you had been the modern kind of mother who not only tells her children All but keeps on patiently reiterating All to make certain that it becomes as familiar as the plumbing (a system not always possible to carry out, I found, when I tried to explain in appropriately scientific terms the uses of his body to my then small son and he said: "Please, Mama, don't be disgusting!"), even if my sister had been less in love with love than she was or more discreet with me about it, I would have caught from my schoolmates both the worm's view and the moth's.

I was not, and was never to become, popular at school. Though I had nothing untoward on my face, nor any external disability; though I was neither so scholarly as to become a social leper nor yet so successful at anything as to arouse envy, there was something— and I will not be trapped into describing it—that, as crippling as if it were visible, set me apart from my peers. Because you still thought in those days that my unsatisfactoriness was probably more the school's fault than my own, you went on trying me out in new ones. But at least in the third, the highly fashionable school, reputed to make silk purses out of the least promising and grubbiest of sows' ears, I managed to erupt from anonymity, to stand out, not as you would have wanted me to stand out, nor even as I myself would have wanted to stand out had I foreseen the consequence of eruption, but to stand out all the same.

Perhaps because I, and no one else in that school, had been to Japan and China, I was invited one Friday night to supper with a classmate I hardly knew. There were three of us there. The others, a year or so older than I, had the touch of sophistication that commanded my respect.

"What did you do in Japan?" one of them asked me.

"For one thing," I said, "I went to see prostitutes."

Was there a flicker of surprise in the four eyes watching me? If so, it went out as a firefly vanishes. In silence, they waited for me to go on. And I did go on. Heaven alone knows with what details about prostitutes and prostitution I regaled them or how I managed to create out of what has always been my singularly uncreative fancy enough verisimilitude to convince. But I had my moment of triumph, during which the four eyes did not leave my face, and it was not till a few days later when, on returning home from school for lunch, I was met by you, and taken upstairs to your room where you spoke to me more stonily than I had ever been spoken to before, that I knew how convinced my school friends had been.

This incident was a milestone for us both. If it is true, as I believe, that you henceforward considered me, while not exactly delinquent, then potentially so (as I probably was, and as who is not?), it is also true that from then on I never again counted either a schoolmate or you as friend.

Yet I was not without a friend. Indeed, I would be as thankless as you so often called me if, now that I have lost her, I were to pass over her in silence. For I had a best friend, and went on having her for some thirty years, until not death, which would have been a clean and therefore acceptable intervention, but money, mere money, parted us.

It is one thing when there are many friends and out of them, almost by accident, one happens to be the best. It is quite another when the best is at the same time the only friend. You would have remembered, I know, my best and only friend, though not, of course, as I do. You would have remembered her as the gangling, overgrown child with a velvet band across her straggly

hair, with her long feet that flapped over one another
even in the flat gym shoes she had to wear, the extraordinary earnestness of her nearsighted look, and the tilt of
her head as she bent in your direction her good ear. And
you would have remembered her as she became much
later, still earnest, but suddenly dashing, and in the first
years of what you referred to as her brilliant marriage
(for her husband was rich, while the man I had married
was not), rather more radiant than any other young
woman you or I had seen. And you would have remembered her very much later than that, not in fact so long
ago, as a mother and grandmother, no less earnest than
at the start, but with radiance spent. You grew to like
her, you would have had to like her for the unmistakable,
almost frightening innocence in her face though you
could not have altogether liked her because she trusted
me; in the same way, she must have liked in you your
mastery of narrative in conversation and your quick eye
for beauty, but she could not have actually liked you, for
I had taught her to mistrust you.

Since then I have had many friends, and have even
managed to keep them, despite what time often does to
such confluences. But I have not had another friendship where the accord was so almost mathematically perfect. It is said that in love, one person does the loving
while the other lets himself be loved. This is also true,
for the most part, I believe, in friendship. But curiously
enough it was not true of my best friend and me. I say
curiously enough because, having as she did a mother
who held her wings outspread and who would, like the
pelican, have allowed the child to devour her piecemeal
had it been necessary, she might have been so sated with
devotion as not to want what I had to offer or be able
to meet what must have been, considering how frugal

my own fare, rather rich demands. And yet she met them.

I have no doubt that I was fatuously sentimental, for although all my life I have respected the Anglo-Saxon phlegm which, whether assumed or natural, gives such an impression of invulnerability, I have not been able to hazard more than an amateur facsimile of it and it has taken me patient toil, egged on by rebuffs, to entomb my sentimentality and at the same time erect upon it a façade that conceals its grave.

Was it you who, quite unwittingly, gave me my first inkling that it must be concealed? Was it perhaps in part because of your cult of your own sensibility that I slowly, though too slowly, began to realize that to be hypersensitive is not an asset nor, necessarily, a virtue in itself? Thin skins come by the dozen, I have observed, and while they are thin to the point of transparency where the self is concerned, they seem singularly impervious to others. Indeed, it is more often in the pachyderm whose hide looks as though no arrow could pierce it that one finds hidden the real, the two-way sensibility.

But sensibility, at least the appearance of it, was in your day the hallmark of a lady. The more quivering her sensibility, the more of a lady the lady was thought to be. It was perhaps for this reason that you often chose, when you could persuade us to listen to you read aloud, a scene or passage or verse in the reading of which (always slow and dramatic) your voice would be sure to have to break; that you often recounted to the assembled family at table an incident or anecdote which would not fail to bring ready tears to your eyes and necessitate dabbing them with the tiny handkerchief that somehow made you seem so frail. I do not know whether or not I should be grateful for this early exposure to pathos which has rendered me impervious to the show of it, if not quite impervious to the thing itself. But I have often been grateful since, though I was not at the time, for your remark on the occasion when I brought home to lunch the first of the teachers upon whom I was to lavish a purity of devotion I never succeeded later in bestowing on any man. As I sat absorbing her face across the table, you said, with an apologetic smile: "My daughter wears her heart on her sleeve." The shaft of these words sank into me. I saw with a shock for the first time that I looked and was a fool.

But my best friend, though doubtless as sentimental as are all but the wickedest females in the budding season, had learned before I knew her to keep her sentimentality hid. If, intellectually, she already felt drawn to the aestheticism of the Athens we learned about, it was still in the asceticism of Sparta that she found what, emotionally, she most admired. She wanted us both to be Spartans. Not I, but she, initiated the exercises we practiced on the floor of her room or mine, lying on our backs and drawing in our belly muscles till we nearly burst with the effort to make those comfortable convexities concave; not I, but she, introduced what became for a while the daily practice of holding our hands under the hot water faucet, turn by turn, and watching them redden without yielding by so much as an "ouch." It was she who recognized self-mastery for that arch-weapon that it is, and not I, who, though now past my Indian summer, am still engaged in a struggle with it.

Nor, may I say, did my best friend evince a flicker of interest in the Facts of Life. Though, as my sister imparted them to me, sometimes in a trickle and sometimes in a headlong stream, I hastened to share them with her, she listened with polite indifference and refused to speculate about them. I remember how, on one of the long visits she paid to the Farm when you had offered us each five dollars to learn *The Rubaiyat* by heart and I, having heard that a cow was due to freshen, suggested we take out copies of *The Rubaiyat* and go sit in the barn, she simply walked away. I do not include this now in my narrative either as a confession of abnormal curiosity or because I am ashamed. If I had known then what I know now—that birth, any birth, is an incomparable drama and by all odds the closest to a proof that God exists—I would have stayed in the barn for as long as it took that cow to come to her term.

But most sharply I remember an afternoon in the city when, because you were no longer able to believe that any of my intents were pure since you had heard of the tall tales I told my schoolmates about prostitution, you threw a first shadow across my best friend's innocence by including her in your suspicions.

The windows of the room in which she and I were spending that afternoon had been closed against the rain. Though so far on our way to growing up, we still liked to make what we called houses, in trees, in corners of rooms, anywhere that suggested itself; so we had made a house apiece out of stacked-up pillows. It was hot and stuffy. We had taken off our dresses and were curled up in our slips at opposite ends of the sofa, reading aloud by turns the book of my choice, a book neither she nor I had heard of before, but one in which, because I had found it on my sister's shelves, I hoped to find love. Our faces felt flushed and we were growing restless when the door opened and you came in. For a long moment of silence, you simply stood and looked at us. Then, with tight lips and eyes ablaze, you seized our pillows and tossed them on the floor. "Get dressed at once!" you rapped out at me. To her, on a gentler note, you said: "It is time you went home." "I would like to know," you went on, as we scrambled back into our dresses, "what you have been up to." I stole a look at my best friend. She looked away. Neither she nor I ever spoke of that afternoon again. And as before, though the slime of your suspicion stuck to my memory, it was only long later, from the unsolicited confidences of a half-amused, grown-up friend, that what we might have been up to swam across my ken.

What did evoke far more than a flicker of interest from my best friend, however, and would perhaps never, or at least not for many years to come, have engaged me at all had it not been for her, was the universe. It was she who bought out of her pocket money and read aloud the little book in which was explained Einstein's theory of the relativity and simultaneity of time. It was she who suggested, as darkness fell, that we go up to the roof of that Park Avenue apartment building, from over the parapet of which in our less serious moments we used to spit and then try to see fifteen stories below us whether our spit hit the ground, to look at the depths and distances in the night sky. It was she who fired us to compose a parable of man's journey through an imaginary land, she who made the map of this land, and she who planned out the chapters. It was she, in those years when vision was as yet unobscured by the desires that befog adult eyes, who launched us both into the kind of speculation which, while doomed to die for lack of enough sustenance, nevertheless so stretches the mind along the way that it can never again be quite as small as it was at the start.

She taught me without knowing that she knew it that we were at one and the same time specks and watchtowers, slaves and masters, and what else is this, after all, but the measure of man? I cannot help but wonder, now that I no longer see her, whether she has found for herself again that place in the universe, so small in fact and so infinite in fancy, that was hers long ago.

YOU WROTE AND RECEIVED MANY LETTERS IN THE COURSE of your eighty-eight years, and with your sense of language, your unerring ear for syntax and your natural style that contrasted so oddly with the artifice of your speech, you were a master of letter writing and a judge of it. It is true that your familiarity with the essays and journals of the most didactic as well as the loftiest professional travelers sometimes trapped you into writing descriptive passages in which the molehills you passed on your way to the mountains were so laden with superlatives that your peaks, when at last you reached them, had crumbled away. But when you were writing, not from Kuala Lumpur or Auckland or New Delhi, but from home, your letters had a surprising grace of heart.

Of the letters you received, however, I find it less easy to speak. They were by no means all from family or friends. I do not fear to speak of such exalted letters as those from the poet who was your closest woman friend; of the simple, tender letters from your father (those from your mother you evidently did not keep); of the almost illegible but nonetheless magical little notes from my father (the only ones of which I found when you had died had been written before your marriage); of the sometimes professionally smooth and entertaining and sometimes wild and venomous (though always neatly penned) letters from my sister; of the breezy letters in handwritings in various stages of development

from your several grandchildren, all of which you kept;
or of the three letters from me which alone remained out
of my weekly communications to you during the six and
a half years I lived in Poland and which, when I reread
them, astounded me not because of what I had managed
to put in them but because of what I had managed to
leave out. Why should I fear to speak of all these written
acknowledgments, some long since yellowed and others
yellowing, of the ties that willy-nilly bound us to you?

It is of the other letters that I can bring myself only
with anguish to speak, of the letters you mentioned to
me seldom but with an emphasis and an awe, when you
did so, that showed you prized them most. They cannot,
therefore and alas, be ignored. Do many letters of this
kind exist? I doubt it. Paradoxical, ambivalent, explicable
only to people prepared to explain the inexplicable, these
letters were written by, and written to, yourself. Hour
after hour, year after year, sitting either in bed or at your
desk, in trains, on boats, on terraces and in hotels, you
spelled them out with what you claimed were automatically guided fingers on that Ouija board from which you
were not parted for as much as a day or a night. They
were letters from the dead. Most often, they came from
one particular friend whom you constituted as your liai-
son with the other world. But some of them came—in a
simultaneity of time so simultaneous as to startle all but
the least earthbound—from Shakespeare, Beethoven, and
Henry and William James. And others, on a very few occasions, I concede, came, you were apparently certain,
from One whom you designated simply as "A" but Who,
from their context, could have been none other than the
Almighty Himself—though which Almighty I cannot
say, since who your God was you never defined.

Were you really so engrossed with the hereafter as

you did not hesitate to claim? Were you really so certain that from the portals of death you would need only a step to reach some Valhalla where all the choicest spirits, or at least all the spirits of your choice, freed from their scarred carcasses, still kept their identity undisseminated and intact? Had you really, beneath your fretful and seemingly almost uncontrollable anxiety about the death of your body, such a warm certainty about the survival of your soul? Have I then been guilty, in the excess of unease and embarrassment that your belief in your extrasensory perceptions caused me, of a blinder injustice to you than the blindest of your injustices to me? Perhaps I ought to have kept my door open to your experience, rather than slamming it in your face.

If I measure my attitude against my father's, that I failed you is quite plain. How hard it must have been for him, I can only surmise. But whether or not he thought you were in flight from the realities around you; whether or not he believed you to have made use of a mechanism to escape into a world where nothing was demanded of you but which at the same time would give your authority a weight you could not otherwise have claimed; whether or not he understood better than you what you were doing when you transmitted messages, explanations, and even orders from the dead—my father never showed you or anyone with whom you shared your strange preoccupation, by so much as the echo of a smile, a single doubt. I am inclined to believe that this was on his part a perfect example of the noble duplicity of love.

Perhaps, if you had gone about sharing with me in some other way this world you obviously preferred to ours, I might not have unalterably stiffened against it. But when, on that tour of Italy which was the only jour-

ney I ever made alone with you, you consulted the Ouija
board wherever we went as to all that concerned me
from my right to buy a Florentine gown to my right to
be engaged to a Polish aristocrat, was it not logical that
I should resent the board? And was it not inevitable that
I should hate it when, one evening in a hotel in Venice, I
returned to my room to find you standing with the love
letters you had taken from my drawer and you fell into
a fury with me for having "allowed" such letters to be
written and then, after telling me that I had killed you
(that was one of the first times you made use of death
against me, O my Cassandra), locked yourself in your
room while I stood—was it minutes or hours?—in that
hotel corridor begging to be let in and I saw as at last
you opened to me that you had been consulting the
board again? It seems to me now that, if having found
that by terror you could manipulate as stubborn a creature as me, you had voluntarily laid down your arms, I
too might have laid down mine. Or am I once again seeking in rationalization some solace for a loss I should be
blaming alone upon myself? Where is the truth, supposing that in such imponderables as these the truth exists?
The new priests of personality may well have an answer. But I, whose religion, if I have one, stands on the
mystery of the soul, say frankly that I do not know.

I am not speaking, at this point in my narrative, of
what for so long I have held to be unspeakable merely on
impulse or out of malice, but from necessity. Now that
I am about to retrace the road I was henceforward to
walk alone, I must make sure, or as sure as my selective,
biased, still raw memory will let me, that I have dug up
all the ancient sites of our misunderstanding. I am aware
that in this dialogue in which I do the speaking for us
both, I take what some might call cruel advantage. But to

be fair, you would have had to admit that I have said little so far that I did not try, and try often, to say to you viva voce (how insufferable my attempted explanations were to you, I know, for nothing is more insufferable than an exacerbated ego to the ego that exacerbates it). From now on, however, my road was to be largely hid from you, although it never took me as far from you as I thought it was taking me and, after describing an arc so prolonged that it seemed to remove me beyond your reach for good, it led me back to the point where I had started.

Whether, as I have alternately sped or dragged myself along my road, it has been my conscious, subconscious, or unconscious self that chose the turnings; whether my stars have in concourse concocted this road for me; or whether in its obscure but undoubtedly infinite wisdom Providence has worked out what It knew would be the only way to teach so unteachable a creature, I refuse to guess. I am not a necessitarian. I admit that we have no more than what is given us at the start. But what I will not admit is that we cannot do what we choose with it, any more than I will admit that the drunkard cannot turn down his first empty glass. We are more than the pots the potter shapes on his wheel, and it is this more for which we can and must be held accountable. However, at the start of the road, it was neither I, nor my stars, nor Providence, but simply you who set me on my way.

"CONGRATULATIONS," READ YOUR TELEGRAM, "ON ADMISSION to boarding school this fall. Come home at once."

It was a Labor Day weekend when the telegram came, and I had been discussing with my best friend and the girl we were both visiting in an Adirondack lodge what to do with the crisp afternoon ahead of us.

"Did you want to go?" asked my best friend, frowning. I shook my head. She recognized as readily as I the word "congratulations" for the device that it was. Nevertheless, as you well knew when you wired me, there was nothing I could do but go.

Looked at from your point of view, boarding school was the obvious solution to the problem I had by that time become. You had tried me out in four day schools, the last of which, diametrically differing from its fashionable predecessor, was considered wildly experimental, though of its experimentalism all I now remember is the experiment my chemistry teacher made upon me by refusing to help put out a fire I had started with my Bunsen burner and the experiments that the boys (chief innovation so far as I was concerned) carried out in my locker, with brews of hydrogen sulphide and odes to my eyes. It was at that school that the headmaster, appointee of a learned foundation and hence infallible, told you at the end of my only year there that I was not born to lead. It was, in fact, never clear to the heads of the schools I attended, nor indeed to you, nor for that matter to me either, for what I had been born, and I suspect that only in the case of gurus, saints, and victorious generals can one ever be clear on that point. On the day when, diploma in hand, I was to put schools behind me for good, the last of those awesome figures ever to rule over me said, in parting: "You will come into your garden late in life—if at all." In presupposing the existence and accessibility of gardens, she went farther than I have ever gone.

Another, and to you no doubt the most convincing reason for putting me away, so to speak, behind those distinguished walls, was that my sister and the young man whose picture she had been keeping under her pillow and whom no amount of distraction and dissuasion could make her forget, had been married in a war wedding three days before he was to join the American Expeditionary Force in France. Did either she or you ever know, I wonder, that in the midst of preparing for that wedding I heard her ask you: "Does that child have to be there?" Had either of you known that I overheard her, would you have understood or cared how deeply those word stung? He had come safely home again, not too many months later. Now a baby, as you would have put it, was on the way. Taking this Fact of Life into consideration, together with my unconcealed interest in it, how fitting it was, from your point of view, that I should be sent away.

"I CAN CALL SPIRITS FROM THE VASTY DEEP," MY GRAND-mother used to quote, a gleam in her pale Swedish eyes, and then answer herself with an ironic smile: "But will they come?"

Mine is no vasty deep, but a narrow and cramped one, and I am only afraid, as I begin to call the spirits I have consigned to it, that they will scramble out all at once and so overwhelm me with the remembrance of things past that I will find myself unable to choose from among them those whom I must attempt to reincarnate for you and those whom, from this vantage of retrospect, it looks as though I had best, after all, discard. If moreover, as is maintained not only by our modern fishermen but by the ancient fishermen on whom they depend for nearly all they know, my deep has a life of its own, with its own submarine battles for power and prestige, I may

be shocked to discover that the spirits I summon follow
another order of priority than the one I recognize. Indeed, already, so soon after embarking on my narrative,
I have begun to suspect which of the spirits in my deep
will prove to have been all along in power. Yet I still
hope, I still like to believe, that my suspicions are unfounded.

I have referred to my first, my real, my forever-to-
be-remembered love, and I so named him who was one
day to become the father of my children in good faith,
for I remember that as soon as I came to love him, my
earlier loves fell out of my consciousness headlong, without a sound. But how I then felt I could only have told
you, had I ever been able to tell you what I was feeling,
at that time. Now all I can say is what I feel at this moment about what I felt then. Between then and now,
across the floodtide of experience, the bridge I am building serves the one-way traffic of memory. If, in the eye
of eternity, the past, present and future are reflected
simultaneously as one, in my poor field of vision the past
is so mantled in the present and the future so obscured
by it that, like an insect, I can span but a single day.
Therefore, remembering back still further and in equally
good faith to the time before I had met my first, my real
love—to the time before there was supposed to be any
question for me of that kind of love—I will have to recognize that I had another love which was not unlike the
love I was not supposed to be ready for, in the sense that,
although I demanded nothing from it except the right
and privilege to serve, I gave to it all my hope.

Was it love at first sight for her, standing there in her
orange sweater, her smooth iron-gray hair fastened tight
at the neck with a brown velvet bow, the not altogether
friendly flame leaping up in her eyes, and her voice so

dry that it almost crackled as, facing the row of new girls in her classroom, she said: "I suppose you all know as much Latin as you need to know, already?" Or was it when, before the end of that hour, I read aloud a Latin sentence with a Spanish accent and she quelled the laughter this provoked with a glance, that I fell in love with her? I no longer remember. What I do remember, however, and what, had you known it, must surely have given you a few of those wakeful nights with which mothers, even I suspect the least devoted of them, pay for being mothers, is that during the two years I was at boarding school there was not a lesson I prepared, not a hymn I learned, not a ball I ricocheted or plumped neatly into the basket, not a poem I composed (for of course, once away from my family, I tried to become a poet too), not a last swift thought before I slept, not in fact a beat of my heart that was not dedicated with my whole being to that sarcastic, middle-aged Latin teacher.

But I was not as innocent, when I first committed myself to this love, as I would prefer now to think. There had been, after all, those nights in the tent by a Maine lake when I had discovered in my restlessness that the counselor in the next cot was awake too and had buried my face in her abundant gold hair, and during a successive summer in that same camp the wholesome routine of which was evidently not the right prescription for what ailed me, another counselor whose hand I had pressed in the dark. No, on this evidence, I was not innocent, unless the impulse, as inextricable from the heart as from the head, can be called innocent no matter where it leads. I am almost certain, though in this I know how totally, and I might even add how instinctively, you would have disagreed, that the impulse to love is neither innocent nor non-innocent, that it exists outside the moral sphere, and that only by the uses to which it is put can it be judged.

But if I am to judge my passion for my teacher in boarding school by the uses to which I put it, I still would be unable today, in the full knowledge of the range not only of my own but of many other passions, either to exonerate or condemn. For I put my passion to many uses, all the way from reading, on my own initiative and in order to stretch my mind to meet hers, the *Metamorphoses* of Ovid, to surmounting my horror enough for her sake to remove a mouse from its trap in her room; all the way from sitting up half the night in my closet after lights were supposed to be out to correct examination papers for her, to kneeling by her chair in her little, orange-curtained room and murmuring over and over, as I leaned against her, the "I love you" that I heard myself saying for the first time. There was nothing, absolutely nothing, that I would not do for my teacher, I was certain. Yet the time came, and why I did not see it coming I shall never understand, unless this lack of foresight was in itself my innocence, when she made, very gently, very tentatively, a demand upon me to which I could not respond and which, to give her credit for the subtlety and generosity she was capable of, she never made again. It was later, when I had ceased to be a schoolgirl and had become a college woman, that I learned from a classmate enamored of Sappho the name by which my teacher, unknown to me, had perhaps been known.

HAD YOU READ THIS FAR, YOU WOULD SURELY HAVE NOticed and no doubt pointed out that I seem far too often to have discovered the meaning of what I was doing only long after it was done. You would, of course, have been right. For hopefully as I search my memory, I cannot unearth a single one of the Lessons of Life (those reverse sides of the Facts of Life) that I learned, when I managed to learn them at all, in any other way than by direct experience. "Do as I say," you used to tell me, "not as I do." But it is not from what our authorities tell us that we learn, but rather unconsciously from what they do, more often than not, from what they themselves do unconsciously. And how seldom we emulate their best. But if they pick their noses, lose their tempers, give in to irrational compulsions, betray one another or betray us, we are almost certain to find ourselves sooner or later, with or without provocation, doing the same. If it is difficult enough to profit by our own experience, it seems to be quite impossible—not just for the shilly-shalliers but for everyone—to profit by that of others. A weightier argument against the belief that God has created us in His Image could hardly be found. For surely an Imagination seminal enough to have invented such an infinite variety of living substance—the elephant and the atom, the amoeba and the man—would not have repeated throughout the ages, *ad absurdum* and *ad nauseam*, the same mistakes. How can we hold poor God, Whom we beseech in behalf of ourselves in the very acts we must suppose most unacceptable to Him, Whom each side of opposing forces beseeches on the eve of battle for a victory which would destroy the other, responsible for our monumental, truly extraordinary incapacity to learn, an incapacity so irrational that to call it His handiwork is blasphemy? Unless, of course, God has foreseen, and by making us so unteachable has forestalled, the eventuality that if we could learn by experience the day might come when there was nothing left for us to learn and thus bring an end to His whole experiment.

SOME, HOWEVER, ARE BETTER ABLE TO LEARN FROM EXperience than others. I do not refer alone to those supernaturally or just naturally illumined saints and prophets who constitute our justification for claiming more likeness than tigers and jackals to God. I refer also, and not only unabashedly but with pride, to those throughout recorded time who have made use of their education to recognize the forest from the trees it encompasses, to deduce, to synthesize, to assemble the parts of their vision and make it whole. Of such, there is a long and honorable genealogy. If, separately or together, they have not succeeded, no matter what their weapons, in razing the wall of our common stupidity, they have breached it, here and there, and now and then, just often enough to keep us, so far at least, from an emasculating and hence mortal despair of our educability.

Among all the men and women I have known, none, I believe, put more emphasis than you and my father on education. It is true that in the play my father wrote together with your friend, the lady poet, he saw us chained to three balls of equal weight: heredity, health, and environment. But the cornerstone of his philosophy was his belief in our educability. "There is no habit," he told me, "that cannot be broken in two weeks, if you work at it every waking moment." "There is no one," he said, "without talent. It need only be sought to be found." And in his little book, *Creative Re-Education*, he showed again and again by example that not only upon the plasticity of childhood but upon the petrification of age, not only upon the sound but upon the already damaged personality, education can be grafted and bear fruit. He was, by profession, more aware than most of human folly. Yet he believed in mankind.

And as for you, who were inclined both by nature and by my father's tempering of the wind to an even less sceptical view of humanity, you put education on a veritable pedestal before which you were always ready to bow your head. What else was it but your unquestioning faith in education that spurred you to work for those causes of woman suffrage and child health that you espoused so wholeheartedly as to almost empty my father's pockets for them? What else was it, for instance, but your veneration for learning that enabled you, when once you asked a Nobel prize-winning physicist how he measured the speed of light, to listen in silence while he gently, but inexorably, explained for the rest of the afternoon? Or, to take the opposite extreme, what else was it but that same respect for the educational process that made you always willing, even when it was wholly counter to your convenience, to listen to me recite a lesson or a poem? Both to you and to my father, education was knowledge itself.

Never before in history, I suppose, had the acquisition of knowledge for its own sake seemed so surely the key not just to progress but to happiness as at the turn of this century, when you and my father were planning an education for my sister and me. Science had flung open the gates of impossibility. Deserts were to be made to flower; pestilence was to be wiped out; the bandy legs and dropsied bellies of the hungry nine-tenths of the human race were to vanish; literacy was to be removed from the sphere of privilege and extended to everyone, at least to everyone white and Christian; children were to be born on order like custom-made dresses; labor was at last to receive proportionate respect and reward; war was to be reasoned out of existence; and God was no longer to be sought outside and beyond, but within, ourselves. Essentially, it had been concluded, men were good. The evil they did stemmed only from ignorance. The iron that was to flatten out the great furrows on the world's brow was knowledge. And so in knowledge, you and my father put your trust.

You yourselves were both, by any standard, knowledgeable, and so by your own definition, educated. Moreover, except in the field of my father's special competence, his knowledge and yours—of nature, of man's history and handiwork—were not unequal. Yet while my father's knowledge irradiated his vision, yours, which you knew so well how to exhibit and impart, seems to have shed no light on your own. Must there not therefore be something outside of knowledge, some tool without which knowledge is barren? Might it not be this something else that turns out after all to be the key to salvation? For it is clear that by knowledge alone we are not saved.

My father, I think, would have agreed that such a tool exists, though in his selflessness, in his objectivity, he would not even have known, let alone claimed, that he had this tool himself. You, on the other hand, would have insisted that to light more light must be added, that to know must be enough to live. And how diligently you sought to know more. Often, I found my father sitting up in bed at night with a paper-backed Western, such as *Bring Me His Ears*, concealed within the learned tome he held propped on his belly. But you, in your room across the hall, I never found reading anything that would not be conceded educated fare. Indeed, every night in your life, even at the end of it when for you to see the printed words required not only a special lamp at your bedside and special lenses in your glasses but a magnifying glass with a light bulb attached to it, you read yourself, if not to sleep, then to exhaustion. You had some knowledge about nearly everything. Yet it was not to you that people turned. It was not to you but to my father that derelicts and friends and strangers, maids, chauffeurs, doormen, gardeners and farmers, aunts, uncles, and cousins; the several sons-in-law with whom my sister and I provided him; my sister until she wrenched herself away; and I, until the last moment I was ever to see him, turned for the help, as often intangible as tangible, that he did not fail to give. But it was not his knowledge that drew us to him, not his knowledge that enabled him to help.

Yet I am too much your daughter still, as well as his, to belittle knowledge. If it was only later that I came to value the kind that you and my father, in his way, valued so much, I began nevertheless as far back as I can remember to search for the kind I felt the need of for myself. It was not for nothing that I was born to readers. Cortez could scarcely have had a wilder surmise than I, on the day, long before I first went to school, when it swept over me that HEN-PEN spelled Hen-Pen and TURKEY-LURKEY spelled Turkey-Lurkey. The sea to which Hen-Pen and Turkey-Lurkey were the gateway is bottomless and has no bounds. Just as no one could wrest that book from my hand till I had finished it, so no friend, no lover, no one with the possible exception of my children, has ever as naturally and ineluctably captured my attention as whatever book I happen to have in hand. But, of course, I see at once the gap in my logic. A book is a part of, but not necessarily synonymous with, knowledge, as knowledge is a part of, but not necessarily synonymous with, education.

Even today, a book need not be good to capture me. But for a long time, for as long as I had not experienced what I was reading about, a book, to capture me, had to be about love. Yet books about love were conspicuous mostly for their absence on the shelves of the family library. Had there been, on those shelves, *The Rosary*, *V. V.'s Eyes*, and *Lavender and Old Lace*—romances I eventually read in a rented summer house and found sweeter than any lollypop I had thus far licked—I would probably not have been compelled in desperation to read the poetry of the Brownings, Ernest Dowson, John Donne, Swinburne, George Meredith, and Matthew Arnold (it mattered little to me which), and even Shakespeare's sonnets, for the food of love. It was fruitless to look among the sober bindings that encased Macaulay, Ruskin, Plato, and William James for love stories. Among the few contemporary novels we possessed were those of Galsworthy, largely because he had named "The White Monkey" after a Chinese picture in our house. It was equally fruitless to expect to find what I wanted in the *Atlantic Monthly*, the *New Republic*, or *Asia*, the latest copies of which always lay neatly ranged on the library table. And it was also fruitless to suppose that either you or my father were, or had ever been, or would for a moment understand my being absorbed in the question of love. But if my attempts to find a source for the Facts of Life in your library were fruitless, how much more so was any attempt of yours to distract me with Scott or Dickens or Irving or Cooper or Oliver Wendell Holmes. Once when I complained to my father, in the presence of all our books, that there was "nothing to read," he went to the shelves and took down *The Shaving of Shagpat*. "I think you will find this exciting enough," he said, with a glint in his smile. I never asked him for something to read again. No doubt an analyst would say that it was because of this disillusionment that I have never yet brought myself to read *Pilgrim's Progress, Robinson Crusoe,* or *Gulliver's Travels,* all of which at one time or another my father proffered me. To these, even now, I suspect I would still prefer *Dusty Answer* and *The Green Hat.*

But if I mortified you, and sometimes intentionally, with the bubbles of literary opinion I blew in your direction, and if to disagree with you for disagreement's sake always tempted me and, though you are gone, tempts me still, at this point in my narrative and on this subject of books where there was far more than a mere possibility that our minds might meet, I will not pretend that I consider *Dusty Answer* and *The Green Hat* Olympian. All I say is that such novels, which you would no more have considered reading than you would have considered reading pornography, set off in me an echo that has never quite died away. And in saying this, I am only trying to establish that I do not believe that it is always and inevitably the purest, the loftiest, or the most authentic voices in literature that speak most directly to the heart. Nor, for that matter, is it always or even necessarily from the masterpieces of art or music that we receive these shocks of recognition which break the surface of our consciousness, ripple across it in ever widening circles, and then drop beneath it to change, if only by a fraction, the contours of the subconscious for good. They can stem from the light some unknown painter has caught on a face or a parasol as well as from the El Greco Apocalypse, from some refrain or shred of popular tune as well as from a Beethoven symphony. To call this taste is not to define or explain it. To ascribe it

to education is absurd. No amount of education or accumulated knowledge can create this capacity for shock,
if it is lacking. What prompts the shock does not matter.
It is the shock itself that counts.

My father, asked what is the object of education,
would probably have answered: to serve mankind. To
the same question, you would undoubtedly have said: to
know and to behave. By neither of these definitions, as
indeed by no official definition I have ever heard, could I
be said to be truly educated. Yet I do not concede that I
am not.

It would be no mere presumption on my part but outright madness to measure my little Latin and less Greek,
my academic gropings, against the trained minds I know.
Compared to their orderly interiors, in which one well-
furnished room succeeds another with never an anach-
ronism of style or a hodge-podge of misplaced bibelots,
mine is a mere tent pitched on an oasis in the shifting
sands of irrelevancy and housing only what I need for
the night. It is as hopeless for me to try to measure what
I know against what I do not know as for me to try to
compute the stars. And while this would probably also
be true of all but that handful of practical visionaries
who have actually computed them (and these have found
out that their task has scarcely begun), it is truer of me
than it is of most. It is therefore not by measuring myself upward toward those above me that I can establish my claim. On the other hand, to look down at those
clustered below is dangerously easy and misleading.
What would it prove, if I were to point out that I speak
five languages whereas they do not; that I know by
heart *The Rubaiyat* as well—incidentally—as a number
of better poems, whereas they may not; that I am paid
for my literary guesses, while they are not; that I can

harangue and hold an audience (not in the palm of my hand, to be sure, but by the skin of my teeth), whereas they cannot; that I am beginning both to grasp and relish an abstract thought, whereas perhaps they do not? It proves nothing, unless to be able to make a wearable shoe when one is given the last, the material, and full instructions, is proof of education.

If you had asked me by what right I dare claim to be educated, and you would have asked me had you heard me make the claim, for you did not neglect either to remind me of all the opportunities you and my father had given me or of how little I had managed to profit by them (I doubt if there has ever existed a parent who forebore to send this barb, as I myself have too often sent it, winging into children's tender flesh), I would have found it hard to answer you, whom of all those I have failed I have failed the most, that I stake that claim upon my heart, and not my head.

I do not say it is a heart such as my father's. How could I say so, in view of how often it has flagged, pouted, shrieked, betrayed, and turned to stone? But if a heart can lift as swiftly at the sight of an alley cat as at the sea's moon-silvered roll, if it can respond as immediately to a debasing confession as to one of love, if it can feel even for a moment the pinch of another's misery as it feels its own, if it can rise to danger and also knit the dust, if it can both bleed and refuse to bleed, if it can recognize and wrestle with its rancors, if it expands before the spectacle of the smallest heroism to include the heroism attained by all who simply live, if it quails more before the death of others than before its own, it can be called an educated heart. For these are the uses of education. There are fewer such hearts, I am convinced, than there are heads stuffed with knowledge.

And my heart, I am struggling to make certain, will end as one of these.

IN THE HEADINESS THAT COMES FROM THIS EXCURSION into memory, I must not so lose myself among countless and contradictory conclusions that I forget to carry out what I conceive to be my purpose—namely, to explain (now that I need fear no reprisal) as objectively as I can how and why I did what I have done and how and why others have done to me as they did. There are many pitfalls to this task, some obvious, and others well hid. Into some of them I am conscious of already having stumbled, though I think so far I have managed to claw my way out again without altogether losing either my compass or my truth. But pitfall after ever more treacherous pitfall lies ahead and none can be skirted since the road I took is the only one I can retravel.

The road of memory is, of course, dotted with milestones, but it is not distance that they are set to mark. Some of my milestones are so far apart that I wonder, since in those intervals I appear to have noted nothing, whether perhaps I slept as I walked. Others, as close together as the stones in a family graveyard, constrain me to linger over the inscription on each one. And of these the most thickly set, on a longer part of the road than I like to confess, are the milestones of what, for want of the words to describe its varied and by no means always kindred hues, I must designate as love.

My love for love had led me blindfolded, and very soon after I could walk by myself, to the edge of a cliff from which, still guided by instinct, I had turned back in time. Until then, however, the love I found I had not consciously sought. It was after that that my search began.

I remember, how well I remember, though with my head and not my heart, the beginning of that search. Fittingly enough for a day when properly brought-up New York girls were kept not only from tempting young men but even, save in the presence of their elders, from meeting them until the day they were launched for society's inspection, I had my first, longed-for opportunity to taste, surreptitiously and briefly, of the experience for which I was sure at the time and indeed until relatively recently that I had been born, on the night of my own coming-out party in our house.

We had moved into that house at the start of the prosperous 1920s and with the two lots it preempted, which doubled the width of the usual city house, it gave you the scope to create what was agreed by all who came to it to be your masterpiece. That it was a masterpiece of its kind was never before or again more obvious, however, than on that night when the rugs had been taken off the brilliant parquet floor of the long front room, the stiff folds of the Chinese silk curtains had been drawn across the tall windows on the street, and the standing lamps at the four corners shed through their lotus-shaped, up-turned shades a diffused and lovely light upon the blue Kwanyin over the mantelpiece (which replaced in importance the copy of Tintoretto's Bacchus, long since relegated to my father's office), upon the other less breath-taking but even subtler Chinese paintings on the pale walls, upon the ivories, bronzes, and porcelains unobtrusively placed here and there on small tables pushed back to make space for the dancers, and upon the handsome faces (handsome, because young) of my guests, most of whom I did not even know by name, but whom

you had culled with due consideration from the lists kept
by social secretaries for this purpose.

I might easily have forgotten the dress I wore that
night, as I have forgotten many I liked better, were it not
for the fact that I had for once been allowed to have
a say in the choice of it. I had bought it in Paris
the summer before, with the advice and consent of a
worldly companion, and I had thought that, though it was
not what you would have called artistic (it was ivory-
colored, made of velvet, and shaped, with its mildly
scooped neck and no sleeves, like a distinguished nightgown), you approved. But when, the night before the
party, I came down from college, I found that you had
had sewed into it a pair of long lace sleeves. If the tears
of fury that caused me to wake up on the day of my
debut with a puffy, distorted face seem as uncalled for to
anyone else as they seemed to you but do not even yet
quite seem to me, let whoever has had to face the
thought of appearing in sleeves before a sleeveless world
throw the first stone. "You will see," you had answered
my protests. "If you lead the way, others will follow."

That might perhaps have been true in the town and in
the time where you were born and where, as the daughter of a leading citizen, you may well have set the fashion in dress as you set the fashion for Browning. But
this was New York, and who, after all, was I? And who,
for that matter were you, or my sister, or even my father, in New York society—except one more family assembled from other places and other rooms, and trying
to make this place, this room, our own?

It was not my tears, as indeed it had not been nor
would ever be my tears, that changed your mind. But
your mind was changed. An acquaintance of yours was
the one to change it. "How much prettier the dress is

with those sleeves," she said to you, soothingly. "What a pity fashions change. But after all, dear lady, we must swim with the times. You would not want your daughter," she added, smiling, "to look odd."

So my bony arms were bared like the others, and despite the ravages to my face (since ravages, at eighteen, are relative), and also because I was after all the hostess, I had someone to dance with every moment of the time. But there was only one young man who kept coming back, kept cutting in on my partners, kept leading me away from the rest of the dancers and into the shadows of the hall where I was almost certain he was holding me closer and almost certain his mouth was on my hair. The older people along the walls and in the library had left. The drawing room gradually emptied of dancers. The musicians took up their instruments and disappeared. My father, for whom the whole evening had been a test of endurance, had vanished. The extra servants had been paid off, our own maids had gone upstairs. You must have thought the last guest had departed, for you were nowhere to be seen when I led the young man who had made no move to say good night down into the darkened kitchen for a familiar, wholesome glass of milk, between sips of which I discovered in myself an unfamiliar, but perhaps not altogether unwholesome appetite for being kissed. Remembering my sister, I had closed my eyes until, with the sharpened sense of the quarry, I opened them again to see my father standing in the door. "I just came down," he said, with a smile, "to look in the icebox." He did not even know, and he knew that I knew that he did not know, where the icebox was. But he was to make more than one nocturnal visit to it before the end of my vacation when my young man and I had to part.

When today I see my daughter effortlessly draw to her, by a mere flutter of the long thick lashes which she did not inherit from me, the most supercilious young men, and when I see with what comfortably maternal and domestic arts girls fasten unto themselves my son, I look back in amazement upon the uncertainties and anxieties that accompanied my search for love. It was not that I capered inanely or tried with false blandishments to gather scalps (I was not the scalper but the scalped), for coyness had by that time gone out as a method of conquest—north of the Mason-Dixon line. But I still felt compelled, like generations of women before me, to pretend. The only difference was that the pendulum of pretense had swung the other way. Instead of pretending ignorance and innocence, I had to pretend sophistication; instead of pretending helplessness, I had to pretend never to need help. Instead of appearing soft, I had to appear hard; instead of elusive, direct; instead of timorous, bold and brave. I could swear, smoke, drive a car, discuss passion, go to nightclubs, and exchange kisses (though my slippers never stuck out of the taxi window as I had seen other slippers sticking out) on the ride home through the Park. These were not privileges, however; they were imperatives. It was not enough to have been emancipated. One had to prove, so it seemed, that one was free.

Fittingly enough in that day of general acceleration, we of my generation, or at least we of my city and my place in that city, were trying to be what we called fast. To have been fast only a few years earlier might still have been a risk, but by then to be slower than fast was to be too slow to count. A girl such as I could no longer afford not to be, or not to appear to be fast, unless she could face being stranded on ballroom floors when there was no longer a row of chaperones among whom to take shelter and the only recourse from standing alone was to hide in the ladies' room and try not to let the gimlet eyes of other girls detect the humiliation. Not to have developed this style, or at least a passable imitation of it, would be to have joined battle on the high seas in a sailboat when all other ships were ironclad.

But you could not have been aware, I am sure, since no older generation is ever aware until too late, that my striving for worldliness—my rouged cheeks, my then almost unheard of scarlet nails, and the wicked touch of Roget et Gallet's pink lipstick (kept hidden at the back of my dressing-table drawer)—was no more than a token indication of the powerful social current in which I was being swept along. What you could have been aware of, however, and I have not ceased to be surprised that, considering your suspicions, you were not, was the number of lies I put myself in the position of having to tell. When I said that I had been brought home by the youth who, perhaps just because of his blotches, you so often appointed as my escort, you seemed to believe me. When I said that I had not left the party I was supposed to be attending, whereas in fact I had been dancing in Harlem cheek to cheek with some youth you had never seen, you also seemed to believe me. Even when, early one morning, you met me at the top of the stairs still wearing, to be sure, the headdress of artificial grapes you had insisted that I wear to look—as you said—poetic, but with all the grapes on one side of my head now crushed in, and I told you that I had fallen down, you seemed to believe that too. And indeed, when I said I had fallen down, I had said not the literal but the real truth. For not just on that occasion, but on many, in that first winter of my emancipation, I had made certain that there was no one, or at any rate no one tall enough and sober

(I have always hated drunks) who wanted to kiss me whom I did not kiss. By your standards, to kiss was in itself to fall down. By mine, falling down was the use of a kiss to purchase what I saw as social survival.

I used to think, with my unfailing flexibility in self-excuse, that it was because you mistrusted me that I lied. But I feel constrained to admit that, even when you apparently did trust me, I went on lying. I used to think, because you consulted about me behind my back and because I often caught you manipulating me, that I had to lie out of self-defense. But now, belatedly, after having found that although I have made a point of not lying to my children and not plotting any more than was imperative behind their backs, they have in turn lied and continue as a matter of course to lie to me, I conclude that there is no other way to allay the instinctive suspicion between the generations, at least until both are old, except with lies. For the lie, and perhaps the lie alone, however ugly it is in theory, however offensive in the eye of God, enables the old to withhold as they feel they must and the young to discover as they feel they must the Facts of Life.

IT HAS OFTEN STRUCK ME IN RETROSPECT, THOUGH OF course at the time it did not strike me, that for you, with your deep-scored fear of the sensual, to have chosen out of all the poetry you knew *The Rubaiyat* for me and my best friend to learn by heart when we were twelve was so far beyond irony that it must have been an accident. Was it possible that you saw only the pretty metaphors, heard only the tinkling cadences in Fitzgerald's approximations of the Persian's naughty thought? Is it conceivable that you, who yourself deliberately let every rosebud you might have gathered wither on its stem, could have missed the bee-stung lust in those honeyed lines? More likely, you simply told yourself, as you handed us the book, that it mattered little what we incanted providing we underwent the discipline of incantation.

For pride's sake, I will not say that the coy and leering vade mecum of those verses insinuated itself into my soul. Besides, that particular message does no more than weakly echo the roar in all fresh blood. But what you could not know, of course, was how smoothly the Victorian Fitzgerald was to lead into an American Fitzgerald of my own vintage under whose banner we adolescents were to come, if not of age, then into a bright, taut semblance of it. I do not suppose you ever heard of F. Scott Fitzgerald, living or dead, and moreover I do not suppose that, even if you had, his legend would have seemed to you to warrant more than a cluck of disapproval. Neither his appetites, his exacerbations, nor his despair were kin to yours. He might have been the man in the moon for all you could have understood him. But he was no man in the moon to me. Although his tender nights were not the ones I dreamed of, nor was it for yachts, sports cars, tall drinks, and swimming pools, nor yet for money or what money buys that I burned, I too was burning and watching myself burn. The flame was simply of a different kind. It was symbolized (at least for those of us who recognized ourselves in the image) by that self-consuming, elegiac candle of Edna St. Vincent Millay's, that candle which from the quatrain where she ensconced it became a beacon to us, but which in point of fact would have had to be as tall as a funeral taper to last even the evening, let alone the night. One should not, of course, pluck the head off a flower and expect its perfume to linger on. Yet this passion for passion, now that I look back on it with passion spent, seems somewhat overblown and operatic, though as a diva Miss Millay perfectly controlled her notes. Only what else was she singing but the old Song of Songs, that most ancient of tunes that nature plays with such unfailing response upon young nerves? Perhaps this is not so little. Perhaps the mere fact that by plucking on the nerves nature can awaken in the most ordinary of us, temporarily anyway, the sleeping poet, and in poets can discover their immortality, is the most remarkable of all the remarkable phenomena to which we can attest? One can see it as humiliating that an extra hormone casually fed into our chemistry may induce us to lay down our lives for a lover or a friend; one can take it as no more than another veil torn from the mystery of the soul. But it could also be looked at from the other end of the spectrum. One could see this chemical determinant as in itself a miracle. In any case, Miss Millay's sweet-throated bitterness, her variations on the theme that the world was not only well lost for love but even well lost for lost love, her constant and wonderfully tragic posture, so unlike that of Fitzgerald since it required no scenery or props, drew from the me that I was when I fell upon her verses an overwhelming yea.

But all this, I am well aware, is the *bel canto* of love, and although I have always liked to think that it was to the *bel canto* and to that alone that I listened, I know well enough that it was not. If I am to speak the whole truth about my knowledge of love, I will have to stop trying to emulate the transcendant nightingale. There is another side of love, more nearly symbolized by the croak of the mating capercailzie, or better still perhaps by the mute antics of the slug.

Whether you experienced the passion of desire I have, of course, no way of knowing, nor indeed have I wished with even the most fleeting fragment of a wish to know, for the fact that one constitutes by one's mere existence so to speak the proof of some sort of passion makes any speculation upon this part of one's parents' experience more immodest, more scandalizing, more deeply unwelcome than an obscenity from a stranger. I recoil from the very thought. At the same time, I am aware that my recoil could be interpreted by readers of the tea leaves at the bottom of my psyche as an incestuous sign, since theirs is a science of paradox: if one hates, they say it is because one loves; if one bullies, they say it is because one is afraid; if one shuns, they say it is because one desires; and according to them, whatever one fancies one feels, what one feels in fact is the opposite. Well, normally abnormal or normally normal, neurotic or merely fastidious (do the tea-leaf readers, by the way, allow psyches to have moral taste?), I have never wanted to know what you knew of passion.

YOU PROBABLY WOULD NOT REMEMBER, SINCE YOU NEVER seemed to remember even the same moments as I, much less their intensity, one sunny midday on Fifth Avenue when you had set out with me for some final shopping less than a week before the wedding you staged for me with such reluctance at the Farm. I can see us now. We had been walking quite briskly, for despite your being so small and me so tall, your stride in those days could easily match mine. We had stopped before a shop window to assess its autumnal display, when you suddenly turned to me, looking up from beneath one of your

wrong hats, and with your nervous "ahem!" said: "There
are things I must tell you about this man you are marrying which he does not know himself." If you had
screamed right there in the street where we stood, I
could not have felt more fear. With scarcely a mumble
of excuse, I fled. I fled, however, not from what might
have been the natural fear of being unable to disguise
from you that the things about my bridegroom—in the
sense you meant the word "things"—which you had been
galvanizing yourself to tell me as a painful part of your
maternal duty were things which I had already insisted
upon finding out for myself (despite, I may now say,
the unspeakable awkwardness of making the discovery
on principle, yes, on principle, and in cold blood) because I was resolved, as a modern woman, not to be a
mollycoddle waiting for Life but to seize Life by the
throat. I had developed too foolproof a façade to be
afraid of self-betrayal. What I fled from was my fear of
what, unwittingly, you might betray, without meaning
to, about my father and yourself.

But I can see from this latest trick of memory how
much more arbitrary and influential it is than the will.
While my memory holds with relentless tenacity, as I
cannot too often stress, to my wrongs, when it comes to
my shames, it gestures and jokes and toys with chronology like a prestidigitator in the hope of distracting me
from them. Just as I was about to enlarge upon my discovery of the underside of the leaf of love, memory, dis-
pleased at being asked to yield its unsavory secrets,
dashed ahead of me, calling back over its shoulder:
"Skip it. Cut it out." But I will not skip it or cut it out. It
is not my intention in this narrative to picture myself as
a helpless victim moored to the rock of experience and
left to the buffetings of chance. If to be innocent is to be

helpless, then I had been—as are we all—helpless at
the start. But the time came when I was no longer innocent and therefore no longer helpless. Helpless in that
sense I can never be again. However, I confess my hope
that I will be innocent again, not with a pristine, acci-
dental innocence, but rather with an innocence achieved
by the slow cutting away of the flesh to reach the bone.

For innocence, of all the graces of the spirit, is I believe the one most to be prayed for. Although it is constantly made to look foolish (too simple to come in out
of the rain, people say, who have found in the innocent
an impediment), it does not mind looking foolish because it is not concerned with how it looks. It assumes
that things are as they seem when they seem best, and
when they seem worst it overlooks them. To innocence,
a word given is a word that will be kept. Instinctively,
innocence does unto others as it expects to be done by.
But when these expectations are once too often ground
into the dust, innocence can falter, since its strength is
according to the strength of him who possesses it. The
innocence of which I speak is, I know, not incorruptible.
But I insist upon believing that even when it is lost, it
may, like paradise, be regained.

However, it was not of innocence in general that I was
speaking, but of perhaps the frailest and surely the least
important side of it which is innocence in romantic love.
Here, if anywhere, it is not wholly incontrovertible. To
you, for instance, the word innocence, in this connota-
tion, probably retained its Biblical, or should I say technical sense, and therefore I suppose I must make myself
quite clear by saying that I lost—or rather handed over
—what you would have considered to be my innocence
two weeks before I was legally entitled, and in fact by
oath required, to hand it over along with what other

goods and bads I had. But to me innocence is far less tangible. I had long since begun to lose my general innocence when I lost my trust in you, but this special innocence I lost before ever I loved, through my discovery that one could tremble with desire and even experience a flaming delight that had nothing, nothing whatever to do with friendship or liking, let alone with love. I knew this knowledge to be corrupting at the time I acquired it; today, these many years later, after all the temptations resisted or yielded to, the weasel satisfactions and the engulfing dissatisfactions since endured, I call it corrupting still.

You, I could swear to it, remained innocent in this sense until the end. Yours, but not mine, was an age in which innocence was fostered and carefully—if not perhaps altogether innocently—preserved. You had grown up at a time when the most distinguishing mark of a lady was the *noli me tangere* writ plain across her face. Moreover, because of the particular blot on your family escutcheon through what may only have been one unbridled moment on your grandmother's part, and because you had the lean-to kitchen and trundle bed of your childhood to outgrow, what you obviously most desired with both your conscious and unconscious person, what you bent your whole will, sensibility, and intelligence upon, was to be a lady. Before being daughter, wife, or mother, before being cultured (a word now bereft both socially and politically of the sheen you children of frontiersmen bestowed on it), before being sorry for the poor, progressive about public health, and prettily if somewhat imprecisely humanitarian, indeed first and foremost, you were a lady. There was, of course, more to the portrait of a lady you carried in your mind's eye than the *sine qua non* of her virtue. A lady, you made clear to me both by precept and example, never raised her voice or slumped in her chair, never failed in social tact (in heaven, for instance, would not mention St. John the Baptist's head), never pouted or withdrew or scandalized in company, never reminded others of her physical presence by unseemly sound or gesture, never indulged in public scenes or private confidences, never spoke of money save in terms of alleviating suffering, never gossiped or maligned, never stressed but always minimized the hopelessness of anything from sin to death itself. A lady kept intact her pride by her circumspect manner with her betters, her way of making her equals feel superior, and her condescension to those beneath her. A lady, that is, an enlightened, cultivated, liberal lady—the only kind to be in a time of increasing classlessness—could espouse any cause: wayward girls, social diseases, unmarried mothers, and/or birth control with impunity. But never by so much as the shadow of a look should she acknowledge her own experience with the Facts of Life.

By this definition, carved on the portals of my mind before I knew how to open them, I was not a lady at the time of which I am speaking nor am I now. But at the time toward which, despite seeming circumlocutions, I am moving in closer and closer, I cared not a fig for ladies. What I sought to make of myself, from the angle of my hats to the disposition of my kisses, was a *femme fatale*. It did not occur to me then that *femmes fatales* are not fashioned in a designer's studio, but in heaven or hell. I had to learn that they are artifacts of nature. I had to learn that no bedecking or bedizening, no sedulous aping of known models can make a young girl who wants to be loved more than to love the kind of woman for whom men gladly lay down their lives, their fortunes, and their sacred honor. The sow's ear is easier to convert than such as she.

CATECHUMENS OF THE CATHOLIC CATECHISM ARE TOLD TO avoid the circumstances of temptation, a piece of advice than which there could hardly be a cannier. Before Eve did bite into the apple, she had first to be alone with Adam under the tree where the apple grew. But I had not then been exposed to any catechism, Catholic or other, save that of your own creation, and I daresay even if I had, the promise that gleamed in those circumstances would, like the gleam in the Lorelei's hair, have swept me off the course you set. Countless as are the circumstances of temptation, however, and I have tried to count them both in literature and in life, I would be hard put to it to find any more tempting than those within a great formal city stripped down to summer dress. The heat itself is suggestive enough. Bemused couples lean against the stoops or move along the sidewalks in a dream. New wildness creeps into the children's voices. Women lean out over windowsills and gaze down into the street with vacant stares. Strangers have time to smile at one; doormen, so hostile in winter if their door is not one's own, make almost wistful comments on the weather as one goes by. The façade of the city has come down.

But it is in an empty house that temptation hums loudest in the ears. Not only the hangings and rugs have vanished, but the servants and masters too. Freedom seeps in through the windows discreetly opened behind protecting shades and wells up from sofas and chairs with their familiar contours softened and changed by light covering. The long, hot twilights separate themselves from the rest of time and reality, and images which on a brisk day or in a crowded hour one would have resolutely banished at first appearance fill one's unresisting, indeed one's tremulously welcoming mind. No calculated *mise en scène* of seduction is more sensual than sooty New York when the summer sun is down.

Anywhere, anywhere, that is, in the northern hemisphere where under its snow blanket the pine dreams always of the palm, summer is that wonder of wonders —an event that never lets one down. If it is true that summer is greener with hope for the haves (like everything else, for that matter) than for the have-nots, it is nevertheless as much better to be too hot than too cold as to be quick than dead. Summer was one of the few things you and I agreed on, since even as I, you feared and hated cold. But your summers were always privileged, whereas I have known summers that were not. Yet all the more I can say that, while there exists no unmixed blessing except as a figment of human longing, the most nearly unmixed of blessings, not the least blessed part of which stems from its certainty, is summer.

Ungrateful as I have been for so much that I was expected to be grateful for, I abound in gratitude for summer's first excitements: bare feet on the grass, salt-tasting stones left behind by wave's withdrawal, moss as live to the touch as a furry animal, the awesome antiphonal of insects in the night. I did not want to know then, nor do I now, how grass grows, what makes the sea salty, why moss curls as it does, nor how the insects sing. But, perhaps because neither you nor my father nor Mademoiselle who so often bade me "sit still and enjoy nature" had pointed out these particular excitements (which in no case would you have described by the word "exciting" since excited was what I was to be kept above all from being); perhaps just because I happened upon them

by myself and had not been told to experience them, I
treasured and treasure them still. I am grateful too for
the later excitement of finding that I could breast the
waters unafraid, dive through a snarling surf unmauled,
ride in on the waves' crests triumphantly. I am grateful
for the sometime swift whang of a tennis ball well served
or well returned; for the powerful elation of steering
my first Model T down the seven long hills I knew best
in Connecticut with the motor turned off, my foot removed from the brake, and the words of "My Lord!
What a Morning!" bursting from my throat. These excitements were not self-enkindled, nor dreamed up. There
was, therefore, no gap between the anticipation of them
and their reality. Would that the same could be said of
the quest for love.

Now that, with Life safely tucked away under my
belt, I look back upon that first phase of it in tranquillity, I see that its excitement lay just where the worldly,
the wicked, and the sated—as also, oddly enough, where
the unworldly, where the moralists themselves—have
said it lay: in anticipation. For in reality, even when that
reality reached fever pitch, there was always something
wrong.

IT IS NOT HARD TO IMAGINE YOUR FACE, HAD YOU HAP-
pened to return to your dismantled house on one of those
weekday summer nights when I and the friend who inhabited it with me were investigating Life. The semi-
darkness, the whispers, the murmurs, and especially the
silences would have alerted far less acute eyes and ears
than yours. But what, had you been able to switch on all
the lights without in turn alerting us, would you have
found? To you it would have seemed an orgy, as in-

deed it seemed to me. Yet neither she with her young
man in the library, nor I with mine in the drawing room,
had lost more than a hairpin or two; neither she and her
young man nor I and mine had partaken of anything
more aphrodisiacal than milk. I can vouch for her as for
myself, since I well remember how upon the wildest of
these occasions she rushed into the room with loud sobs
and cried out on a rising note of hysteria, and to my own
shock as much as to hers: "He wanted to take me upstairs!"

What would have surprised you even more, perhaps,
than to find me huddled in the arms of the son of your
old friend; what I never could have made you believe,
was that I had at that time, if not for precisely the same
reasons, precisely the same sense of sin as yours. For although I did what I could to persuade myself that I
loved this summer love—in which case for me there
would have been no question of sin—I knew that it was
not true. In fact, so little was I in tune with him when
he did not have his hand upon me that I failed to recognize, when he said "I want you to be able to hold your
own with gentlefolk and scholars" that he was offering
me his hand for good. I did not love him. I loved what
he made me feel. Each time the door closed on him, I
knew it.

Frankly, and how little courage it takes, with the certainty that your eyes will never fall upon these pages,
to be wholly frank (though let me not fool myself that
frankness is a synonym for truth), I have always suspected that your morality, unquestionable as it was, was
rooted more in fashion than in conviction, more in form
than in faith. Yet in this I have become like you. As you
in your time were shocked, so I am shocked in mine. Today, when the nature of love, laid as bare as the intestines

of an experimental corpse, has been so probed and palped
that no rift or tumescence or deflected contour is hid;
today, when the fulfillment of desire has been stripped
of its moral swaddling and flaunted, not as the means to
an end, but as that end itself; today, when to satisfy the
senses no matter how deviously, and even with hatred,
is said to be still better than not to satisfy them at all; today, when the nimbus of chastity has become as old hat
as a boater—I find myself just as hostile to these times
that surpass me as you were to the times that surpassed
you and that were mine. Is it merely that I am outraged
by the death of propriety? Is my first concern, after all,
a concern for form? Am I then so shut away, if not in
what I am pleased to call my morality, then in custom
and prejudice, that I cannot hear the tone of revolution?
Have I, with the years, become such a fossil that I see
only corruption in change? Perhaps so, since there is no
reason why I alone could expect to escape the hardening
of opinion's arteries. Besides, it is possible, even probable,
that in this hour of my supposed maturity I do not see
that the adolescent I was for so long is still caught, like
any poor fly, in the amber of my decay.

Yet still I believe what I believe. I concede that passion
can flourish, can even nourish—though only briefly—
without love, as I concede that love is a weary load to
carry without passion. But I know that love is hardier
than passion, that while passion can sicken and die in a
twinkling, love can live on with the death rattle in its
throat. No matter how long science broods on the nature of love, no matter how many learned doctors batten
on it, no matter how many experiments are tabulated in
its name, love, like God, will never become wholly manifest. Moreover love by its presence, like God by His,
makes everything not necessarily clear or right or even

good, but acceptable, whereas in its absence, as in His, there is no hope.

ONCE AGAIN, HOWEVER, I SEE THAT MEMORY HAS UNCON-sciously tricked me out of my determination to be forth-right about that pursuit of pleasure which I like all the same to call the pursuit of love. In presenting so emi-nently presentable a partner in temptation as my summer suitor, I have given myself the appearance, if not of an innocence, then of a fastidiousness I did not have. For none of the other young men I saw in that period of ambivalent flowering had the same honorable intentions as he. I would not say, however, that their intentions were dishonorable, since for such the penalty was still in those days too high. They had, in fact, no intentions at all. Rather, like me, they were buzzing about in the gar-den of the senses, heedless and greedy, no more than I as yet at their ease. I demanded of them neither love nor friendship nor, of course, what you would have called respect. What I demanded was that they make advances, but that they advance with skill, with the most precise instinct about when to accelerate and when to brake, and above all about when to turn off the motor altogether. Yet, as I learned more about my own senses (to theirs I gave not so much as a thought), my pace insensibly—if I may so put it—quickened, so that what had once seemed heady enough began to seem slow, what had once seemed precipitous began to seem flat and plain. As I look back now upon their forbearance, I can only explain it by the fact that they too had been brought up with a set of barriers and that they too, for all their masculinity, were still afraid.

It was not in the deshabille of a New York summer,

but in London, where you sent me to spend a month
with a chaperone who had the "right" connections, that
I encountered for the first time someone who had forgotten the very existence of barriers and who was no
longer either young or afraid. He had invited me to dine
at his house alone, and either because my chaperone was
certain that he was too old, or because she had been convinced by the bona fide English poet to whom she had
introduced me and to whom I had had the temerity to
show my verses that my mind was more fixed on the
congress of stars than on that of men and women, or
simply because she longed for an evening free of my
charge, she let me go. When, after a meal served on a little table by the fire in what I now realize to have been
echt Hollywood style, not excluding the device of cham-
pagne, and after the long approach on the inevitable sofa,
followed by a scuffle which all but destroyed my aplomb,
I found the little door to the only place where I could
decently recover it, the box from which the roll of paper
was suspended suddenly burst into song. Across the hall,
I could hear my host's laughter. I seized my wrap and
ran. It was then, I think, that I first understood that a lit
match can burn.

By all this, had I told you of it even in your last years,
you would have been no less scandalized in retrospect
than if—oh, inconceivable thought!—I had told you of
it at the time. Yet how playful, I had almost said how
amateur, it looks now by comparison with what was to
come when, deflected from the true course I had set
myself by a chain of pressures of which your power over
me was no less a link than my lack of power over myself, I reaped the whirlwind of the senses that, as carefully as it had been unwittingly, I had sown. But, whether
because I now have a grown daughter of my own for

whom I tremble far more than, even if you had loved me, you could have trembled, since I know as you did not know the manifold reasons for trembling, or simply because I have acquired the twenty-twenty vision of hindsight, I too, as I unwind the reel of those fumbling experiments, am scandalized. For once, had we been able in this post-equinoctial to speak of it together, we would have been in accord. I was wrong. I was taking a first step in that wrong direction toward which I would return, as though hypnotized, again and again until such time as I plunged so far into it that I could not turn back by myself. That it was wrong physically I have had proof enough, but let me pass over as less than secondary the loss of bloom and the nerves' blight. That it was wrong morally, wrong from my vantage point as well as from yours, I suspected all along, and perhaps it was this recognition, or at least this incapacity not to recognize wrong from right, that was to prove, when it was almost too late to prove anything further, enough of a salvation to raise me from the dead. But where it was most wrong was on a plane of which I had no inkling at that time: it was most wrong philosophically. For I had listened neither to reason nor to the heart.

II

THE TIME OF MY LIFE

NOW THAT IT IS POSSIBLE TO GO TO JAPAN FOR the weekend, or to San Francisco or Paris for lunch, all my ocean passages, not to mention all yours, seem almost as quaint, if not as venturesome, as my Swedish grandmother's crossing of the sea by sail. Is it only another sign of growing old that, when I see my children bridge the distance in less than a night's sleep between the Europe where they were born and the America where they have taken root, I am convinced that they are foreshortening both a historical and a psychological experience of some magnitude? To me, still, it seems necessary, if one is to grasp the extent of the gulf that exists—notwithstanding the theory and hope of "one world"—between the old world and the new, to cross the wastes of water as they were crossed the first time, sea mile by long sea mile, feeling the swell beneath the feet, seeing the white wake of the ship trail off and vanish, learning how relative is the splendor of the most splendid ship compared to the splendid emptiness it traverses, gauging by the tension in one's own fibers the temerity it must have taken to head out for the first time into such loneliness with no assurance beyond the wild surmise that it would end, and coming to realize by the taste of the spray and the sound of the waves and the boundlessness of the horizons how truly estranging are these waters that divide us. How can those who now wing their way from world to world through the neutral and impassive sky ever guess, as we can guess who have ridden the ocean, what old fears were washed clean and what new hopes had time to germinate during that long suspense? Whoever is now borne unconsciously and in such a twinkling across the distance from continent to continent, to buy a frock or attend a conference or meet a lover, has lost irreplaceably that sense of time and space without which there can be no just sense of man's measure.

Of the thirty-two times I have crossed the ocean, only those that took place when I was three and six left no mark on my memory, and while certain of these crossings marked more than mere memory since they carried me to points in my life of no return, all of them, swift or slow, calm or stormy, no matter how frivolous or routine or bitter some of them seemed at the time, I now look back upon with wonder. I have left New York, Southampton, Cherbourg, Hamburg, Genoa, and Gdynia both in laughter and in tears. I have arrived at these ports in joy or terror. I have sailed together with you and my father and sister; alone with my father; alone with you; with a chaperone; with my college roommate and her mother; with my first husband; with a man who was not my husband; with my then best friend and her husband, and with her alone; with the father of my children alone, and with him and my daughter and her nurse and my unborn son; and with, on the last of these journeys—the last, I suspect, that I shall ever have taken—my children's father and both children, then six and two; also I have crossed and recrossed alone.

I have had small stifling cabins and ample airy ones; I have crossed without exchanging a word with my fellow passengers and have crossed with a seat at the captain's table. I have played shuffleboard, swum, and gambled in the bar, as I have danced all night and stayed up to watch the light steal over the sea from a lifeboat. I have spent midnight hours on the bridge in deep fog, sounding the horn while the ship's master strummed his guitar inside. But I have also walked the deck by myself with a lump in my throat too hard to swallow or sat in my cabin conning Polish verbs to keep from going down in the leaden sea of my griefs. And sometimes, I have been able to sleep more deeply, more sweetly than anywhere else ever, with the wind from the open porthole slapping at my face. But no matter what the purpose or climate of the journey, I did not lose the sense of being suspended, as between future and past, between inexorably separated worlds.

You could not have known, of course, any more than you knew how wicked I felt years later when I traveled from Brooklyn to Hamburg with a lover you did not dream I had, how lightheartedly, a year after I had left Grenoble, I sailed away from you with my father on that only journey he and I ever took alone. Nothing, not a dandelion puff or a feather, is so light as the heart from which a stone has been removed.

It had not been you but an Act of God that had placed the stone there by paralyzing me for several weeks from the waist down and leaving me, once my system had scotched the polio itself, with a permanently weakened knee and ravaged nerves I could conceal, but with a dragging foot which, if I could not restore it by the relentlessly minute exercises I was to do eighty times a day, would brand and hobble me for good. The full weight of the stone I had only come to feel in the aftermath of the illness, as I endured irrational sweats and fought an impatience set aflame by new limitations. Whether you understood the ignominy of such dependence I never knew. I did know, of course, by the presents you brought me, by your intermittent hovering at my door, that you were anxious. Yet with what has always seemed to me a quite inexplicable persistence, you held me down. I could recognize, despite the fret of it, a protective impulse in your refusal to let me walk out alone when I found I could and your careful explanation to what few friends tried to pry me from the house that I had not the strength to go. But why, oh why did you continue to present me, each time anyone came to call and until the very day I left the house, as "our little infantile paralysis case"? Were you or were you not aware that in so doing you almost crushed me under a load of pity I neither sought nor could accept? I could not have felt dizzier with relief walking free out of San Quentin than I did when, after eight months, my father and I stood together on the ship and watched it turning and heading for the sea.

I never knew how my father managed to convince you not only that I was well enough to go but also that I should be allowed to see again the Polish prince to whom I had considered myself engaged through that whole first dark year of our separation, despite the refusal of his parents to recognize the fact and your own reiterated doubts first of his suitability and then of mine. But overriding all objections, my father had invited him to London to meet us, and although I was anxious about that meeting, about whether my father would like him but still more about whether he would love me less or no longer now when I had, as it were, a clipped wing, my anxiety cast no shadow on the boat trip. Every morning my father and I lay side by side in our deck chairs and exchanged winks and jokes about the other passengers as they paraded past. Every afternoon at six, after looking at his watch and, with exaggerated care, shaking it as though to make sure that it had not stopped, and exhaling the sigh of one about to perform an unpleasant duty, he would say, "Time for my medicine," and move off in the direction of the bar. On the last night of the voyage, as we stood at the deck rail with our eyes on the gray-looming land mass of England, my father, always more liberal with jokes than gestures, took my arm and said: "I don't know if you knew, but I thought we might lose you. It was then that I realized what I had."

But among all the crossings and recrossings, the one that was to engender most of those that followed, the one that was to lead me into a future so improbable at the time and, now that it is becoming the remote past, somehow so improbable again, was the journey to spend my junior year at the University of Grenoble in France. Yet of this ultimately most decisive departure, since it was a departure from which I have never completely returned and never can, I remember only, ironically enough, that I had no sense whatever of impending fate.

Although it was less usual in the 1920s than today for college students to break into their regular courses for a year abroad, it was not unheard of either, and to you who so venerated cultural opportunity, my plan had not seemed for once ill-timed or ill-considered. Had my roommate's mother not been ready to accompany us, you would never have let me go, but with her presence, enhanced in your eyes no less by her own brilliance than by her physicist husband's world renown, you doubtless felt quite certain that my untoward impulses (already so much more untoward, after that summer in New York, than you suspected) would be curbed and might even possibly be cured. What from your viewpoint must have capped the plan and served to convince you of its advisability was the fact that her husband, who had been exchange professor at various European universities and who knew, as my father knew too, how much sharper, how much more invigorating was the climate of learning across the sea, desired this experience for his own child.

What you could not have known and what neither my roommate nor I knew until the knowledge was borne in upon us was that, sharper and more invigorating as these universities were for anyone seeking the knowledge they had to offer, they also provided a perfect cloak, in their godlike indifference to students and students' problems, behind which one could be as flighty, as harum-scarum, as irresponsible as one pleased. No record of attendance was kept at the Faculty of Letters where we signed up. There was no system of questions and answers at the lectures. The professors developed their subjects as they pleased, one of them pausing, if it happened to catch his fancy, to consider for as long as the class lasted whether Corneille did or did not use a comma at the end of a certain line, another hurtling through William James's pragmatic consideration of the medulla oblongata in an hour's output of rhetoric. No students there received, as so often they received at home, a little note in the mailbox suggesting that, since their papers had fallen off surprisingly in the last month, they might like to come to tea and talk it over. Indeed, when I once stopped at the desk of the philosophy professor at Grenoble to ask him to explain a reference I had not understood, he gazed at me in genuine surprise, arched his eyebrows over his glasses, and replied: "But Mademoiselle, one is not here to answer your questions!" Only when it came

time to be examined did one actually have to make an act
of presence. For both oral and written examinations one
paid special fees, and at this season there appeared, like
mushrooms in the rain, students whom none of us had
seen before. I sat, for my first examination, between two
Italians whose pockets contained small dictionaries and
scrappy notes, and when I paused with my pencil to de-
liberate, one or the other would nudge me and gallantly
offer to help. They did not understand my refusal. Nor,
when I met them a week later on the street and they
hailed me victoriously, shouting *"Passato! Passato!,"*
could they understand why I laughed. In the whole
crowd of our fellow students at the Faculty of Letters,
one could count on one's fingers those—a few Japanese
and the rest French—who moved silent and pale and
book-laden among us, their purpose emblazoned on
their brows. The others—the flashy Canadian girls, the
Tuscan who kept saying that he would have been a
monk were it not for the concupiscence of the flesh, the
skiers, the Alpine climbers, the sons and daughters of the
local glove manufacturing families, the Neapolitans who
were also registered for the same term at some other university at home, and the Americans among whom my
roommate and I could at least claim the advantage of not
murdering French—all had what I am sure, could we
meet again, we would agree was not precisely what we
had enrolled for, but precisely what we wanted—the
time of our lives. The University did not care. It had
been there for centuries; centuries later it would be there
still. It did not stand or fall by averages, aptitudes, quo-
tas, or benefactions. It was the bastion of an elite.

That stretch of seasons, from the fall of the leaves off
the lindens on the quays that bordered the Isère, through
the winter when sundown after sundown set the sur-

rounding white peaks aflame, to the slow, tender bur-
geoning of the European spring was, not just in one way
but in every way, the time of my life. I was freer of you
and of the gloom of your disapproval than I had ever
been before, and to be free of you, or at least to believe
that I was free of you, was always the west wind of my
internal weather. But after this clearing sky came liberation upon liberation. In my roommate, whom I had
spotted our first day on the college campus two years
before (and with whom still today, close to forty years
later, I can speak in the language of mutual trust), I had
a companion who saw with my eyes, and in her mother
I found the first older person to show me that friendship
can actually exist between the ripe and the still green. If
the pomposity of the lectures I attended did not fire me
to become a scholar, there was all the same in the approach to learning of these professorial professors a style
and a flavor new enough to me (for whom all that was
old was new) and marked enough to get at least a toehold on my mind. Moreover, there was more than learning to be learned in those months at Grenoble. Ours was
a crowded, casual manner of living in the three sparsely
equipped rooms on the second floor of a villa high above
the town, a manner which though to me it seemed so
Bohemian struck most of the friends we made there as
quite extravagant. From them, I discovered what Americans always seem to discover with recurring surprise
when indeed they discover it at all—that the accouter-
ments with which one's house is furnished are not necessarily an index to the furniture of the mind.

Of the winter sport of skiing, which undoubtedly ac-
counted more than the repute of the university professors for the flocking of so many foreign students to the
town, I cannot sing wholeheartedly. While I had not yet

had polio and was still sound enough of limb and not incapable of seeing in the snowy expanses we reached
every Sunday by funicular tram the pristine virtue they
had, I did not relish the tortuous ascents and wobbling
descents, the pervasive smell of wet wools, and the ex-
cursionist spirit of the bands we always moved in. It was
only when, sixteen years later in the spring before
France fell, I returned to spend a weekend in these same
mountains above Grenoble with my Polish husband, an
American war correspondent, and a Frenchwoman who
not many months thereafter was to die at Buchenwald,
that I realized how wonderfully clean-swept and care-
free had been those skiing Sundays of our youth.

On that wartime occasion the hotel, which had not
yet been dreamed of when I was a student, was full, not
of jostling, shouting young people, but of paunchy,
middle-aged profiteers with their hard-eyed mistresses.
All day I sat on the terrace watching the profiteers, who
had themselves hoisted up the face of the mountain by
ski lift and then sped down again, bent double, swaying,
often falling, but persistent in the effort to sweat off
their fat, and their mistresses who lay on deck chairs
with furs across their knees and their breasts bared to the
glare of the sun, while at fixed intervals and with a hum
that sounded so innocuous at the great height at which it
flew, a silver reconnaissance Messerschmitt would cross
the sky. At night in the tight-packed dining room, red-
faced from sun and wine, this company, which within
two months would be stripped of all it possessed and
running for its life, sang with voices coarsened as much
by desire as by the smoke-heavy air the brassy songs that
are no less French in their brassiness than the clarion of
the *Marseillaise*. On the eve of our return to Paris, the
smallest of the small fat men got up on the long dining

room table before all the other hotel guests and, howling the lascivious *"Forgeron"* song in time to the drum of his audience's fists, stripped off his clothing piece by piece till he got down to his long, unbuttoned, woolen underwear. The whistles of the men and the high laughter of the women who had discovered the pitch of his excitement were still ringing in my ears when, with scarcely less fright and disgust than the first time I heard a crowd of Nazis ejaculating their *"Sieg Heil!,"* I went to bed.

By the time of the Nazis, however, quite incredibly slow as I had been to look past the end of my nose, I had learned, not through my own effort but by *force majeure*, that not only my needs and the needs of the two children upon whom I had bestowed the dubious gift of life, but the needs of any and all individuals, those needs which you and my father and my native air had taught me to consider sacred, were in fact no more sacred than the blades of grass the hail whitens or the elephant's foot stamps down. By that time, I had seen the homeless flee across darkling plains to escape an inescapable enemy; I had seen an old woman and her cow strafed by a rain of bullets from a sunlit sky; I had seen a whole nation, a whole history, a whole concept of life wiped out in the time allotted a worker for his summer holiday. I had seen and been compelled to understand at last that the injustice of a woman toward her child, of a man toward his wife, of the loved toward the loving, of the powerful toward the powerless, of the old and the young toward each other, bitterly as each may sting, is no mere accident, no mere misfortune, no haphazard mishandling of any one of us by destiny. For if I ask which of us has not been stung, I must in the same breath ask which of us has not also done the stinging? To be unjust is as much the nature of human nature as to love. But I had to have the

dogs of organized injustice yapping at my heels to find it
out. Now I know. Still, I am not resigned.

BUT IN THAT FAR-OFF TIME, WHEN I WAS STILL A
student at Grenoble, the world was my orange, as it
was the brightly dyed, forced orange of the privileged
young everywhere, though most especially of the privileged young in America where my generation was coming of age with the conviction that war was to be out-
lawed forever; that one could always make a living
provided one was foxy enough and knew how to pull
the right strings; that politics—though apparently necessary as a token fighting force was necessary—could never
be more than a rather embarrassing game played (except
at the ambassadorial or presidential level) by classes lower
than one's own; that women were not just equal to but
possibly better than men since it was they who hoisted
and kept flying the flags of culture on Main Street; that
while there was more civilization on the Left Bank in
Paris than in the whole of the United States put together,
the smart thing was to go over there and pick up the
civilization and bring it back where it could be com-
bined with plumbing; and that happiness was, like a sitting duck, waiting to be hit by all but the clumsiest
marksman. How could I, or anyone else with a successful father and a house in the silk-stocking district of
America's arch city believe that my choices were anything but unlimited, that it would not be enough to
know what I wanted and reach for it to find it in my
grasp?

One of the articles of American faith was at that time,
and is still, I suspect, today, though by now it has paled

somewhat with an anemia brought on by the divorce records, that when the Right Man or the Right Woman appears, the sound of music accompanies him or her, music so soft that no one can hear it but the person for whom it is intended, and also so authentically sweet as to be unmistakable. As the doctrine went, this could happen only once in a lifetime. There was only one Mr. Right for the right kind of girl and only one Miss Right for the right kind of young man. On the other hand, it was axiomatic that the course of true love, like the course of the salmon, ran upstream. But if the swimmers had the strength and tenacity to breast the current of family query and opposition, if they could hurl themselves past all their difficulties and attain the quiet mating pools beyond, theirs would be a future so edifying in its serenity as to justify however much it had cost. This was not a class doctrine. It cut across the classless classes. It belonged to that American public best defined as everyone else except those who happen to be speaking of it. It even belonged to such an upper-class philosophy as yours. But this much can be said in behalf of your generation: at least you abided by it after, presumably, the fog of illusion had lifted. Whereas we of my generation, lacking that vein of iron which enabled you to go on beyond and without romance, have chased this bubble through marriage after marriage like the child in the Strindberg play whose pursuit of his toy balloon brought him under the wheels of a train.

There may be, indeed in some lives there is, as I well know, one image, one face, one form for love that no other loves can displace. But that this is the image, the face, the form one must marry does not any more necessarily follow than it follows that, even when one goes through fire and flood to possess it, with possession will come surcease to longing and to pain. The idea that romantic love is the only basis for marriage and that only a marriage born of such love can succeed has never been held by the other peoples in the world to be any more substantial than a Cinderella myth. Why then has America swallowed it whole? Why have Americans helped to perpetuate it by a conspiracy of silence on the part of each generation as it discovers the fallacy too late? Why, for instance, did you wait until I had stumbled upon my Mr. Right to tell me, who was by then so far beyond heeding, that marriages were not made in heaven? Why did you never tell me—or perhaps you never knew?—that they are made on earth, and by women willing and able to make patient, ungrudging compromises; that the rightest of Mr. Rights, if one did not continually strive at no matter what price to one's ego to please and promote him, might overnight as it were become Mr. Wrong? Why did I not find out for myself until now, after so much havoc, that more often than not one can, if one puts both mind and heart to it, turn Mr. Wrong into Mr. Right?

No soft music, I may say, sounded in my ears when I first saw my particular Mr. Right handing the two Canadian girls out of their legendary Rolls-Royce on the street by the Faculty of Letters.

Dark-eyed and slender, the Polish prince was neither tall enough nor rugged enough to make the impression at first glance of a commanding presence. If I gave any thought at that moment to his being a prince, it was because it evoked a fleeting memory of my fascination as a small child when an Egyptian lady smoking a long cigar on the balcony of the Swiss hotel where we were staying was pointed out to me as a princess. Undoubtedly the idea of meeting this prince crossed my mind, but only as an impulse of curiosity, half-hearted and short-lived.

Nor, strictly speaking, did I ever meet the man whose language I was to learn, whose religion I was to adopt (insofar as without grace a religion can be adopted), whose country I was eventually to inhabit till its enemies drove me from it, whose children I was in the fullness of time to bear. Had he not happened one day to board the same tram as I, taken a seat from which he could not help but see me, and seeing me, disapproved of what he saw, the whole future—not the world's, I admit, but ours which has become now the past but is still the future of who knows how many of our descendants not yet born —would not even have been written on the sands from which it will so soon be wiped out.

He got off the tram at my stop.

"I hope you will forgive me," he said in his English English, falling into step beside me, "but I must tell you, you should not wear your hat on one side. Allow me," he said, and with a firm little jerk on the brim, he straightened it. "There. That's much better. You are not angry, I hope?" he added, with a sudden, luminous smile.

I was not angry. By the time he left me at the gate of the villa, I had agreed to have a cup of chocolate with him in town the next afternoon. But by morning the episode seemed absurd. I was prepared to break the appointment when I realized that I had no way to let him know. I did not know his name. One did not make people wait in vain. I went.

Many meetings and many partings later, since the years of our marriage were largely composed, it has always seemed to me, of meetings and partings, he once remarked: "You wanted an eagle; what you got was a sparrow."

If the sparrow were a bird with panache, a graceful

colorful bird, a bird tame on the surface and wild underneath, a bird of both warmth and independence, a bird of
unalterable purpose and conviction, a bird that flew high
and bravely to battle with hawk or hurricane, a bird
which—however well one learned his habits and studied
his habitat, however closely one held him, however familiar his heartbeat—yet kept the secret of his self inviolate; and if among all existing birds there were but a single sparrow, then he was a sparrow, and it was a sparrow
that I wanted.

I HAVE ALREADY APPRISED YOU, WHEN APPRISING COULD
no longer matter, that the road I was to take when free
to branch out from the one on which you started me
would describe so wide an arc that it looked for a long
time like a diagonal. The false starts I had made earlier
were no more than gropings compared to the backtrack-
ing I was still to do and the blind alleys I was still to rush
into before I at last set forth on it. But on that leaf-
strewn, drizzling afternoon of late autumn when I kept
my appointment at the Grenoble *pâtisserie* with the
Pole, I saw for the first time clearly the way the road
would go. Rough-hew my destiny how I would and did,
it was to shape my end.

There are those who maintain that happiness is a habit
acquired in a happy home, that one must be healthy to be
happy, that only he is happy who turns every cloud inside out for its silver lining. They may be right. I cannot
in any case disprove them. But I can and do say that from
a home sicklied over with discontent I wrested—from
my sister while she was still young enough, from my
father when I became old enough, even from you when

I met with a flash of your approval, and most memorably from the thrall of certain books—moments of a happiness so high and bright, perhaps just because of their rarity, that I would not exchange them for any habit, since joy and the habit of it seem to me by definition mutually exclusive. I can and do say, moreover, that in the midst of that only dangerous illness I have had and after nights in a viper's nest of pain, there came mornings when the sight of the sun on the reddening trees outside my window and the shafts it sent across my bed so filled me with happiness that I had to sing. And I will also say that although I could never see silver linings to the clouds in my sky unless their gleam was unmistakable, I have been able to be happy, not always but on occasion, in spite of the blackest cloud until it burst on my head. I have said before and say again that if there were no dark one would not know that light was light as, if there were no light one would not know that dark was dark, and that it is only by the chiaroscuro that we see which is which.

In the months that followed that odd meeting in Grenoble, there was almost constant light. It was indeed the time of my life. I had my Polish beau, my roommate had her French beau, and her mother—soon nicknamed by my Pole La Maréchale—approved them both. Whomever else we saw and whatever else we did was thus irradiated. In the earlier part of the day we had our lectures; in the evenings, when there were no visitors, La Maréchale, who preferred the bitter to the sweet, read aloud from Maupassant or Anatole France. But it was from the late afternoon that life derived its purpose, for I began to go regularly after classes to the shabby room in the *pension* where my Polish beau, his fur-lined coat spread across the only armchair, with the soft red foxes uppermost and a teapot steaming on the table, awaited me.

The first time I went there, he had suggested gently and courteously, that I become his mistress. I was, as you would have wanted me to be, appalled. Still too naïve to realize that to a European who knew much about women but nothing about American girls, the mere fact of my presence in his room gave him every right to hope, I struggled between my immediate bridling reaction of offended virtue and my fear of jeopardizing the adventure. "I can't," I finally found the words, "because I don't love you." Had it been on his part no more than the adventure I thought it was, it would, I am sure, have ended there. It was not to end truly and finally for twenty-six years. But when, by the start of spring, after each of us had declared and redeclared our love and he had asked me to wait for him and I had sworn I would, I offered myself in an overwhelming desire to put this seal on my trust, it was his turn to bridle. "Not now," he answered firmly. "Not when you are going to be my wife."

Only looking back to that first season of joy did I come to realize, years later, how fixed and how far apart had been from the start our fundamental attitudes. The bridge we had thrown out across our differences, solid as it appeared, had been all along but a trembling makeshift span, unable to bear the weight of birth and death and war and loss of fortune and exile with which it was destined to be charged.

If I did not learn more than a fraction of what there was to be learned at the Faculty of Letters, I learned all that I was capable of learning in that twentieth year of mine at the Faculty of Love. I heard (though I could not visualize until nearly a decade later when I saw for myself) what it was like to live in the forests of southeastern Poland. I found out (though I could not grasp) what had been expected of the son of a feudal family who must speak half a dozen languages; ride bareback at a gallop and pick up kerchiefs from the ground as he flew past; shoot pheasant, hare, fox, and boar without first wounding them; master the rotation of crops, the seeding and felling of forests, the selling of grain and wood; doctor sick animals and arbitrate peasants' disputes; play a musical instrument and sing or whistle with absolute pitch; keep a whip hand over his inferiors and a light hand on his ladies; honor all debts, obey his parents, love and worship his God, and be ready, as generations of his forebears had been ready, to kill and to die for his country. I learned (though my imagination boggled at it) what it had been like to have enemy soldiers lay waste one's land and desecrate one's house and how it had felt, at nineteen, to ride to war with flowers beneath one's horse's feet and wind up in a typhus-infected hut with gangrene in one's thigh.

From the snapshots he showed me of sisters and parents and uncles and aunts and cousins, I tried to guess what these elegantly boned, dowdily clad relatives were like, but of course I failed, for what was there in either the circumstances, the expectations, or the principles to which I was born to inform me either of their narrowness or their depth, their intransigeance or their resilience, their arrogance or their humility, the distance of their manner or the gallantry of their hearts? I heard in his voice and saw in his glance what all this—which was Poland—meant to him. But not having yet been swept, as one day I would be, by such a longing for the sights and sounds of home that it even encompassed, though briefly and only at its most severe, the look of your face and the sound of your voice, his nostalgia, as ghostly to me as it was real to him, I could not and did not then understand.

Insensibly, too, I learned from the reflection of myself that he gave back to me that to be sophisticated was not sophisticated enough, that better than to be a good winner was to be a good loser, that reason did not prompt as unerringly as intuition, that the spine stood faster than the brain, that charm unlocked more doors than candor, and that it was not a universally accepted sign of enlightenment to disbelieve in God. I also learned not to bedeck myself with either false airs or false earrings, to keep my elbows down when eating, and to be silent when he held me in his arms. That there was more to be learned at my Faculty of Love goes without saying, as it goes without saying that in time I was to find this out. But what must be said, to my sorrow, is that there was a power to consider and to endure as also a power to withhold and to bank that I recognized, but that I had not the power to learn.

Only once until many years later at the end of your relationship with him did you and he cross swords. You were on your way home from that journey to India on which my father had counted, as it turned out in vain, to dispel the spell of the spirit world which had already by then begun to encroach upon your always frail realities, and he had left you in Paris where I was to join you when my term at Grenoble was done. May had come with all its perennial balm. Not more than two weeks remained to us, before my Pole had to go home for the summer to his alien forests and before I had to go with you first to Italy and then home for good to a house, a city, a continent alien to him. He had not yet told his parents his intention nor had I told you and my father mine. I was afraid, and so, how rightfully, was he. But despite our separate and unspoken fears, and despite, or perhaps because of, the pain we knew we would so soon have clamped upon us, we were finding each day sweeter than the one before.

Suddenly, warning me by belated wire, you appeared. As I sat in your hotel room with tight throat and wet hands, I tried to explain to whom I had got myself engaged. Since to be magnanimous lies so far outside my nature as almost never to occur to me, let me make the most of this moment of insight (undoubtedly due to the fact that I am in my turn the mother of a headstrong daughter—though what else can daughters be but headstrong, if they are to survive?) and say that in that instance I can indeed put myself in your place. You asked me how I knew he was a prince. I can see that, when I answered, "Because he says so, and anyway that's beside the point," you had to think me a liar or a fool. What I cannot see is why, when he called on you to ask you, as he phrased it, for my hand, you parried his request with questions which Molière himself might have hesitated to insert in a comparable scene. Here he was, braving what to him must have seemed a far more impossible situation than it did to you since he had rarely met anyone—until he met first me and then you—who questioned the authenticity of his name. No doubt he expected a few pious questions and a vague inquiry about his ability to support a wife. What you asked him, however, was whether he knew any Shakespeare by heart; if it was not true that Catholics could do as they pleased since confession relieved them of responsibility; whether there was, as you said you had heard, a high incidence of social disease among European aristocrats; and if he was not likely to abandon me, once I was with child? You did not ask if he were sure it was I whom he loved.

"Never mind, darling, never mind," he said, holding fast to my hand as he steered the Ford he and I had borrowed on the evening of your return to Paris to celebrate not just the fact of your departure but also the fact that both our birthdays and our hearts' desires had met at the same hour by chance. He was still making sure I did not mind; still saying that our parents would end by recognizing the inevitability of our marriage; still telling me that the future, modest in scope but splendid in depth, was secure for us; still pointing out that separation in time and space, however bitter, was no more than a nightmare from which we would soon awake, when, hours later in the night, after a dinner on the edge of Lamartine's Lake during which he had drunk Swedish punch out of my slipper, and while we were as yet many miles out of Grenoble, the Ford bounced over into a graveled shoulder of the road, and two tires blew out with a single bang. Rattling and shaking on battered rims, we reached town only at dawn. I could not walk up the mountain to reach home in an evening dress and silver slippers. Fitting myself out in his clothes, tucking my hair under his cap, and arming myself with his cane, I was soon on my way across the river and up the hill, the golden May light so filling my eyes and the golden hours just spent so filling my mind that the jeers of the peasants I met on their way to market and the look I got from a priest as he sped past me on his bicycle with the black sail of his soutane bellying out behind made no inroad on my consciousness. The landlord was already up and digging in his garden when I reached our gate and to the "good morning" I proffered him made no reply. Upstairs, I found La Maréchale, who had not gone to bed all night, awaiting me. It was only when I saw her face that I understood how much more important can be the appearance of reality than the reality itself. Seldom since have I appeared more culpable; never since have I been so entirely, so wholeheartedly innocent as in the first rays of that Alpine morning and in that first spring of love.

THERE IS A GAME WHICH I SUPPOSE NO ONE WHO HAS EVER lived has not played. It is the "iffy" game of hindsight. Some play it sooner, some later; and some, the Hamlets for whom there is no such thing as no alternative but who on the contrary are always finding themselves impaled on the two horns of any one decision, play it continually. Even more surely than in the interstices of their living, people are lured into this game of hindsight in the interstices of their dying. The living play it out loud, laying their cards on the table and explaining to anyone who will listen that if they had just led with this card instead of that one their fate would have come out. But the dying play it in silence, play it deep within their own echo chamber as it grows ever quieter, ever more soundproof to all tones save their own. One can see them shuffling and reshuffling, arranging and rearranging the hands they dealt themselves, hoping to discover, now that no new cards can be drawn, what they might have made from what they had. I have seen in the watching eyes of a woman prone on a bed in the garden of an Italian tuberculosis sanitarium how, as I passed with my hand in that of my Polish husband, she calculated that but for the grace of God I would have been in her place and that if grace of God there were, she would have been in mine. I have seen in the terribly unsmiling eyes of a mortally afflicted young friend, in the rows of tor-

mented eyes in a cancer ward, in the hooded eyes of my
father as he tentatively palped the treacherous swelling
at his throat, and I have seen in your fearful and angry
eyes as you listened within your body for death's approach, the solitaire of hindsight being played.

I will not therefore be singular, but infinitely plural in
giving rein for a moment to my "ifs." If you had not
been my enemy (which is as good as saying if you had
not been you) on that journey to Florence and Venice
which I had to make with you after parting from my
Pole on the station platform at Lyons and traveling toward you locked in the smelly little room at the end of
the car where for the first time, but not the last, I knocked
my head against the wall to give pain a name with which
to combat the nameless one; if, when at last we reached
home, I had not been felled with the polio my father had
feared would be fatal ("I never saw your father cry but
that once," you told me years later with undiminished
wonder); if you had not bored into my confidence in my
Pole and in myself with the relentlessness of a wood-
pecker; if, during my instruction by the Catholic priest
whom I had asked my father to find for me, I had
thought less about my separation from the Pole and
more about my separation from God; if I had been less
provincial, more sceptical about the moving-picture
myth of lovers who jump walls and swim seas and shoot
villains and defy all opposition to gain their objective,
and had understood that a young European aristocrat, an
only son whose brother had been killed, whose three
sisters were yet unmarried, and who still depended on
his parents would not and could not cross the world to
fetch himself any bride at all, but especially not so quixotic a choice of one; if, above all, I had gone along with
the tide as it was then flowing, knowing that all tides

turn, rather than flailing against it with impotent impatience; if, in other words, and at this point comes the confluence of my game with all other games of hindsight, I had not been I but another, my solitaire ought to have come out. But would it? For is it not in the very cards themselves that, however free one is to play them, there is only one chance in a million that they come out right?

If, and I admit that the word "if" has for me a reptilian fascination, if in the summer after our first year of separation when we met again in London my Pole and I had married despite the dread of his parents (made obvious in the telegram they sent us announcing "urgent military circumstances" which they had invented as an excuse to recall him and which were not to become true till fourteen years later) and despite the promise not to marry that I had given my father and that I suspect he did not think I would keep; if I had gone then to live in Poland at a still tender twenty-one (tender at least by comparison with the scar-tissued toughness I had acquired by the time I went there at twenty-nine), would the story have ended another way? Had I gone there still fresh from a house where social justice, public health, and educational opportunity were gospel, would I have found, as later I only half-heartedly sought to find, less patriarchal ways to help those "souls" who flocked to our door with their feet tied in rags for lack of shoes, who borrowed salted water from each other in which to boil their day-in and day-out potatoes since in that country of salt mines they had no money for salt, whose children were bluer in May than in December because by May no food was left from the year before and no new food had yet grown? Or would I even then have stood by shocked and helpless while the masters—handing out wood for coffins,

cloth for skirts, and permission to gather up faggots for
fuel—exhorted them to pray more often and more truly
for the love of the Virgin Mary and the mercy of God?
Fresh, as I would have been had I gone to Poland when
first we planned it, from my Catholic baptism which,
despite my father's sardonic warning and your patronizing smiles, I had arranged and carried out not, alas with
the fervor of conversion so much as with the fervor to
please my Pole, might I still then perhaps have been
more than merely impressed, more than merely amazed
by the faith of both master and servant alike who,
though struck again and again by God's lightning, never
doubted that His goodness had sent the flash? Might I
still then have accepted and not been antagonized by the
candles and promises with which they sought to bribe
God's attention and bargain for His good will? Might
I have accepted for the heresy they said it was the Prot-
estantism that proclaims that He helps best those who
help themselves? Might I perhaps still then have been
singed by Almighty Fire, and from hating its heat have
learned first to endure and then to love it, rather than go
on watching, as for so long now I have watched it, from
outside its lambent pale?

Surely, I tell myself, whenever I give my game of
hindsight full play, if I had married my Polish husband
first, not having known so to speak another man, not
having yielded enough to the circumstances of temptation to have discovered my secret itches, not having
hardened youth's sensibilities with rebuff after rebuff
both given and taken, not having stowed away aboard
the still untried vessel that was my twenty-one-year-old
self the cargo of opinions, prejudices, tastes, and demands with which my holds were already laden by the
time I finally set sail on that marriage, surely my heart

would have informed me of what every woman is supposed to know, that I was to be, or at least to make sure of
appearing to be, the sounding box and the strings, while
it was he who was to call the tunes. But is it so sure that
I would have discovered this, even then? For in the marriage I knew best, the marriage I had always known
without knowing that I knew it, it was you, the American woman, and not my father, the American man, who
called, and called openly, the tunes.

There can of course be no doubt that a difference in
chronology, had I gone to Poland fourteen instead of
six and a half years before having to leave it on that
September midnight when the Nazis were a few miles
from our house, would have at least qualified the events
of my story. Even if I had not been able to extend new
roots into that alien subsoil, the longer habit would have
given me more protective coloration. Even if I had not
succeeded, with so much longer a time of trying, in
beveling my edges enough to keep them from grating on
the Polish family, I would have established firmer bonds
than a mere *modus vivendi*. Even if I had not found out
how to master the restlessness that drove me at times to
roll unseen in the leaves of some forest bypath or plunge
through the wintry underbrush till the iced twigs had
drawn my blood, I would have learned some resignation.
Even if I had not lost, or having lost, had not known
how to recapture, the love of the man upon whom I so
absurdly sought to depend (as no one should ever seek to
depend on another for the weight of such dependence is
too heavy for anyone but God), I would have had to
accept in the end my loss. There would have had to be
a different story, since after all the children would have
been so much more nearly launched had they been born
that much sooner, and being that much less helpless,

might well have helped to give the story another end.

When I wrote, almost immediately after escaping from the Nazi invasion of Poland, my account of the years I had spent there, there was of course no question of having achieved that tranquillity in which the remembrance of things past is supposed to be bathed. Now, however, twenty years later, it stands to reason that memory should have been tranquilized. Yet that so often what appears to stand to reason eludes reason altogether, I seem always to be in the process of rediscovering. Not so long ago, and only a few weeks before you died, I had occasion to rediscover it again.

On one of those later winter afternoons, made grayer and more chill for me by the daily visit which, in spite of dragging heart as well as feet, I exacted of myself with that consciousness of virtue which is actually virtue's antithesis, I found you holding my book, *Polish Profile*, closed on your lap. I well knew that you had never liked it; you could not have liked it, not liking me. And so, as you leaned back on your chaise longue, I shrank from the expected comment. You sat up then, and looked at me. "I never knew," you said, "how hard it must have been for you." How simple those words, how simple they were, and how good! I have racked my memory for any other moment between us when you held out to me such balm. There is none. Yet no sooner did I feel the healing touch upon me than I answered: "Not any harder than at home." That it was true does not excuse me for loosing an arrow I would now give much to have withheld. Thus does the custom of the bow so train the thoughtless fingers that, rather than let one bird go free, it shoots the dove of peace.

*   *   *

IT IS NOT ONLY IN FICTION, I SUPPOSE, THAT A WEDDING day is for the willing bride her most tightly kept, most cautiously evoked memory. Like a bouquet of flowers each one of which has been culled for its perfection, she carries the best of her hopes to this occasion. For a willing bride, the climate of her wedding day is no more marred by the tears and scenes which may have preceded it than by the mischance of a rainfall. Even the compressed lips of parents and the jeremiads of those who know they will always have been at least half right in prophesying failure, no matter how painful they may be immediately before and perhaps forever thereafter, cannot score her on that day. Beneath her raiment she wears a coat of mail forged in the white heat of an anticipation which, unlike joy itself, is proof against outside attack.

Yet, undetectable to the beholder and often unknown even to the bride, there is always a rift in her armor so perilous in its invisibility that if probed even lightly the wound may be fatal, for it lies above the heart. I have no way of knowing how often, by the fear in his face or the reluctance of his manner, by a cliché jest or by the sheer clumsiness with which honest males tend to meet their solemn moments, the most willing bridegroom pierces the rift by instinct or by mistake, since this is doubtless the best kept of all secrets. I only know that, on the three wedding days when mine has been the star role, my armor did not hold.

Let me not hear you say, even in my imagination, that three wedding days is two too many for any woman to have if she is to be taken or to take herself seriously; that a bride is a bride but once; that to wed three times is to make of the wedded state a cliché more stale than any joke about it; that if one marriage bespeaks that courage of conviction which is the prettiest of courages, three marriages in one lifetime speak more of caprice than of holy purpose and in their embarrassing repetition can only elicit guffaws. Let me not imagine that I hear you saying it, for you would be echoing what I have said all too often of others and have thought still more often of myself. And if, as the law has it, there exists extenuating circumstance; and if, as our modern rationalizers of the unreasonable and unreasoning impulse have it, there need not necessarily tread upon the heel of one marriage the failure of another, these are loophole provisions, arguments to be used in drastic cases of ill-mating, to save lives that might otherwise be lost or thrown away, but loopholes of immeasurable danger to those not steadfast enough not to take advantage of them at a first sign of discord. Only when the advantage has been seized does the heedless but determined seeker after a dream poppy find that a forget-me-not has appeared in its place.

More than another year had gone by since my father had taken me to London. From month to month after returning home, I had expected my Pole to set the time of his coming, but from month to month he had remitted it with reasons which, incontrovertible as they seem now that the world has at last somewhat seasoned me, seemed then to be made of straw. Doubt, born of his hesitations, but nurtured, too, by your hints that he might well be reconsidering marriage with someone as ill-fitted for a prince's wife as I, bloomed venomously, together with a no less venomous pride. It had not therefore been impossible to convince myself, when the laughing American, who had sat out an evening with me because I could not yet dance, began dancing serious attendance, that what he offered me was not an escape but life itself. It had not even been impossible to convince myself, when I wrote my Pole that I no longer loved him, that it was true. Nor was it at all impossible, now that I stood at the altar with this sandy man, to believe the responses I gave him.

"Remember to smile nicely at the servants!" was the blessing with which you sped me to the pine-festooned playhouse at the Farm which was the scene of my first wedding. Waiting for me at the imitation altar behind which stood the New England minister coralled to perform the marriage was my large, sandy-haired bridegroom who, though almost notoriously gregarious, had arrived pale and tense the evening before and greeted my eager descent upon him by an abrupt "Leave me alone," and was now paler than ever as we met again before the small assemblage of relatives and friends who had come to witness our union. In his wide-set eyes, as they fell on me, there was only unimaginable distance. It did not occur to me then that he must be mortally afraid.

This was neither the bridegroom nor the wedding I had once envisioned. Here was no church, no bridal veil; here was no loving approval on familiar faces, nor benign smile of the world upon successful worldlings; here was no moment of awe before a dream fulfilled. Alas and alack for my impatience, the man who placed the gold band on my finger was not my Pole, not he to whom I had first pledged my troth. But I was not dying for lost love, nor even sick for it. I wanted to marry this man as much as, or almost as much as, I wanted to leave home and you. My intentions, for whatever they could at that time have been said to be worth, were honorable. That they did not remain so could have been foretold. Given what I was and what you had helped to make me, given what I sought and what I found, given the custom of my country and the habit of my heart, it could not have been otherwise.

Driving down the steep hill and along the river and away, away from my father who looked faintly puzzled and sad and from you who were patently glad to see the end of this wedding between a young man whose provenance lay outside your acquaintance and a daughter whom you had not succeeded in molding to your heart's desire, I felt a vast relief. I scarcely heeded the continued silence of my new husband as he drove our two-seated Ford runabout with its freight of rice-sprinkled luggage and the old shoes the farmer had insisted on tying on behind. My mounting excitement was not solely enkindled by the prospect of the first night I would spend alone under one roof with a man. It was more, as well as less, than that particular and sweet excitement. It was the excitement of having someone to call one's own.

It lasted through the jouncy ride over country roads in October's gala setting; through the long ferry trip across Long Island Sound; through the shock of the fat, gray, rotting melon I found in the icebox which, together with the slanted fourposter and a few battered chairs and bureaus, constituted all the equipment of the old shingled house my husband had borrowed the money to buy; through the night during which he slept so soundly; through my struggle the next morning to turn, with the witch's wand of good will and a flick of a match on the wick of the oil-burning stove the like of which till then I had not seen, into the housewife that from that day forward I planned to be. That flash of my excitement even carried me over his departure in the Ford forthwith after breakfast to gather, as he told me, the free peaches available at a farm some miles away. I waved him off with a smile. I tidied the house, and then for hours I watched from the bare porch the empty road. But the day had worn down and darkness had come before my bridegroom returned. By then, though the smile was still fixed on my face, it was crooked. The flame of my excitement had guttered and gone out.

But if the first matrimonial weekend, in its dearth of frills not to speak of thrills, was something less than typical of that era and that milieu, the general *mise en scène* of our marriage was quite a classic of its kind. We had our car, a house (ramshackle though it was) on Long Island, and a two-room apartment on the roof of a converted mansion on one of the good streets in New York. My husband, who had a job writing advertisements for golf balls, had also written a novel about a Yale man coming of age in a copper mine, while I, who had been educated not to earn a living, knew how to dust the new furniture you gave us, how to light the gas in the closet that was our kitchen, how to make a perfectly groomed bed, and how—if one liked it hard-boiled enough—to cook an egg. We were poor. Indeed, before every pay day we were penniless, having spent what we had on the ingredients for Alexander cocktails with which to ply his friends. However, young, tall, and distinctly presentable, we dined out night after night. With his one-man band of cymbals and drum and ukulele and little, befeathered team of dancing dolls to manipulate on a string, and his repertoire of altogether decent songs, he could put any party on its feet. Meanwhile, I was learning not just to hold my Prohibition liquor but the far headier stuff of freedom in an amorphous society to which there were, I had discovered, no bounds.

What did money matter either to him who had never had it or to me who had never not had it? In the ever-widening circles of New Yorkers we frequented, there was more than enough to go round. I was quite sure, for a time that I look back at not without pride, that money did not matter a tinker's dam. What did matter was people. I could not then have enough of them. I had not known, and if I had not left home when I did I would not have found out, how many people there were, and of how many different kinds.

Not so many years ago, when I complained to the headmistress of the fashionable school my daughter was attending despite my inability to meet its bills, that the confines from which she drew her pupils were too cribbed for our times, she replied, with the edge of surprise in her voice: "I wonder why you say that? Why, this year we have a furrier's daughter!" In your day, and in her position, you would have given the same reply. Then and even now, when the ground rocks and swings beneath society's feet, the invisible walls that shut out the furrier's daughter unless or until an invisible door is opened for her still stand fast.

But what I was learning in that early time of my first marriage was that the society in which you had gone to such pains to place me ("Just think, Daddy darling," you had written to far-off Texas, "she has been to the Rockefeller ball!") was only one milky way, that there was a literary society, a theatrical society, a musical society, an artists' society, a Jewish society, a Greenwich Village society, and beyond these a society of individuals individual enough to be free and welcome to any or all of them, and that in none of them would a furrier's daughter stand out as such. Who you were or what you had was of no matter; it was what you were and what you made of what you were that counted.

Can it be that I, who have never owned a pair of rose colored glasses, am looking back upon that long past day in New York through eyes grown rheumy with sentiment? Or was I then merely naïve in seeing and judging others with a tolerance with which I was not being seen and judged myself? Was there never as happy-go-lucky and disinterested a society as the one I thought I had found? Were the ideas that seemed to me so passionate and the passions that seemed to me so ideal no dearer than the coinage of any other social congress, no more substantial than the balloons sent up at midnight from a ballroom floor? Was I, like the village maiden, too dazed by the baubles at the fair to see the short-changers and thieves behind the counters or to look for the skulduggery going on inside the booths? If so, that too does not matter. In my fancy, at least, that direct, unhampered, unprejudiced, uncalculating, roomy, person-to-person communication did exist.

That, if it ever did exist, it does so no longer I have had more than sufficient time to learn. None but the most sanguine of young aspirants to the arts dares walk today into such drawing rooms and expect, because they can play a one-man band or because they have written a novel that did not sell, to have anyone pause long enough even to inquire how they are unless they have a name. None but the most daring hostesses can risk inviting to a party more than a handful of people without a name. To be gracious to the nameless is an art left to politicians. Under the aegis of equality, the equal are equal only if and when and as long as they have a name. Elsewhere, perhaps, to be what one is, if one is something, still suffices as a passport for any social frontier. But today, in the New York I speak of, frontier officials will not lift the barrier for a face, a manner, a mind, a character, or even—if one happens to have it handy— for a sizable list of achievements, unless to these are added that crown of crowns which is a name.

The cult of names is, of course, hardly new. History

has filed away in its attics more names than it could ever have hoped to preserve in the limelight to which it briefly accustomed them, and in its back yards, the dump piles of those too short-lived to be recorded have become funeral pyres for fame. There has never, I fancy, existed a society anywhere that did not automatically turn its febrile attention on this most ponderable of imponderabilities. Moreover, the names that command its attention have not always been of like distinction. Oscar Wilde no less perhaps than Julius Caesar, Lady Diana Manners no less than Cleopatra, Houdini no less than Marco Polo would have created a furor in any drawing room. That a name, per se, acquires special value is not peculiar to this present time and place. It is what makes the name that today has changed. Whereas it used to be that to have a name one had to have reincarnated a Phèdre or unearthed a treasure, composed a symphony or won a battle, invented a novel or a means of locomotion or a code of laws or a drug, climbed a peak or plumbed an ocean, eloped with a prime minister or sired a queen's bastard, swum the Hellespont or the English Channel, conquered a nation or an audience, or at the very least plunged a dagger in someone's back, today, when reputation moves like brush fire, one has only to advertise oneself to enough people to establish one's autograph, for the time being at least, as a collector's item.

What's in a name? The answer lies not in its scent but in its price. How much does it cost on film or screen or stage, on playing field or platform, or at the speakers' table? How good an investment is it? How long is it likely to go on waxing, how fast is it likely to wane? For wane it must eventually, no matter how much capital is invested in it, else there would be such a glut of names that the market for them might itself be swallowed up.

As you were not unpleasurably aware, though you took care to conceal from me the pleasure others told me it gave you, I have myself had a name, not to be sure a name out of the display window where no one could pass without noticing it, but rather a bargain-basement name. Yet, however low its price, it was all the same, since it had to be paid for, a name. When first I acquired it, it was still the name I had borrowed from a feudal history in which I had played no part and was so plumed and beribboned with tradition that it sat on my head, for as long as I wore it, as inappropriately as a Gainsborough hat. After I lost it, or as you and my other critics so readily said, tossed it away, I fell back among the nameless and trudged my anonymous way, no longer—I admit—so content with anonymity, until quite by chance I was singled out for myself and given this time a name of my own. Inconspicuous as it is, not to say plain, it has proved none the less serviceable. When it was new it even brought me compliments from strangers. But a name must be constantly reshaped and refurbished to suit the fashion. Mine, by now, has become too weathered to catch the eye.

However, I know enough now about having and being a name to estimate its corroding power over self-esteem and self-doubt, and its drive toward fruitless preoccupation with how one is viewed from without instead of toward the fruitful preoccupation of how the without looks from within oneself. To all but the inviolate few whose beacon is so bright that it blinds them to the distraction of lesser beams, a name is like a mirror on the wall, drawing the glance over and over again to the reflection, now from this side and now from that, of a self with an apparently implacable appetite for its own image. A name, to him who has one, assumes its own identity; it becomes more real to his mind than that mind itself. The reality becomes the name. He no longer has, but is a name. There may exist a world where a name is still only a convenience, a world where a rose by any other name would smell as sweet. But in the world I know, the smell of the rose is as sweet as it is only because the rose is called a rose.

At the slippery point in my narrative that I am about to reach, however, when I was twenty-five and had been married three years, I had not a name. It is true that from time to time there appeared in a Sunday supplement a review of some novel under my name and that the sight of my paragraphs in print so flattered my image of myself that I easily forgot how much closer the reviewer is to the vulture than to the lark, how paltry is the risk of the reviewer compared to that of the reviewed. But the toehold I gained among professionals with these early reviews, and with the occasional profiles of personalities commissioned by magazines, seemed far less important, since it did not then occur to me that I either should or could or would ever have to live on what I earned, than the fact that as a dinner guest, as a dancing partner, as a woman, I was at last in some demand. Moreover, I began to see myself as a modified but still not unauthentic version of those heroines of the new fiction (so memorably incarnated by Greta Garbo and Katharine Cornell) who, because they had been deprived by fate of their true love, were ready to give what was left of the rag-and-bone shop of their hearts to any lover of love who happened by, since they asked nothing more of love than the prodigality of its caresses. With the pallor of my face, my by then merely slightly unusual gait, my rather better than wieldy figure, and a certain over-all intensity, I had, or thought I had (which is as good as having) the appearance at least of the *femme fatale* I had so long before set out to be. I knew now what Life was. I proposed to live it.

Even if it was you who first, however unintentionally, appointed the road down which I henceforward hastened by myself, I would not hold you responsible for where I went. I walked as I walked from choice. Whether the first link in the chain of choices was forged by you as the handmaiden of my fate, or whether it was forged in a concatenation of genes and circumstances as much more complex than you as nuclear fission is more complex than an arrowhead, the ultimate responsibility has, from the day I first chose alone, been mine. I can only absolve you *in absentia*, but herewith I give you unqualified absolution from any share in my guilt.

THE SERPENT OF EDEN WAS NO MORE OBSIDIAN, BRIGHT-scaled, and hypnotic to Eve in her ignorance of creation than was to me, who had thus far been safely running the gauntlet of temptations, the blazing creature who entered my sitting room one morning to suggest improvements in an article I had written about him but who remained there beside me on the sofa in the wintry sunlight just long enough to discover whether, if he condescended to call, I would come.

"Who are you? Where do you come from?" the Maestro murmured, his voice pitched as only a man made of music could pitch it. "I know who you are," he went on then, since to this dumbfounding approach I had no suitable answer. "You are Agni," he actually said, "the goddess of fire."

As the guile of the original serpent, so his method,

transparent enough now in retrospect to make one wonder how even the most embryonic eye could fail to see
through it, had exactly gauged the clarity of my vision
at that time.

At the end of his brief visit, or should I say visitation,
when he took my hand at the door, he must have felt
in the touch of it that I not only did not expect, but
did not want him to go.

"Not now, Agni," he whispered. Then, dropping my
hand, he moved over to the clock on the vestibule wall
and gave it a little tap. "The tick was not right," he said,
and with a smile, and shaping his lips to form the word
"Soon!," was gone.

My first appointment after this, it was tacitly but un-
misunderstandably agreed over the long-distance telephone, was to last the night. Only someone who has
been completely possessed by the dream of such a night
can imagine what I, who had not been allowed one with
the man I had first loved and had not succeeded in having one with the man I had married, was now imagining.
Enflamed no less by the great adulteries of literature—
Anna and her Vronsky, Emma and her Rudolphe, whose
pleasures had been left with a now vanished art to the
reader's private surmise—than by exact information, my
imagination, when the appointed time came, exhausted
itself in arabesques of flight. The necessary lies all told
and for the moment well forgotten, the short train trip
finally accomplished, my minutely scrubbed and per-
fumed person encased in a borrowed velvet skirt and
fur jacket, and with only a book to carry besides the
discreet handbag on my arm, I paused for a long breath
before I rang his bell. At some less eventful moment
I might have been surprised by the lack of surprise with
which his secretary greeted me and, her face frosted

in impersonality, led me up the stairs. In the study, the light from a brisk fire was playing on the elbows of two grand pianos and on the unclad limbs and above them the short scarlet tunic which was all the Maestro had on.

Some hours and one of Life's more envenomed lessons later, as I lay sleepless, as much perhaps because of the hunger that a supper of wheat germ and honey had not been able to still as because of any other unstilled hunger, I watched while the moon crept round till it shone on the pistol he had brought to bed. "Anyone who enters, I shoot!" he had said, as he prepared himself for the night. For him, now, the night was over and he slept. The moon moved slowly. At last its light fell on his face. I reached out my hand and waked him. "I can see you," I whispered. "I arranged that," he murmured, and with a smile he turned and slept again. When day came, I gathered up the paraphernalia of sin, took one more look at the source of all my imaginings, and with a step made heavier by the weight of the new knowledge it bore, I left.

NOW THAT MY TELESCOPE IS TRAINED UPON THAT MAR-riage which I found easy, once betrayed, to go on betraying with ever shallower ripples across the surface of my conscience, I should make clear that I did not practice the religion I had espoused in much the same spirit as I had espoused my first husband, seeing in it not the end that it is but a means to my particular end. I could not, of course, have gone to confession since I had married outside the Church and to have confessed not only without repentance but without the intention of regularizing my position would have been unacceptable. No more profound error about Catholic doctrine is ever

made by outsiders than the assumption, so generally
held by the very intellectuals whose profession it is to respect intellectual discipline, that the confessional is a kind
of privy where the soul can relieve itself and, once relieved, can resume with impunity its diet of forbidden
fruit. It is true that the priest on the other side of the
grilled window in the little box must believe that the intent behind the whispered *mea culpa* is pure unless he
sees proof to the contrary in the quality of the confession or the nature of the sins confessed, just as in a secu-
lar court the judge must believe the oath of a witness
who swears he is telling the whole truth and nothing but
the truth unless that witness can be proved to have lied.
But in the camera of the confessional the priest is not the
ultimate judge; he is only the mouthpiece for a Supreme
Justice in Whose Presence, if It is felt and recognized,
there is no use in even attempting to lie. To offer God,
if one believes in Him, anything less than the truth as
one sees it and anything less than wholehearted remorse
is to make, not of God, but of oneself, a mockery. Let
no one who has not prepared his own confession make
light of it, for in the ring where the mind wrestles with
the conscience it is not always the conscience that wins
the match. However eager the desire for absolution, to
be truly sorry—what with our genius for self-excuse,
our pride, our appetites, our temper, and those resent-
ments which have such a stranglehold—is more than
hard. Yet confession is nothing less.

"Was it in bed, child, or on a couch?" the priest asked
me when I returned after so many years to knock at a
Church which, no matter how often or how far one
flees it, never refuses to open its portals once again. This
was, after a period in which I had known almost every
temptation except the temptation to confess, my general

confession made at the time when at last I was to go to Poland. I had prepared myself for it with a care more superstitious, I confess it, than religious, for I was convinced that if I did not accuse myself of all that deserved my accusation, God would not give me a second chance, not at Him, but at my Pole. Yet with all the care I had taken in preparation, for this question that the priest threw out at me I was not prepared. Before I could lay hold of my mind, so quick and sly at subterfuge, it was prompting me that, rather than say both, I had best choose the lesser of two evils and say bed. I could not have been more ill-prompted, not because I did not know that on a couch adultery could conceivably be construed as an accident while in a bed it could only have been engaged in by design, but because on my own scale of values, to sin by design was more honorable, if I may so paradoxically put it, than to sin by accident. Though this was not at the time I speak of my *maxima culpa*, since the most grievous fault one can have is to have been knowingly exposed to God's love and knowingly reject it, it was a fault, according to the priest, so grievous that it led him logically into asking me further whether I drank and played cards for money, upon my denial of which he seemed quite baffled. Yet still today, at the canonical age from which I look back at my ages of turpitude, I have to believe that to sin by accident is less forgivable in matters of the flesh than to sin by design.

In the world in which I move today, once more for me the non-Catholic world, the word sin, the very concept behind it, has been castrated by the medical metaphysicians. It is no longer a lusty demon to be exorcised by evangelists or by the sinner himself; it has become a bedridden patient constrained to a routine of drugs. For

the fact that you managed, despite having brought me up
to believe that the story of Jesus Christ was no more
than the most touching fable and that He Himself was
never more than the most remarkable of men, to incul-
cate in me a sense of sin, I cannot be too grateful. If it is,
as is now so generally said, unhealthy, then I prefer my
unhealth to the health that knows neither the squirm nor
the bite of conscience. It did not keep me—as it does
not of course keep anyone except the saints—from sin-
ning, but it gave me both the pain and the pleasure of
knowing, when I did it, what I did.

For I have no doubt that adultery, no less than treason
or murder, is a sin, even if all it betrays is dignity and all
it kills is pride. The pity is that in the so-called emancipation from dogma, a man now has no more right over a
woman in our society than a woman over a man, and
adultery has therefore lost its sting for those committing
it. Not long ago, in a much discussed work by a contemporary French novelist, this lady enumerated the
places—fields, roads, beaches, bushes, forests, mountain-
tops, decks of ships, not to speak of hotels, *cabinets parti-
culiers,* and other people's bedrooms—where her heroine rejoiced in flagrant delight. Topographically, the
list, in its variety, had a certain *élan vital.* But psychologically, I would maintain to my last breath that it is impossible to bring to so many chance acts of love the excitement that each such act demands, and that when
adultery becomes a commonplace it is at its most sinful,
for it sins against sin itself.

Principled as you were, not to say prudish, about the
sins of the flesh, I do not think I would be maligning
you if I were to suggest that, had you known about my
affair with the Maestro, you might almost have been
able to stomach it, since the luminosity of his name did

so much to mitigate the darkness of his morals (a frequent effect of light and dark in the world of the arts) and a little of that light might therefore have appeared to you to reflect on me. But that you could not have stomached the further sensations that I sought with such stubborn recklessness after the Maestro, beelike, had buzzed off to another still unprobed flower, I have no doubt.

It was on Thanksgiving eve, I remember because of the acute unease with which I partook of your family turkey the following day, that an art collector, husband of a friend and one of the few such acquaintances who had never attempted to test the limits of my resistance to extramarital advances, led me up the musty stairs of a building on a Harlem side street. "How tough are you, anyway?" he asked, as he rang at an apartment door. "Tough enough," I said, and followed him into a dingy parlor where, on straight chairs arranged in a circle as though for a boarding-school dance, there sat half a dozen dark-skinned girls in such pink or blue taffeta dresses as one might have seen of an evening at the Danbury Fair. "We want a party," my escort told the lady of the house. Turning to me then, he said: "You choose." The two gazelle-eyed maidens I selected took us down the narrow hall and into a room furnished only with a washstand, a large brass bedstead, and a strong, unshaded light bulb hanging over the bed on a cord. Unsmiling, unhurried, they let their dresses slip to the floor. Naked, they lay down together and began the play. In the hot room there was only the sound of the girls' rapid breathing and from one or the other a little moan. I found I could not meet the eyes of the guide with whom I had descended into these nether regions, so I fixed my gaze on the bed. "Come over to this side," he suggested.

"Look at that angle! What a Gauguin! Don't you agree?" With the acceleration, on the bed, of sound and motion, I must have paled, for his voice was gentle as he remarked: "You're not enjoying it." I managed to hold back my tears.

But even this venture into such circles of hell as, for certain, you could not have surmised would have been easier, I think, for you to grasp than the occasion—the only occasion of its kind—when I myself ventured into an entirely casual bed. I had met the stranger whose bed it was at a gathering of people almost none of whom I knew, had discovered behind his silences the brain and humor that I found it so hard to resist, and had accepted his tentatively put invitation to stop by at his apartment for that nightcap which, since the liberation of women, has become a threadbare euphemism for the love that is supposed to cap the night. I had undressed in his room and stretched out in his bed when, still dressed himself, he came in and sat down on the edge of it. It seemed a long time that he sat there, looking at me. "You have no business here," he said, finally. And in a tone as cool as his look had been kind, he added: "Get up, get dressed, and go home!"

To you, who could hardly have regarded this first act of a play that was never finished as other than appalling, it would have seemed still less excusable than the moonlit tragicomedy I had played out with the Maestro till the final curtain. But to me, oddly enough, it was a milestone. It marked the first, and if my memory mistakes me not, the only time when a man, stranger though he was to me, looked at me with the eyes with which I should have been able but could not or would not see myself. And it marked the first time that I had been the recipient of a man's generosity.

* * *

FOR SO LONG I USED TO WONDER HOW MY NARRATIVE would sound in your ears, had I had the tongue to tell it. So often, on the road I chose and which I wanted to think and wanted you to think I traveled alone, you have willy-nilly accompanied me as an unwelcome but inescapable *Doppelgänger*, casting your shadow now behind and now before. What would you have said had you known where your feet must tread to follow mine, through what dark streets and into what for you unimaginable situations? Would it have comforted you at all, in the anxiety a thousandfold multiplied had you realized the extent of the grounds for it, to have known that more than once when I had just come out of a door through which I should never have entered, when I had just parted from someone with whom I should never have been together, I would see some little figure in the crowd that I was suddenly convinced was yours and rush with my heart in my throat in the opposite direction, and that one twilit hour when the aging figure I had spotted stopped and stood still, I ran blindly towards it, calling: "Mother! Mother!" and only checked myself, shaken and aghast, when I reached the unknown woman and saw the surprise on her face? Would the bitterness of your disappointment in me have been mitigated? Might you even have found some salve for the wounds I undoubtedly inflicted had you known that it was you, and you alone in the coronation hall of my conscience, who reigned supreme?

Readers of psychological tea leaves may be right in their claim that conscience does not come wrapped, like the viscera, in the original human package. They may even be right in their claim that the small voice the ancients heard in the stillness after the storm is no more than the poetic expression of their own loose anxiety. Their educated guess should be at least as good as mine. But if they should be right, if conscience is an external fixture arbitrarily fastened upon the helpless babe before it can defend itself and then so well hammered in by parental tyranny that it can never be pried out, how explain its presence in those who grow up among drunks and lechers and thieves and murderers, in the Romuluses and Remuses left to be suckled by the wolves? How explain, for instance, the sickness in the eyes that look out from the pictures of those wanted for crime and in the eyes that look out from between prison bars? From where else stems the sickness, if not from the soul? And what else is the soul's sickness except a troubled conscience?

But even supposing the conscience to be superimposed, supposing it to be no more than a mechanical device invented by man to dog himself with warnings he knew he would not otherwise have had, no more than a brake he devised to curb the headlong pace of his instinct for destruction, it would still have to be conceded that no matter how often it fails, falls into disrepair, and even appears unreparable, conscience, acquired or inseminated by artifice, would still constitute the last best hope we have.

If the small voice could be simultaneously amplified and broadcast across the world, its reverberations would be boundless. Everyone who stopped long enough to listen would recognize it, since its speech is a lingua franca which ears need only be open to understand. As it is, however, I must concede that there seems not to exist a brotherhood of conscience, or at least that if such brotherhoods do exist they are unorganized. There was once a Man who sought to organize a communion of brothers under the banner of conscience, but in the two thousand years since He raised it, too many have failed to see it above the heads of the crowd, and of those who saw it, too few were willing to follow it, and of those who did fall in step behind it, so many quarreled over what it stood for that they tore it apart between them and went off in separate and warring factions with the shreds they had managed to salvage, never to march together again as one. Obviously, to bring about the union of conscience, neither precept nor example is enough, nor is it enough to raise the brightest banner that the world has seen, nor is it enough to be crucified for it. Yet what more could that Man have done?

The trouble with conscience therefore must lie in the nature of its role. In the human drama, it is designed for stardom. But there are many other aspirants for stardom in the theater where conscience has to act, and the competition is always grim. Though it can audition for hero or heroine, it does not follow that it will be allowed to play them. Moreover, dependent as it is both for its stagecraft and its interpretations upon the scope of the play itself and also, to a measure not predetermined, upon the behavior of the rest of the cast, it may, even when happily appointed hero or heroine, forget its lines and muff the part.

Still more confusing about conscience is the *prima facie* evidence that to the selfsame problem no two consciences respond in the same way.

Take, for example, two consciences within one family and assume for the sake of the argument that they were not born each within the individual and circumscribed by that individuality, but that on the contrary both were fashioned and foisted on them by the same parent, the same authority. Would not these two consciences be stamped, if not identically, then at least with an unquestionable family look? If they had been sensitized by external process rather than by the secret processes of their respective souls; if they had been taught all their responses to good and evil by a common teacher rather than being prompted by their own intuitions as to how to respond, would they not have grown up to admire more or less the same virtues and recoil from more or less the same sins? Would they not have had, and have suffered as much from, a same sense of guilt? Yet you knew, we all know, kindred consciences which do not.

But to say that conscience is inborn, as I believe it beyond a doubt to be, is not to say that, like the lungs, the spleen, the heart, and for that matter the brain, conscience knows from the start of life its appointed task and goes about it automatically, growing with the growth of its fellow organs and gaining as the body gains in which it is housed. This is of course not so. Conscience is not as necessary to the health of the body as any one of the body's other parts; a body can achieve full stature despite conscience's delayed, disturbed, or even quite arrested growth. Yet however perfectly for a time the body may seem to conceal the failure of that seemingly most supererogatory of its parts, it cannot conceal it forever either from others or itself. And when the moment comes, as it must, when the body is forced to descend, as it were, into its own cellar and confront that too long etiolated and neglected organism, the conscience, its confrontation can be terrible, for no matter in what condition conscience has been left, it is always still alive. So instinctively does the body dread such a belated meeting, so eager is it to avoid such a meeting at any cost, that it will even, if afraid enough, prefer to die. This I can vouch for. I know it, as you would have had to find it out had you been able to read my narrative through to the end toward which I am heading with such determination. I know it from my own experience.

IN A NOVEL BY RUMER GODDEN I FIND ONE OF THOSE BRIEF candles of a writer's mind for the sake of which readers read and for which they go gladly and permanently into debt for a lifetime. A child speaks to a trusted adult. "Is everyone unhappy?" the child asks in despair. "Everyone," the adult replies, but adds after a moment, "That doesn't prevent them from being happy."

Today, when I bear on my shoulders the full weight of accumulated error which, while heavier no doubt than many, is still the kind of load carried by all who reach my age, being unhappy does not prevent me from being happy. This was just as true when I was a young married woman with no more responsibility (as I then saw it) than to be faithful in my fashion, if not to the man who so kindly had given me his name, then to the image of myself as one who might have been true to her true love if she had stayed true to him long enough to make that love come true. I was grown up, or at least so considered by those other growns-ups of my generation who, no more than I, stopped long enough in the rush of new experience to ask themselves: grown up to what? And since I knew by then that being unhappy was part of being grown up, I would have felt a kind of *noblesse oblige* to suffer, even had I been unable to think up a reason for it. At the same time I could not help being still young enough to be a little happy in my unhappiness and I might have gone on enjoying it in this peculiar sense, with my heart only sporadically and never more than halfway engaged, with my mind just distracted enough by the occasional writing I did and the occasional visit to an exhibit of paintings or afternoon at Carnegie Hall with Bach and Beethoven and that Brahms whose peculiarly sweet turmoil so suited me, and with my conscience safely stowed away in a corner where I would be least likely for some time to stumble on it. I might have, but I did not. Outside the front door of my apartment, one morning as I bent to gather up the mail, I saw on the topmost envelope a writing I had not expected to see again. The letter was addressed correctly to my married name. It was postmarked Africa and came from my Pole. He had been shooting elephants, he wrote. Except for his escort of Pygmies, he had had no one to talk to. He wondered if I was happy. I had only to read the question in that familiar, precisely trained hand to know with a suddenly focused certainty that I was not.

THERE WAS TO COME A TIME WHEN, AS AN AMERICAN princess who had escaped from war in Poland and had written a book about it, the story of how my Pole and I had met and been parted and met and been parted again (bowdlerized as much for the sake of box-office appeal as for discretion) would enable me to sail, under somewhat touched-up colors, from lecture platform to lecture platform without fear of being snubbed no matter how inadequate the lecture itself, since romance, provided it is romantically enough presented and with neither the pumpkins nor the mice nor above all the glass slipper left out, comes even before money in the pecking order of popularity. "I want to tell you a fairy story," the program chairman would begin, and as I sat listening to the invariably and indisputably improved version of the major fact of my life, I could see in the soft smiles of acceptance that appeared on the upturned, listening faces along the rows of women before me a benevolence I had never seen on yours. Though I knew that in allowing myself to be so smoothly painted as to obliterate the cracks and lines that were there, I was a hypocrite, and though a hypocrite was never what I had wanted to be, I found myself easily resigned to the make-up. Indeed, I am not sure that it has not been for the fortification of this multiplied and somehow—despite my age—quasi-maternal approval from my audiences, rather than merely for profit, that I have made myself a professional daughter, as it were, of the platform and have gone on lecturing these many years since the bubble of the fairy story burst.

However it was not as any Juliet, nor as any Cinderella either, that I visualized my story while I was living it, nor did I look upon the man I had so long longed to marry as a Montague or indeed a prince as such. From that first letter that bridged the gap between us by then so wide that I had resigned myself to believing it no longer bridgeable, I saw that he was still my friend and, though in those days I scattered confidences freely enough among the various women I called friend, the only friend besides my father whom I could trust. I answered his question as to whether I was happy truthfully, and truthfully also, though with an eye to making the truth as palatable as possible, I wrote him what sort of woman I had become. When I showed my father his letter and told him how I had replied, he looked at me gravely. "Remember," he said, "about the frying pan and the fire."

But if with this counsel my father had unerringly guessed, as he always did, where the wind was rising and which way it would blow, I was myself still convinced, and for some time thereafter would remain convinced, that marriage between me and my Pole was now impossible. It was not for marriage that I asked my stars but merely for the chance, which then seemed equally impossible, to meet again. But as if the wish were in itself magnetic enough to alter even the predestined course of the stars (and it is curious how often the power of the wish is thus proved, though more often than not only after one has abandoned it for a new one), the chance came.

It was in the Vienna station, as I leaned out of the railroad carriage window from which one is requested in three languages not to lean, that I saw him again for the first time in six years. Dressed, not as the tweedy student I had known, but as the plenipotentiary of a Central European coal empire that he had now become, and with two new grooves that descended from the flare of his nostrils to the newly compressed corners of his lips, he was not the same. Yet to my companion, the best friend of my childhood and still then my closest woman friend who now stood at the window too, her cheeks aflame with anxiety, I almost shouted: "Look! There he is! He's just the same!"

Just as neither the words we exchanged in the few days of renewal accorded us nor the fervor with which we exchanged them were the same, nor even the promises they encompassed (for we did exchange promises, though more to break through the unreality of this improbable reality than because we had any real hope of carrying them out), so too neither of us was the same. Yet just as the sunlight, the poem, and the phrase "I love you," no matter how different they look and sound from day to day or year to year, have always the same genesis, so too was our love the same. Whatever life's mutations, and they are apparently illimitable, its impulse is constant. It is this continuum of impulse, and only this, that is the same.

IT WAS AGAINST WHAT YOU CALLED YOUR BETTER JUDGMENT, more against it, oddly enough, than against that of my father despite his warning about the frying pan and the fire, that three long years later, and after not only the most legitimate hesitations on the part of both my Pole and me, but also after (and how loath I am to confess now to you what I was loath enough to confess to the priest) still another and this time most illegitimate excursion into one of those seemingly luxuriant bypaths which I used to find irresistible, I set out, with an acquiescence on the part of my husband surprisingly and touchingly rueful and with, on my part, a pang so short-lived, that our seven years together were all but exhaled in the sigh that ended them, to obtain a Reno divorce.

Main stop for commuters on the streetcar named desire, Reno is perhaps the most American of American institutions, for by its mere existence as a divorce capital, it underwrites that right to pursue happiness and that conviction of human perfectibility which together form the cornerstone of our fondest national dream. In Reno, there is always a bull market, never a bear market, for the stocks and bonds of happiness. Men and women who have left or been left by their wives and husbands come together like so many anodes and cathodes caught and compelled to continual circulation in the current of their desire. There is no hiding place in Reno. No cap of discretion is enough disguise. "Got a good lawyer, dearie?" asks the drugstore clerk, when one ventures to buy soap. "Have a drink?" asks the mufti-clad flatfoot, rocking on the porch of the boardinghouse next door. "A letter from your sweetheart?" asks the landlady, as she scans the envelope for which one is holding out one's hand. "Care to go to the movies?" asks one's shirt-sleeved fellow boarder at the end of the evening meal, and then with a shrug, putting on his jacket, goes whistling down the street to pick up a real good time.

That there is another Reno I would not have discovered had I not been given the penance, after my general confession, of attending Mass every morning and saying the rosary every evening for the six weeks I was there. This other Reno does not play the one-armed bandits, frequent the bars, or loiter on the streets. Homebodied and homebound, it appears in full panoply only on Sundays when, hatted and gloved, it attends High Mass. If one has suspected that one was out of place among Reno's transients, one can have no doubt that among these natives one has no place at all. When from his pulpit the priest lets his practiced eye travel along the familiar faces of the congregation until arrested by the face of the stranger and then, with a rising inflection declaims against the presence of all strangers darkening the town, one feels as shorn, as shamed as must have felt the women whose heads were publicly shaved for consorting with the enemy during the war. Nor is this Reno so proudly mounted on its steed of righteousness any less America than the Reno that cavorts among joyless joys. They are the two sides of the national coin.

*　　*　　*

LATE ON THE NIGHT BEFORE AT LAST, AT LAST I WAS GOING to Europe, and this time going for good, the Japanese baroness who happened to be your guest at the so long awaited moment of my departure, knocked lightly at my door and came in with the gift of a flame-colored kimono which, even on my tall frame, fanned out in great, soft folds of shining silk beyond my feet on the floor.

"It was one of the wedding garments when I too was a bride," she told me, adding in her meticulous English: "I hope for you it will also be fortunate." As I thanked her she turned to go and then stopped. "You are not afraid?" she asked. "Why should I be afraid?" I answered. "Oh, perhaps you should not," she said. "But Europe, it is not the same as America. Here you are safe, are you not? You do not think of war?" "War?" I can still hear with what certainty I said that one did not give up a marriage because of war. "And anyway, why should Poland go to war?" I asked, but if it did, I told her, I would simply sit there and wait while my husband fought it and be there when he came home. "I do not wish to presume," she said then, keeping her back to me as she looked out the window. "But it is true, I think, that you do not know his country or his people? It is not easy to enter a strange family and a strange land. It is not easy, sometimes, to understand each other, or to be alone." "But I will not be alone. I will have my husband. Besides, I don't ask that it should be easy. Nothing is easy," I reminded this lady who seemed so gratuitously concerned, "and what is worth most is always hard." I found it more than easy, when she had left and I was folding and packing away her flaming robe, to banish almost at once the uneasy questions that, stranger as she was to me, she had been so much more easily able than you or even my father to waken in my heart.

It must be said at this point that upon neither of you could be placed the blame for what I can only call now in retrospect my well-nigh matchless, my quite unbelievable indifference to all the outside world that did not involve books, pictures, symphonies, friends, lovers, or myself. By then twenty-nine years old, older than have been many men and women who by their willing assumption of responsibility or by their single-handed exploits have changed the contours of history, I was still coasting on the gusts of my fancy, still flying head on toward whatever light caught my eye, still bruising on window panes and singeing in fires the frail wings of the apparently ineducable moth I had been from the start. It was not because I had not heard public events discussed, but because I shut my ears against them that, though aware, I was no less than oblivious of not only the threats and posturings of tyrants on the European scene where I was now to take my place, but even of the collapse of our own American economy which, long before I left home, had brought heretofore undreamed-of numbers of apple and peanut vendors into our city streets, had cluttered our park benches with heretofore undreamed-of numbers of desolate, hungry unemployed, and had melted away with heretofore undreamed-of rapidity the savings of so many who, like my father himself, did not know how they would live when their earning power was gone. Because I had not felt the lash of the times on my own back, I ignored the welts on the backs of others. To the shadow of the whip that had already fallen athwart my world, I gave no need.

Yet I felt as I left my native shores that I was more European than American. Be it said in extenuation of this perhaps wildest of wild illusions that no one, not even the Europeans themselves, felt as European in those days as did certain Americans. We sons and daughters of the Jamesian tradition had imbibed with our pasteurized milk a respect for American hygiene and American convenience but at the same time an almost equal contempt for what we considered American barbarity and American Babbitry. If this was an attitude hung over from the nineteenth century when New England and Virginia looked upon themselves and were looked upon by our kind in our milieu as lonely citadels withstanding in almost tragic isolation the attacks upon their refinement and culture by the savages who constituted the rest of their fellow citizens, it received a new impetus from the twentieth-century Sinclair Lewises at home and from that lost generation abroad whose patron, if not progenetrix, was Gertrude Stein. To all who were of this mind, and not to have been of this mind was to lose caste and hence unthinkable, America was the waste land and Europe the Atlantis of civilization.

As I grew up, you, with your love for every stone of Italy, made no attempt to counterbalance this attitude with any such comparable love either for the high skies and gold landscapes of your native southwest or for the domineering towers of our metropolis. If my father, with his ever-sensitive nose, detected within Europe's intellectual climate the unmistakable whiff of decay, you sensed in it only the musty perfume of tradition, and in this you were no less American than he. I had therefore at least come honestly by my admiration for a Europe I thought I knew.

Between admiring Europe and becoming a European, however, there lies a pitfall visible enough to those with the eyes to see it. But myopic as I was, I fell into it. To become a European, it is not enough to have a better than the usual American knowledge of Europe's lan-

guages or even a better than the usual American knowledge of Europe's arts. To speak another language exactly as it should be spoken, it is not enough to know
the grammar and vocabulary; the very articulation of
tongue and lips and larynx must be learned. To understand another art, it is not enough to recognize style
and content; the climate around and inside the artist must
be understood. I had yet to learn that one cannot learn
a nationality. I had somehow convinced myself, with no
one to push me and well before that falling in love with
a European which was to complete my fall, that I was
as European as I was American. My face, it seemed to
me, was European. What I took for my sophistication,
my taste in poems and nightclubs, my preference for
fancy manners, even my immoral morals, I believed
were European. It never occurred to me until many
years later in the retrospect that follows failure that it
was doubtless not because I was so European but, on the
contrary, just because I was not European at all that I
had caught first the attention and then the heart of that
eminently European gentleman whose life I was to try
to make my own.

All my sojourns in Europe, until the one that I intended to be for keeps, had served to entrench me further in this conviction that only my passport, and not
my identity, made me American. In the shops and cafés,
on the streets and dance floors, in the galleries and
churches, wherever my feet took me in Europe, it had
not struck me that I did not look as natural to Europeans
as I did to myself; that when they took me for granted,
as so often they seemed to, it was not as one of themselves but as an American curiosity. It had not dawned
on me, as it was to dawn on me with tropical sudden-
ness after I went there to live as a European, that, when

what I said was not what had been expected of me, they were not only not pleased with its unexpectedness but were able to master their displeasure only by reminding themselves that as an American I could not be expected to know what they would and did expect.

But still more than my sojourn at Grenoble, where the reactions of my professors, my colleagues, and even of my Pole himself might have forewarned me—but did not—of how unalterably American I was, the winter I spent shortly after my first marriage in Portofino somehow convinced me of my transmutability. I never thought, when we rented the tiny villa overlooking the ancient gourd-shaped Mediterranean harbor that its belonging to a Fascist official might affect our standing in that anti-Fascist village. I never thought, either, that our standing might also be affected by our Saturday habit of joining the fisherman at the waterfront to raise the hackles of the night with Chianti-inspired song. Nor did I ever think that when we attached to ourselves the American bachelor, who thereafter went everywhere we went, my role in our trio would become the subject of tirelessly salacious speculation, nor indeed would I ever have given a moment's thought to what our cook told her audience in the village square about my husband and me having separate rooms. That I was a *forestiere*, a creature from another forest, and therefore an object of as much suspicion as ridicule was an idea I could not, because I would not, entertain. I was living in Europe, and since I was happy living there, I must be, I was, as good as European, and Europe might just as well, might indeed still better, be my home.

Today, when my children who after all are half European if not by experience then by birth, speak with shining eyes of how much more livable life is in Europe than in America, when they insist upon how flat, stale, and unprofitable are the ways of Americans who have not lived or are not living abroad, impatience at the sound of what to me has become such an outdated refrain overwhelms me. But it is then that I force myself to remember that, in their attempts to rationalize their feeling of superiority to American ways and to Americans, they are keeping alive, albeit unconsciously, one of the oldest of American traditions.

THERE WAS NO ONE TO REMIND ME TO SMILE NICELY AT the servants at my second wedding, since neither you nor they were there, and the "Gawd bless ye" from an old woman at the door of Westminster Cathedral was the only wholehearted, unofficial blessing I received. In the five weeks that had elapsed since, alone with such lares and penates as I possessed, I watched first you and my father and then the silhouette of the city itself fade out of sight from my outbound deck rail, I had already begun to see both Europe and America with different eyes. Armed with a packet of papers proving my birth, my first marriage, my divorce, and my reinstatement in the Catholic Church without which this new marriage would not have been possible, I had gone to Paris first. There I had tried, quite unaided except by the passive presence of a cousin of my Pole's who dutifully accompanied me from parish to parish, to persuade a French priest to marry us, but each priest, after permitting himself a brief homily on my conduct, had refused. Then, after a last dinner in the hotel with the cousin and his wife and his mother-in-law—for my share of which, as I was leaving the next morning, they had sent me through the concierge a bill—I had crossed the Channel to renew my quest in London. Here, accompanied this time by a lawyer unearthed at long distance by my Pole who was still waiting in Poland till the date of the wedding should be fixed, I made the round of parishes again, while the lawyer discoursed to me on American divorce habits, American illiteracy, and American materialism. I had finally found a priest. I had bought the rings we would need to exchange at the altar, and *en plus*, in the only flurry I had allowed myself, a truly unfortunate white hat. I had safely come through both the importunings of a fellow passenger from my recent crossing who prophesied—not, I believe, with a total disinterest—how unfortunate my proposed marriage was bound to be, and the exhortations of the German husband of an old friend who, just escaped from the new Germany where Hitler had enthroned himself, tried his best to convince me to give up what he was sure would be a hopeless attempt to become a European and to go back where I belonged. I had somehow ticked off the long hours of the days and the still longer hours of the nights of waiting, to rise at last upon the early morning of my Pole's arrival. I had driven to the station where we were to meet, had watched the train glide in and had run the length of it searching among the faces of those stepping off for the face that was not one of them. I had driven back to the hotel with my knees shaking. I had stood, with his telegram saying he had missed the boat train and would be on the next one, outside the hotel on the street awaiting his taxi, and had seen him descend and hand out of the cab his mother whom I did not know and who he had not told me was to come.

During the three days still to be endured before the wedding, I had been alone long enough with his mother to be told, as she gave me the velvet case containing the family pearls, that she supposed I must realize that she would have preferred to give them to someone else, but I had not been alone long enough in those three days with the man I was about to marry to reap even the reassurance of a kiss. In my room in the London hotel which was to be my springboard into a happiness I so tenaciously continued to expect, as one expects, when toiling up the side of a mountain, to be rewarded at the top by a panorama view which it never enters one's head may be obscured by mist or cloud, I was wakened on the eve of the marriage, some time after I had managed to fall asleep, by loud British voices. The light had been switched on, and gathered around my bed were two strange young men and a fair-skinned, mocking girl. They had come, she said, to inspect for themselves the mistake their friend was making. "Such a pity," she said, scrutinizing me, "to marry an American!" Shocked then into full consciousness, I had watched the night pale and risen the next morning with new trepidation to go fasting to the Communion that preceded the later ceremony. I had waited for what seemed an inordinately long time while my bridegroom knelt in the confessional, without being able even for the fraction of a second when he came out of it to catch his eye. And it was here now, in London, and on a sunlit summer street, that my old love and my new husband turned to me at last and said: "I shall not forget what you have done for me and how far you have come."

How far indeed I had come, I can see clearly from this present distance, as I can see too that however far I came it would not have been far enough. But on that day that brought us together it seemed that we never had been or could be apart. Bygones, however recent and bitter, were never more bygone to me who by nature had such trouble in letting any pain go by than on that day that seemed to be laying the specters and bogey-men to rest for good. I was grateful. I was so grateful that the din of the night club where we sat out our first evening seemed like a private serenade; so grateful that when he left me the next afternoon to visit the zoo with some other cousins and did not return till two hours later than he had promised I forgot to worry in the won-der of knowing with certainty that he would be back; so grateful that the lunches and dinners we shared with his mother, the visits to frosty acquaintances, the endlessly tied and therefore unending tennis match we attended, and the trip across the Channel during which, after muttering that he was not accustomed to traveling with women, he left me with his mother till the boat had docked at the Hook, all seemed easily outwaited compared to the tests of patience I had safely passed. I had my reality. The rest had become the dream. And as I see it now, it was better than just as well that I did not share with you then by letter, any more than I would have by word of mouth, either dream or reality, for in giving reality expression I might already then have de-stroyed the dream out of which it had sprung whereas, for a time at least, the two were almost one.

THE FIRST COMMUNICATION I EVER RECEIVED, OR ANYWAY the first that had been actually written and addressed to me—and not merely drawn like a Cro-Magnon graphic to feature a gollywog named Budinsky whom my father had invented as a middleman to go between his complex world and my primitive one—was a postcard from my sister. For a long time thereafter I kept that card as a talisman, until it vanished as so many treasures, both tangible and intangible, have a way of vanishing in the smoke of the years. From the writing which I can still remember and which in no way yet resembled the extraordinarily neat calligraphy of even the most violent of her letters when she was grown, I adjudge that she must have been, when she wrote this card, in mid-adolescence. I have forgotten the postmark, but not the message. All it said was: "Remember, little sister, to be a sport."

Perhaps I owe it to that admonition from her who was still at that time what I wanted to be most, that while I have failed to live up to its spirit so often that the occasions when I did not fail are as conspicuous as thumbs, in the literal sense I have been, not sporting, but a sport. From the swimming race of early childhood when I opened my eyes at the sound of the final whistle to find not only that I had not won but that I had not, despite lunging arms and legs, progressed from the take-off, I have managed not to weep at physical defeats or gloat over physical victories. It is in the metaphysical moments of truth that I have not remembered to be a sport. Since among the couches on which I have stretched out the couch of the analyst does not number, I shall doubtless die as I have lived without knowing why I could never extrapolate from the technique I acquired for the body's endurance to a like technique for the soul's. I assume, though of course I could be wrong in assuming, that an analyst would diagnose the pains of my body as being so many penances inflicted upon it by my recalcitrant and therefore ailing soul, since to so many analysts the soul exists merely as a reflex of the body's nerves or a precipitate from the body's juices or a sediment of the race's experience. But to me, in my uneducated darkness, soul and body, however seemingly interdependent, have independent lives of their own, and indeed are sometimes so at loggerheads that they can be said to be incommunicado. I have found this as true in the confessional as I have found it true in bed.

To be a sport is to put one's best foot forward. No image could be more profitably held before the young, it seems to me, now that for so long I have dragged my best foot behind me and that in my own young it is too late to hope to instill anything. No one can fail to recognize his own best foot. There are some, of course, whose best foot is so crippled before they learn to walk that they grow up to spare it and give the other instinctive preference. But these are comparatively few, one could say miraculously few when one considers how inevitable it is that the most wisely and tenderly administered authority can never always be just and that its least, most intermittent injustices will tend to impair if not actually cripple that delicate best foot of the very young. But most best feet, even if by the time they have reached their maximum growth they are no longer as pristine, as unblemished as they were before ever they touched the ground, retain their spring, and there has never yet been a best foot that could not gain in strength from being used and that did not, if forced to go first, come to do so almost automatically.

But if the habit of putting the best foot forward is to be so established that though there are nails in the road or even though the ground itself opens up it will not hesitate, it must be taught from the start that for putting itself forward there neither is nor can there be expected to be a reward. It must not be applauded when, softly and gingerly, it makes its first move. No matter how hard it may be to look on impassively at the first brave step in the right direction and no matter how tempting it is to the loving spectator to reward the effort, his impulse must be checked as it is being born, for from the moment the best foot begins to anticipate reward, it is lost. Nothing could be more true than that virtue is its own reward, nor could any maxim that sounds so pompous be less pompous than this one, if truly understood. What it means is that virtue has no reward. Virtue is not a means to an end, not a means to win love or enter heaven. But if it is important to make this clear on spiritual grounds, on worldly grounds it is no less important. Once one goes out into the world, one is alone with whatever virtue one has mustered, and while by and large the world cares little which foot is put forward, when it does take note, it is always to approve the wrong foot rather than the right. Moreover, even that tiny fraction of the world one may have cornered for oneself, and even within that fraction of a fraction the person on whom all one's hopes are pinned, may not so much as recognize one's most carefully caparisoned and bravely displayed best foot.

Like everyone else, I have long known how to appear to be a sport when to be a sport was to my advantage, as also, like all but a choice few, I have found it voluptuously easy not to be a sport when not to be one seemed to be to my advantage. Yet, plain as it was to me on that far-off day when I received my sister's postcard, her counsel, together with the card it was written on, faded and cracked and dropped from my sight.

If you could have asked me why at this late hour I put such emphasis on what to you would have seemed not just a childish word but a childish notion I would answer that I so emphasize it, in part at least, just because of the way you lived and died, as also in very great part because of the way my father met the long test of his life and the hard hour of its culmination.

In vicarious form, moreover, I have learned from sampling the literature of all ages and climates, from writers of such different temper that one would have sworn they had not a single common bond, that on being a sport they think alike. But if their testimonial were not in its age-long corroboration convincing enough, I have seen corroboration after corroboration in friend and foe. And above all, I have lived at the side of a man to whom no contretemps was worth a complaint even when that contretemps was the loss of home and country. Yet, stubborn and thick-pated pupil as I was and still am, and reluctant as I was and still am to admit that as a teacher life has been so much more merciful to me than to many others, I was unable to learn from all its vicarious lessons that first lesson which is not to take off the mantle of a sport, no matter how heavy it becomes, and not to hang it up, no matter how conveniently a hook presents itself. I have worn it from time to time, but when the heat is on I take it off. For a great while, I could not even see the use of it except for appearance. Now, at long last, I see it for what it is. It was not living that taught me; it was dying. However one dies, it is then that one most needs the mantle, but if one has meanwhile mislaid it, it will not be there to reach for at the hour of death.

YOU NEVER KNEW, FOR YOU COULD NOT HAVE KNOWN unless I had told you, how gladly, how spontaneously, in fact how almost automatically I set out, in that first season of my life in Poland, to be a sport. And why not, you might well have asked. Why not, indeed? Here I was where I had wanted to be, after traversing the world to get there; here I had what I had wanted to have, after defying the world to get it. The very least I could do, you might have told me, and I would have agreed, was to ignore the concealed but omnipresent doubts of the new relatives, the considerably less concealed hostility of the new acquaintances on their periphery, and the anything but concealed curiosity of such close friends of my husband's as a former Maecenas, then fallen into circumstances so reduced as to be almost non-existent, who came one day in my husband's absence to the mansion on the outskirts of the mining town in Polish Silesia where we were living and, adjusting the monocle that dilated his eye so balefully, remarked point-blank: "Why did you marry him? Surely it was not love. You are too clever for that." Decidedly, he was too clever for me. I still do not understand what he meant.

The very least I could do, too, was to overlook, after our month's motor trip, crossing the Austrian and Italian Alps and descending into a Venice no more gilded for me by the light of the setting sun on its legendary shapes than by the light of our being together, the end of that time of privacy when we had to meet his parents in Vienna for the protracted prayers and processions of a Catholic Congress. I did overlook it, as I also overlooked, when we returned to Poland, his to me inexplicable pre-occupations with everything else, or so it seemed, but me; his airy, unregretted, and everlasting tardiness; and his departures week after week for business in Warsaw, Berlin, Prague, Vienna, and Paris. But I would have overlooked them more wholeheartedly, had they not left me, except for the cook and valet and an elderly maid, with no one to talk to and with nothing to do, except learning Polish regular and irregular verbs and bouncing balls against the backboard of the tennis court. Now, after twenty years in which what I have had to do has so predominated every conscious moment that I can count the hours I have stolen from it, it seems scarcely possible that time was when I counted time a burden instead of a gift. But I did, and if I am to be as honest as I seek to be, I will say that I would not exchange today's stolen hours for those that were heaped on me so abundantly and for which I had no use. However, the hours when he was there at hand were still then so full as to leave me ashamed at the mere thought of fret.

No doubt you sometimes wondered, as my friends must also have wondered until years later when both you and they found out, how little it meant to me—the product of a class so vaguely defined by the word "middle" that it embraced both people I would not have wanted to meet and people who would not have wanted to meet me—to become a princess. From the time I met my Pole, I had had the same disinclination to ask him how he felt about his title as I would have had, had he been Jewish, to ask how he felt about being a Jew. It was no more to be questioned than the arch of his nose. Though when I had first heard his title it had roused my curiosity and when I had first told my friends I was going to marry him I had been aware that his being a prince was of far greater interest to them than what kind of a man he might be, I had come nevertheless to take the prince part of him so for granted that I had never even troubled to search the histories for how it had first come about and was on occasion thereafter put to some public shame by my lack of interest. However, to marry a prince does not make one a princess overnight. When the man at the desk in the London hotel to which we moved the day we were married called me "Your Highness," I admit I thought it was a joke. When I was first introduced to strangers in my new guise, I felt, not that

I must live up to it, but that I must live it down. And when my husband, who had been calling me his "Hobo" for years before we were married replied unsmilingly, when I asked what had become of the hobo, that I could not be both a hobo and his wife, I felt I had been kicked, so to speak, upstairs.

Probably nothing, however, is as seductive as privilege, as nothing is so easy to puff up as the self. Servants make quite a fuss over princesses. Sales clerks abandon their other customers to wait on princesses (perhaps especially American princesses). Ambassadors put princesses on their right at dinner. Clubwomen drive long distances even in snow to hear princesses. Important people treat princesses as their equals, while unimportant people treat them as favored by the gods. Children are allowed to stay up long after bedtime just to look at princesses. I cannot say how all this affects the real ones, but the ones, such as I, who have borrowed their finery tend to forget about the borrowing and begin to imagine that their hats are crowns. But it was not till I ceased to be one that I realized how much of a princess to myself I had become.

In that first winter in Poland, however, the future was still benevolently hid from me. Moreover, it did not occur to me to try to look further into the future than the coming birth of a child, since this event, which I had been afraid to hope for, not having had any reason to be certain that I could fulfill my woman's role and knowing that to the family which had had to accept me only the fulfillment of this role would make me acceptable, was of such magnitude (and never can the magnitude of the coming of a child be overstated) that it preempted my whole horizon.

"You are like the trunk of a tree," my husband said to me on one of the rare occasions when he remarked on my appearance except to suggest an improvement in it and which, no doubt just because of their rarity, have lost nothing of their first echo as they go on echoing down the years. And indeed, as week by week I thickened, I felt as a tree should feel if it could watch its own wonderfully certain growth and know itself to be attending effortlessly yet inexorably to the business for which it was designed.

So few were my distractions that winter that when my best friend arrived unexpectedly from America as breathless as Americans always seem when they are out of America, and said: "But what do you *do?*," I had to answer "Nothing." It was impossible to explain how, insensibly, I was toning myself down to the point where I could find enough in the walks I sometimes took with my husband, trudging behind him on the neat path his feet trod down for me in the snow; in our weekend sets of ping-pong, when it was I who went scurrying after the wicked little balls because, as he said, this would strengthen my muscles for delivery; in the often entirely silent games of halma we played after late dinner and to which, because they kept him so cozily within reach, I looked forward with a longing and an intensity he could not only not understand but found somewhat embarrassing. Euphoria cannot be explained.

It was true that when I had heard over the long-distance telephone from Berlin her familiar voice—the first from my other world to have reached me since our marriage and the first since I had been in Poland to ask to speak to me—I had had to go to my room to swallow my tears. But those tears were no more than dew as compared to the cloudbursts that would, to my own and my husband's horror, come down with such frightening frequency later, and we attributed them at the time and unquestioningly to my condition. There were no tears once my friend appeared, however, and although it seemed to me when she announced her coming that to have her to talk to would round out my days completely, in her actual presence I found I had nothing to say and wanted nothing so much after all as to have no one to talk to but my husband.

I have never again lived so nearly in the present as during the winter that I bore my first fruit. A day was good if my husband was there to end it, bad if I had to end it alone. But good or bad, it sufficed unto itself. Its shadows were its own. The past was too far behind to infringe on it, the future too certain, since I still could not see how our future could be even affected, much less determined, except by ourselves. When, sometimes, I went forth with my husband into the world of the local coal barons or that of the lordly Polish or German squires who formed, though geographically divided, a society of their own, I heard of course about the repercussions of the American depression on European economies, about the bitterness between Poles and Germans, and about the dark deeds (though for these excuses were still being made) inside Hitler's more and more serried ranks. But try as I dutifully would to listen, my attention seemed to be pulled back as by invisible strings and turned in again upon the delight it would be when the luncheon or dinner we were attending was over and my husband and I would drive home together in the leather-lined Austro-Daimler with the fur rug across our knees, or upon the uninterrupted evening with him that I could count on for the morrow, or—looking forward to my private drama—I would think how proud he would be of the child and how brave I would be when I gave it life and how extraordinary it was, after all, that I had life to give. It was a cocoon that I inhabited. That it was spun of dreams made it no less real to me. And now that I would not know what to do with a cocoon if I had one, I am glad that in those brief months I knew and was grateful for its warmth.

I am not yet a grandmother, though through no shilly-shallying of my own, but I cannot imagine, if my daughter were having a child, that I would be so indifferent, no matter what ocean lay between us, to how much she knew about the task ahead. Was it, I wonder, your concept of delicacy that made you withhold such warning as might have changed the course of my life? Or was it a ladylike disgust for the old wives' tales which, in less refined societies, one generation of women whispers to the next with what seems a merciless, but is in fact a merciful, candor? Or had parturition, with its grappling and gore, so scandalized you that you had taught yourself to forget it? Or did you comfort yourself (if in this instance you needed comfort) with the thought, stoutly held by my husband's family, that a woman who has been married and divorced and married again was *ipso facto* informed enough about this elemental crisis to weather it alone? Or were you, after all, quite simply detached not just from my body but from my soul, as I never was from yours?

Even when I brought my husband for his first brief visit to America five months after the child was born and you saw for yourself, or at least could and should have seen, how deep, if unreasoning, were my wounds, you kept your eyes closed to them and lavished upon the, to you, almost unknown son-in-law such a pyrotechnical display of attention that one might have supposed not only that it was you who had found and chosen him but that it was he, and not I, who had given birth. That my father acknowledged no more than you my need of help did not baffle and therefore did not hurt me, for I knew that he knew and that knowing was somehow more than enough for him to bear. But that you did not so much as put your hand on mine or murmur a reassurance, let alone ask the solicitous questions I had thought I could expect, I could neither understand, despite the long history of your failure to understand and my defiance, nor yet forgive. I was lost, as we all are lost when we suffer pain without name or reason. And being lost, I had become again myself a child.

Since I first heard the Chinese saying, "I was sorry for myself because I had no shoes till I met a man who had no feet," I have tried to keep it within reach. I can think of no saying that carries more weight, none more fitting to balance against even the most excusable self-pity in an age which, though it purports to be wholly dedicated to making sure that everyone gets shod, has in fact cut off more feet than any other. Yet such are our fibers (surely I can say ours and not just mine?) that we can endure with at most a passing *frisson* the plunge of a dagger into our neighbor's breast while at the prick of a pin in our sensitive skin we howl. There have of course appeared across the centuries men and women—and please heaven let us not forget them—who preferred to bear their own breasts to the dagger than to see their neighbor suffer from a pin; it is they, and not those who escape both dagger and pin, who constitute the blessed. But the blessed are only blessed because they are so few. For the rest of us, a plane down at sea, a bombed city, a community awash in a flood, or an unknown child under a car—unless we happen to see it—scarcely arrests us long enough to consider that there, but for God's grace, go we. Even a mortal blow to a friend casts no longer a shadow than the setting sun. As the doctor and priest grow a professional carapace from behind which to look at living and dying, so we too, to ensure the peace of mind we insist is a birthright, accept with professional sangfroid all tragedies except our own. Indeed, we not only inure ourselves to catastrophe that does not touch us; we even work out a philosophy of catastrophism to explain and hence belittle the lightning that strikes elsewhere. And so, though in my time six million Jews have been martyred, whole societies wiped out, and the uprooted from every corner wander the earth without a home, I still grieve, now when the story is so long past as to sound almost apocryphal, over that most imponderable of griefs that was the loss of my husband's love after our first child was born.

It does not take more than the unpredictable and unpremeditated roll of a stone to start a landslide. On the day following my daughter's safe delivery into the little world of her family which had anticipated her with such joy, I was lying on my hospital bed, my long finger tightly held in her infinitesimal fist, unaware in the afterglow of triumph, as too my husband and even my doctor were unaware, that for the time being I had given the very pith of what I had. It had been a long birth. Behind it there stretched the years when you had eroded my nerves before ever I knew that I had nerves or that, as the antennae and *sine qua non* of the brain, nerves must be coddled at least at the start if they are not to be permanently crippled. Behind it there were the accumulated years in which I myself had played on my nerves so carelessly. Behind it also lay the immediately preceding months when I had been at some pains to hide every niggling pain and conceal every rooted as well as rootless anxiety; the immediately preceding day when my husband who was tired of idle waiting in the Vienna hotel had arranged with the doctor to give nature an extra fillip; and too the night of the birth itself when, with nature by that time fully alerted to my husband's wishes, we had jounced through street after empty sleeping street in search of a place for me to eat and had shared at last, with two prostitutes and a workman, a Toulouse-Lautrec meal. Now, with the task I had set myself accomplished, I was resting on my laurels, enjoying the first softness of the May air that drifted in through my window and the companionable and approving smile on my husband's face.

"By the time I come back," he said, "I am sure you will both be strong." "Come back?" I repeated, stupidly. "Why yes," he said. "I will go home tonight." "Has anything happened?" I asked, my mind racing over the possibilities of disaster. "But no. Of course not. There is a meeting of the golf club tomorrow. You know I am president. I must be there." With these innocuous little words, and all unwittingly, he had dislodged a stone. It began to roll. I was too weak and unreasoning to stay it. Before it hit bottom, it would have dislodged in turn his pride in me and my pride in myself, his love and my trust, and the bridge we thought stood so solidly across the abyss between us.

SOME ASPECTS OF MY LIFE IN THOSE NEXT YEARS YOU would have liked better than I, for, taken out of the context in which I could not avoid seeing it, that life had a cachet all its own. You always did prefer to play god within even the narrowest confines than to have a minor part on the main stage. To be mistress, therefore, as I had to try to be mistress, after my husband's father died and we left the coal mining town to settle on his estate in the old province of Galicia, of a house which, ramshackle as it undoubtedly was, bore the title, for the hundreds of "souls" on those ten thousand acres, of "the palace" and the outdoors and indoors of which took a staff of thirty-five servants (some barefoot and raggle-taggle, others uniformed and begloved) to maintain, might easily have caught your fancy as it never could catch mine. I have no doubt that you would have flinched at the chocolate paint on windowframes and doors and stairs that still further darkened a house made sombre by prevailingly cloudy Polish skies, that you would have run from the cackle of barnyard fowl so oddly tolerated in the back courtyard and the summer-long buzzing, browsing flies they attracted. You would not have waited a moment longer than compelled to before banishing the dusty, many-pronged hunting trophies that jutted from the walls and stripping the chairs of the black oilcloth with which they had been covered after the waste laid to that house by enemy soldiers in the first World War. You would have scorned the washing facilities which no urban American such as you or I could have called facile and feared the germs, as endemic to that way of life and as staunch as its piety. Nevertheless, without preposterously stretching my imagination, I can see you mustering order out of routine disorder and distributing bounty with a sense of accomplishment which, even if I had mastered the domestic arts, I could not have enjoyed, for I cannot in all honesty bring myself to concede domesticity to be an art and never, not even when it became incumbent upon me to adopt with my own children the tone of authority, have I wanted to play god.

With no effort at all, moreover, I can visualize you in

the *pied-à-terre* my husband took for us in Warsaw, sitting at my end of that handsome refectory table you sent after me when I went to live abroad and introducing one fit topic after another while bestowing your most social smiles upon the ambassadors and fellow princes who came to our dinners, or in turn at their tables leaning brightly forward to greet their gambits with adequate and sometimes sparkling replies. Yes, I have only to close my eyes to imagine you not just keeping afloat but actually swimming in those waters of artifice, less aware even than I of the current of treachery flowing beneath them and hence moving less cautiously, airing your humanitarianisms and liberalisms as another might play the harp or sing. You would have found in the hieratic procedures against which I spent myself trying not to rebel the velvet rope of exclusion and inclusion that to you meant safety.

Above all, I believe, you would have relished the visits to that most fashionable as well as traditional Central European castle which was, so to speak, the jewel in Poland's social crown. With your keen eye and longing for perfection, you would not have failed, as I failed merely because I was not happy in the assembled company, to enjoy the Bouchers and Fragonards smiling their prim, cupidinous smiles from the walls; the mirroring inlaid floors and many-candled chandeliers with their multiple refractions; the gold-braided uniforms of the footmen, one of whom stood behind each chair in whatever room we dined, and the gold plates for gala occasions; the burnished copper fireplaces gleaming from each end of the ballroom; the linens, the tapestries, the high finish of the woods, and the pale, arch-sized flowers that appeared every day in fresh combinations of color not only indoors but outdoors in the beds beneath the castle windows.

What a happy fuss for you, and what a preening, to decide with the maid who would always have been there to tend you, which dress for which part of the day and the night to put on! Even if, in actuality, the talk had drifted as far from your concerns as it seemed to drift from mine, what a widow's cruse of talk those visits would have provided you with, all the same, when you returned home! It would not have mattered to you whether or not you liked the Hapsburgian counts, the small royalties, maharajahs, and duchesses, the aunts, uncles, and cousins-by-marriage lifted out of the pages of the *Almanach de Gotha* and the rich or notorious Americans lifted out of the social columns of the newspapers to fill the rank and file of the guests and with whom, at any cost, cheerful chatter had to be kept up. The fact that they were who they were would, for you, have far more than countered what even you might have come to consider a rather wintry etiquette. And when the evenings were at last brought to an end at the signal of the most important guest, and you were free to retire to the pot-pourri sweetened luxury of the apartment allotted you, you would not have lain awake on the crown-embroidered pillows, fearing almost to breathe lest you miss the light sound of your husband's footfall that might have been crossing, but never crossed, the floor from his room to yours. For you, the pageantry would have been enough. For me, it lacked all drama, lacking the drama of love.

But if it is quite possible to see you as lady of a manor incomparably less well appointed, and indeed almost uncouth in its appointments by comparison with your house at the Farm, and to imagine you coping with servants closer in appearance at any rate to the Bushmen

than to the lace-aproned Irish or Scandinavian minis-
trants to your comfort at home; if it is at least plausible
to picture you making your afternoon calls week after
week on the same Warsaw hostesses or seated among
the foot-tapping matrons at pre-Lenten debutante balls,
and deriving from the acceptance accorded you everywhere for the sake of the name you had acquired and the
husband who assumed responsibility for you a pleasure
that I was not worldly enough in that precise sense to
derive—it is not even conceivable that you would have
ventured into the one world within that alien world in
which, though I could scarcely have been more of a
stranger to it, I did not feel strange. In the forest, I was
at home.

All I had known of forests before were the woods at
the Farm where the underbrush grew up permissively,
cluttering the bases of the trees as it pleased; where the
trees themselves lived and died unmarked and unnum-
bered; where such furry inhabitants as must have made
an abode among them left no trace of themselves or their
habits. No one had planned those woods. They lay on
the landscape by the grace of God, not so wild as to be
awesome but wild enough to offer just that contrast to
house and lawn and garden and meadow that the civilized eye demands. Though they had provided me with a
sometime asylum from your visitors or your vigilance,
I had entered and come out of them without seeing or
hearing or smelling the life inside.

There was nothing haphazard about the Polish forests.
They were as carefully seeded, tended, and pruned as
any garden, some all needles, some all leaves, and some
the magnificent intermingling of both. The dirt roads,
no wider than the width of a cart, and the single-footed
paths that branched out from these were as well known

to the foresters and to my husband as the streets of a town to the people born in it; yet anyone entering the great green town alone and for the first time could be lost within ten minutes of the house. No matter how familiar they became, one could not enter the forests on foot or in a horse-drawn buggy casually. One could no more chatter aloud in their presence than in a museum, a library, a monument, or a church. As one left the clearing behind and moved along between the walls of trees, one's voice dropped, one's feet pressed softly on the ground in obedience to the hush. Of all the sounds that came out of that silence—the rustling and twittering, the crack of a twig, the deep peremptory bark of a buck summoning a doe, even a shot and the ensuing crash through the thicket of a maddened boar—none sent such a shock along the nerves as the sound of an everyday human voice. Here, among the invisible but omnipresent furred and feathered people of this arboreal nation, one was indeed a creature from another forest who had to be silent to belong.

Very soon, I came to belong. I who had never had a cat or a dog of my own because they might have desecrated your immaculate interiors and who till then had no more acquaintance with their undomesticated confreres than a chance encounter with woodchuck or skunk, found in myself a sense I would otherwise never have known, a quite inexplicable sense that I could not call upon at will and that I can only define as a sense of presence. It could not have been born of eye or ear, for long before I saw a shape, and without having heard a hoof that, except in fear, was always soundless, I would know, and know for certain, that something alive was there. Only then, and as though I had been told where to look among the leaves or against the snow, I would see the presence I had felt. To discover this sense and to have it time and again corroborated is a joy to be matched, I should imagine, only by that which a writer or composer knows when from his subconscious, unbidden but prayerfully awaited, a phrase flashes into life. But the writer, the composer can be fooled, can find in the next instant that the phrase is after all stillborn, whereas the fox, the hare, the buck, the boar one does not know how one has spotted is unmistakably alive.

And yet, loving these creatures as anyone must who loves that which in itself is perfect, I sought them only for the most part to betray them. It was because it pleased my husband to shoot them and also because it pleased him that so unexpectedly I could find them for him to shoot that I invited my sense of their presence. Though for no matter what expression of his pleasure or approval would I have shot them myself, I felt no pang to see them die. On the contrary, no sooner had he fired his gun than, like any retriever, I would run to find the warm, bloodied body with eyes glazing over in surprise, and as I dragged the buck or the boar by one pair of legs and he by the other to a road where the coachman could find it, I thought only of the satisfaction on my husband's face.

Curiously enough, however, when it was not he who did the shooting, I hated the death of bird or beast. Taking my stand at a formal shoot beside some guest in our own forest or as a guest in another, I found myself on the side of the hunted, glad when the hunter missed, when the bird winged away untouched, when the buck bounded free, when the boar hurtled safely past bullet's reach. Whether because I wanted to share only in my husband's triumph or whether, more complexly, I wanted all living things to go down before him as myself I had gone down, it was at his side alone that I enjoyed not just the perfection of the living creature but the perfection of the kill.

All the same, I loved them. You who could stand so long before a fresco or a bust, who could not have enough of the view from a hill or a tower, would not have understood, I am certain, since animals when they did not offend you only made you smile as at grotesques, that until today I can go back in my mind with undiminished wonder to the time when I looked for perhaps a whole minute straight into the unblinking eyes of a red fox and the time when a doe fell into my lap where I sat in a trough of snow and pressing her wildly heaving flank against my face as she scrambled to regain her footing, turned, before fleeing, to stare at this other living thing that was myself. You, with your fluttering tempo and quick discomforts, would not have been willing to sit immobile on a tree stump in a swamp for as long as an hour before the northern summer's late darkness descended, waiting, with gaze fixed on the line of the tree tops, for the sudden swoop of the woodcock into the last rays of the light; nor, in the depth of a January frost, could you have forced yourself to stand for perhaps two hours without stirring so much as to catch the drop on the end of your nose before it turned to ice, listening and watching with unbroken tension for the boar to burst from the snowy thicket where he had bedded and clear with a single thrust of his great black chest the path or the opening and vanish. And even if, on an evening of late summer, you had had the patience to attend such a courtship of buck and doe as I was once immeasurably fortunate to have witnessed in a small meadow deep in the forest, I feel certain you would not have seen, in this drama of desire, its lightning, or heard its thunder. The joys of the forest would not have opened to you, for while I was more afraid than you of civilization, you were more afraid than I of life.

But there was one aspect of my life in Poland from which you would have recoiled as instinctively as I. Still less than I would you have brooked the kind and the extent of the pieties expected. You and my father were right, not in your distrust of Catholicism per se, but in your prophecy that I would not truly embrace it. You were right, however, for the wrong reasons. In your prejudice against it, you had the rooted conviction that to be a Catholic was incompatible with being an intellectual. You saw in Catholicism a spiritual corset as outmoded as the *ceinture de chasteté*. You believed that the very orthodoxy of belief was Procrustean, and that belief and enlightenment were mutually exclusive. A mind must be free, you were sure, to be effective, and if you conceded, as I am not sure you did, that in the past there had been effective Catholic minds, you were making a concession to history that could no longer be made after the modern revelation that there was no such thing as revelation. You were therefore convinced that, given the intellectual training I had been given, I would be unable to fit into so doctrinaire a bed. But that turned out not to be the case. It was not my intellect that stood between me and faith. There is nothing so brave, I know now that I have lived long enough to see many forms of bravery, as the courage to take the leap in the dark, to be willing to defy the evidence against God's existence and stake all one has on the chance that He exists. The risk defies description, since what it endangers is one's pride. Niggardly as it sounds, niggardly as it is, I was and am afraid to be fooled. To the sin of pride the gates of any heaven must be closed.

If I had then known what I have since learned vicariously about the heroic argument, the wrestle with doubt, the terrible walk in darkness with perhaps only a single moment of illumination to light the way, that constitute the lot of the believing intellectual, I think, or anyway I would like to think, that I might have accepted the challenge, or at least have recognized its size. But it did not occur to me to raise my sights. All I saw in religious practice was a certain sweetness of manner and custom, and in its strictures, all I felt was the sting.

Only now, I realize that not once either in childhood or later did I behold you on your knees. This might explain in part, though it does not extenuate, the resentment that grew in me with the accumulated hours I had to spend in that position, not only before altars, but in the dust of the road, on bare floors, on the stone in crypts, in the mud at gravesides. Always, it seemed, there was reason for supplication. But the attitude of the suppliant goes ill with pride. Whoever has been taught that above all he must stand on his own feet tends to acquire so rigid a stance that it becomes harder to bend the knee and bow the head than to lie down altogether.

Moreover, like the ubiquitous crows that cawed and flapped on the edge of the forest or hung above the hen roosts awaiting the moment to swoop down and carry off an egg, death hovered over our landscape. It was there, lest we chanced to forget it, in the carved or painted Crucifixions and Descents from the Cross; in the photographs of the bodies of deceased relatives, hands folded over a palm frond and eyes closed for eternity to open; in the commemorative Masses said day after day for one or another of their souls. Not birthdays, but death days were noted and observed. To pray for a good death came ahead of praying for a good life.

However often, and in your last years you made it almost a daily practice, you wielded the weapon of your death, knowing how impossible this weapon was to parry; however sure you were, or claimed to be, of your own particular Valhalla; however defiantly you insisted that you could hardly wait to die—you still would have found yourself, I am certain, recoiling as I recoiled from the black veils, black vestments, black hints of damnation, and black resignation to pain and grief and injustice held to be fit preparation for a death which was not just the end but the goal. No less sombre than the Presbyterianism of your earliest childhood, this puritanical flagellation—practiced, ironically enough, by a society to which the very word puritan was anathema—would have frightened you as much as it frightened me. That it did not destroy, for the people around me, their appetites, their buoyancy, and their capacity for laughter I have never understood, unless it was because, having had martyrdom thrust upon them by history and having found in the religious ideal of martyrdom both a justification and a solace for it, they derived, like those accustomed from the start to bear great burdens on their heads, a certain satisfaction from balancing its weight.

Since martyrdom was no historical or spiritual burden of mine, however, and since as a rebel by nature I could not believe that it might also be natural, I should have been able to observe the rituals, whether necrophilic or not, as objectively as I would have observed the pyres at Angkor Wat. I should have been no more profoundly affected by the prevailing religious gloom than by the prevailingly cloudy sky. Had I been well, my reason might have triumphed. But I was not. Unrecognized by me or by my husband and for that matter undiagnosed by any doctor, I had fallen, following the birth of my daughter, apart. Since the term "nervous breakdown" sounds today as quaint as a guimpe or a corset, let us call it a breakdown of the walls of the imagination which left that intangible inner citadel almost tangibly naked and exposed.

A few days after my return to Poland with the baby, and while I was still dazed by the scope of my responsibility for the new life I now had to hold in my hands, my husband's father had died. If the birth of his child had no more shaken my husband than he would have been shaken by the birth of a foal in his stables, the death of his father shook his very soul. He spoke, when he returned after the week of the burying, of nothing else. He not only did not seek solace from me and the child; he did not wish for solace. Placing in my lap the snapshots of his father's dead face and of himself standing by his father's coffin, he neither knew nor cared that there could have been nothing I would have wanted less to see. At night, he moaned in his sleep. In the few moments of the day when he was not in his office or receiving condolence calls or answering letters of condolence, he addressed me as though I were not there. With the roar of the cataract still in his ears, he was deaf alike to the cry of the newborn and to my own.

Such as my senses were, had I been in full possession of them, I would not have called for help at a time when it was my husband who appeared to need it and not I. Moreover, had he called to me in his bereavement, I would have answered. But what became clear then, and still clearer in every crisis between us thereafter, was that quite simply he did not want me to be there at all.

Just as an experienced swimmer will sometimes drown in what looks to the bystanders on the shore like scarcely roiled waters, so, safely delivered of a healthy baby and

ensconced in a comfortable home, I was drowning, and
too busy battling with the swift cramp in the heart to
tell why I was going down. That I needed rescue did not
occur to him. I could not forgive him for not knowing.
It was then that I ceased to be the me that both he and I
had thought in good faith I was, and became, in turn un-
forgivably, a melancholy, moping bore.

It would have been inconceivable for you to ask me
at any time during or even after the collapse of the marriage what drove my Pole and me apart. Given your
doubts, founded and unfounded, of my character, you
doubtless thought you knew. But if I were to so stretch
probability as to imagine not only your voicing such a
question but my answering it, I would have to say that
I did not, indeed I do not know. Reasons exist, of course,
as I am attempting to prove. But reason itself is ex post
facto when it comes to the heart. One can conjugate the
conjugal failures *ad nauseam:* "I failed you, you failed
me, we failed each other." One can carry the enumera-
tion of failures beyond differential calculus. But precisely
when and precisely why the light went out and the
house, once warm, grew cold, not the patient on the
couch nor the repentant in the confessional nor the con-
fider among confidantes nor the plaintiff in court nor
the mourner at the tomb can say. There is only one certainty: no marriage, when dead to either participant, can
be raised again.

Often, now that I and the friends who are closest to
me have reached the point of no return and I can look
all up and down their lives and my own, I speculate as
to what causes such variation in the capacity to tolerate
stress between one person and another and from one
time to another in the same person. When a building is
being designed, the architect allows for a give in the

struts and girders to enable the finished structure to yield to the play of the wind upon it and not fall. So, in the past, our Architect allowed, in designing us, for stress tolerance. He arranged mutation after mutation to fit us to live in sea and primeval forest. He gave us the brain to withdraw from encroaching ice and the hand that obeyed the brain in striking fire. But unlike the designer of modern towers, our Architect seems not to have taken our greater height and hence our increased need for stress tolerance into account. He has added no new give to our struts and girders although, like the towers, we are now bared to far more turbulence. It becomes harder and harder, therefore, not to believe that when we fall it is because we are not designed to stand, that when we stand it is in spite of being designed to fall, and that whether we stand or fall is an accident.

As stress tolerance goes, yours was as low as any I have observed. Had you not had my father to stand between you and whatever wind arose, you would have blown over with the first gust. Seeing you quail so immediately, seeing you rush for shelter from any outer turbulence, I determined as far back as I can remember that I would weather storms. And so I have. It is not in storms that I fall. It seems to be when the sky is at its stillest, when all wind is suspended, when absolute quiet reigns, that I break down.

How far down I broke, as it were, I have no way of measuring except against the plunge I was to take years later in the false lucidity that comes with desperation. At the time of which I now speak, I was not desperate. I was nowhere nearly yet as near as I would one day come, and for the only time in my life, to being what you were still insisting with almost your last breath that I had always been. I was nowhere near insane.

Certainly, had I been in my right mind (which, when it is right, is no less right than any other), I would have countered the mourning gloom that hung over that house in the forest when we settled in it with the apple-cheeked radiance of the child who brought smiles to the most unsmiling faces; I would have placed on the scales against my several physical disabilities the many physical comforts and the few, the truly negligible demands on me; and above all, I would have recognized their compensatory sweetness in the rare moments when my husband and I watched together the absurdly touching antics of the creature we had called to life. I would have contrasted, as those in their right minds instinctively contrast, good with bad, light with dark, and knowing that at best light is always dappled, would have acknowledged how relatively light was even my darkest dark. But I was not quite, as I knew even at the time, in my right mind. As I lay in my room on the plumply stuffed chaise longue made for me as a special indulgence or lingered with the nurse and child in their whitewashed, toy-filled rooms upstairs or as, in the spurts of fevered energy that alternated so unaccountably with my languor, I covered the doors and windowframes and wall trim of that house with coats of bright new paint, my mind moved back and forth between regret and recrimination with the terrible aimless regularity of the captured beast in its cage. When the nerve specialist to whom I was sent for consultation asked if my husband or his family maltreated me, I was appalled. No one was cruel; no one was even impolite. They were as civilized —if by civilization is meant self-mastery—as any people I had ever seen, as patient and as careful with me as they would have been with a dog not yet housebroken or a horse as yet unbridled. I could tell the foreign doctor how ill at ease I felt, but I could not tell him why. When with a kindly, paternalistic smile he said: "Perhaps your husband does not give you enough attention?," without stopping to think, I replied: "On the contrary, he fusses too much." And for this moment of reawakened pride I paid by being left even more politely even more alone.

ONE DAY AS I WALKED BESIDE THE BABY CARRIAGE THAT the nurse was pushing along a forest path, a tiny peasant woman bent double under the load of sticks and branches stopped, when she reached us, to stare at the sleeping child. "Pretty baby," she croaked in her old voice. "Whose is it?" "Mine," I said. She looked me up and down. "Jesus and Mary!" she said. "Such a mother to have such a child!"

Time has not melted those little icicles of words. In my more than a score of years since then of being a mother to two children who, whatever they are objectively, have in common with every child ever born a merciless vulnerability to the woman who bore them, the sibylline words of that crone have crystallized, and it seems to me now that they have, not just for me but even for the best of mothers, the finality of an epitaph.

When one considers the complex of nerve and vein and fiber, and within and beyond these the secret dynamite of the soul, contained in the frail, puling babe that encases them, how can any woman, her own mystery long since bled out of her, seem anything but prosy and stale by comparison? When one considers what it is that is committed from the moment of conception to her keeping, how can any woman even begin to measure up to her task? If I say this in part at least to exonerate you as well of course as to exonerate myself from the blame I attach to us both as mothers, I am handing out, as it were, a general pardon to mothers good and bad, knowing how imperfect must be the best of them.

But this is only reason speaking, and not the heart. Just as still in my heart I have not forgiven you your failing the child I once was, so too I do not forgive myself my failing, as all too often I have failed, the children my children were. That I find it easier to forgive my failures than yours goes without saying, though failure equals failure whatever the variations in degree. At the same time, I am aware that in principle the heart that cannot forgive other hearts is no more worthy the name than the heart that too easily forgives itself, and hence that it is you who should, I who should not, be forgiven. Principle, however, is reason; forgiveness is of the heart. And unreasoning as I am (at an age when long since reason should have laid firm hold on the helm), I am compelled to say in my own forgiveness that in all but the most furious frustrations of my motherhood, I have remembered what you as a mother forgot—that no child, summoned to existence so imperiously, so arbitrarily, so ruthlessly, asks to be born. For this reason alone, everyone who has ever lived deserves forgiveness. Perhaps that is why we continue to feel certain that if God exists, He forgives us all.

Compounding my debt to my children, as I have no way of knowing whether you compounded yours in that sense to me, I did ask my children to be born. It was not as the chance offshoots of passion that either my daughter or, almost four years later when I was beginning to lose hope, my son, were brought into being. I called them with all the voice I had; I called them, and they came. This in itself is such a miracle that it seems impossible that I, or any other woman who has been thus answered, should forget it. It ought to be impossible for us, however children unfold, whoever they prove to be, and no matter how little they tally with our dream of how children of ours should look and sound, to forget the miracle. It ought to be unthinkable for us to demand that they meet our specifications as tidily as though they were cut from a bolt of cloth. It ought to seem so presumptuous as to be out of the question for us to attempt not just to clear the path for them but to make them walk in ours and go whither we are bound. The miracle should be enough but it is not. Very soon, as soon as the child can open or close the door to itself, as soon as it discovers the power of yes and no, the power of silence when we expect speech and speech when we expect silence, we begin to forget how extraordinary and how splendid is the mere fact that the child is there. We begin, then, that battle for power which goes on, unless we find in ourselves the power and grace to abandon it, until the hour of our death.

Time was when a parent had the right to offer a child's life to the gods; to sell the child into captivity; to live by a child's sweat; to do all but cook and eat a child. But long after such visible exploitation was put beyond the pale, an invisible exploitation went on unchallenged, since, owing its existence to its parents, the child was held to be indentured to them for an advance of sacrifices so great that a lifetime of service could scarcely hope to repay it. This was not called exploitation; it went by the name of love. Even in your time, when it began to be the vogue to set the young free, parental authority was still equated with parental love by all but the few poets and dissecters of the psyche who voiced their doubts. Like patriotism, parental love was considered sacred. But, by the time I became a parent, the pendulum had swung, as pendulums do, completely the other way. In my time, while all other forms of love, however illicit, however perverse, had come overnight to be accepted, the love of a mother for a child came now not merely to be considered ambivalent but potentially lethal. For everything out of line in everybody, mother love was to blame.

Perhaps I may be pardoned my complaint that by having been born when I was and by having given birth when I did, I find myself in double jeopardy. When I was a daughter, it was a crime to resist authority; when I became a mother, it had become a crime to assert it. I was supposed, as a daughter, to give you an unqualified love that you as a mother were not required to give me; as a mother myself, I was supposed to give that same unqualified love to my children, though they were no longer expected to give it to me. By each of these standards, therefore, I stand convicted of that failure of failures, more bottomless than not to have loved at all, which is to have loved critically. Yet how can one love with the heart and not the mind? And if one were to succeed in choking off the mind and in keeping the loved one licked by the warm tongue of unvarying admiration, would not that love be less than human? That was not the kind of love I sought from you, nor was it the kind I offered my children. It was your mind I longed to please, and my mind that I longed to have pleased. What is to distinguish us from other creatures if not the awareness that the mind betokens? What is love worth, therefore, unless it is aware? And indeed, what else is love itself but awareness at highest pitch?

Yet if power tends to corrupt (a theory gladly espoused by all who do not possess it), then there can be no doubt that that first absolute power of the mother over the child tends to be the most corrupting, since it is neither stolen nor preempted but given carte blanche as it were by God to be used at will for the child's survival. The risk of the child, placed so helplessly in the lap of a power that must be accepted for so long before it can be appraised, is greater than any the child risks again until it dies. But the test for the mother is no less of a test than the risk is a risk for the child. More than a test of fortitude, of patience, of the charity that must go hand in hand with love, it is a test of her knowledge of when to wield and when to curb power, how to transfer it and when to abdicate it altogether. It is a test not only of her wisdom but of her essential soul. The test is supreme since it involves a life that is not her own. For a while she must be God. But to be God and human at the same time is impossible.

If I see no reason why mothers, per se, should be sacrosanct (except, of course, for their own advantage), I can at least try, having had and been one, to speak of them objectively. I submit, therefore, that the trap laid for them is preposterous. While they can never be all good, they can be too often (since often is too often) all bad. No matter how serenely sacrificial and loving a mother may mean to be, she will sometimes fail in serenity, sacrifice, love, and even in intention, and the best she can hope is that she will rise often enough to her superhuman role to earn the child's forgiveness for when she fails. On the other hand, quite apart from the debauched, the drunken, the harpies and the she-wolves upon whom, for some inscrutable reason of His own, God so irrationally confers this honor, even respectable, dedicated mothers, mothers who would be capable of dying to save their children, can still be bad. It seems therefore that a mother must be judged not by how much, but by how she loves. Yet if how good or how bad a mother is rests not upon the fact of her loving but entirely upon the quality of her love, it is conceivable, to me at least, that love is perhaps not after all the chief requisite, that perhaps it is more important for a mother to have character, to be dependable, just, even-tempered, sunny and serviceable than it is for her to love. I can conceive of such a woman making a facsimile of love more convincing than love itself. But of course this is a heresy. For today it is generally agreed upon by all who pronounce on the subject of human relations that everything is as nothing without love.

However, lest I make the task of being a good mother appear as difficult as to be beyond any but the highest reach, I should add that every mother starts out with that almost limitless capital which is the child's instinctive trust. The child not only needs but wants to give it. Yet bottomless as it may be at first glance, it is not a widow's cruse. It will not brook extravagant expenditure. That which has been drawn out must somehow and continually be replaced. If not, little by little, perhaps even unnoticed by mother and child alike, it exhausts itself. And once used up, so abhorrent is the vacuum that, more often than not, hate rushes in to fill it. At this point the improvident mother has nothing left to live on but chance charity.

But assuming that love is the *sine qua non* of mothers and granting that it is not the quantity but the quality of the love that counts, what should that quality be? It can of course be defined, like everything else, in terms of what it should not be—jealous, smothering, fearful, exorbitant. Yet the opposites of these negatives do not

make a positive. Nor do even such indisputable posi-
tives as selfless, unstinting, equable, and brave add up to
a definition of mother love on which all would agree.

As though it were not twenty-odd years ago but yesterday, I can see my tiny daughter coming late one
autumn afternoon into the sitting room of that house in
the forest where she got her first bearings from an up-
right position to say good-bye to her Polish grandmother
who was leaving for the winter. "Come," said the grandmother, "give me a kiss." The child stood and stared.
Neither coaxing nor command would budge her. "You
might be sorry," the grandmother said. "You might never
see me again." The child's eyes filled with tears, but she
turned and left the room without bestowing the kiss. "If
you love her," the grandmother said then to me, "you
must break her will." "If I broke her will," I answered,
"what would she have left?" "Submission," came the
reply.

Every instinct I had as a mother recoiled. In the
miniature conflicts that had already arisen between the
child and me, I had felt more pride in the demonstration
of her will than resentment when mine had been defeated. I loved her for herself, and what was her will but
that self's expression? Yet the time was to come when I
would see her stubborn, irreducible will drive her to the
edge of an abyss from which I was helpless to summon
her back, and it was neither I nor my love but chance
and chance only that kept her from falling in. Had it
been after all not the right quality of love that made
me recoil from breaking her will at the start? Had it
been merely my own will not to risk her love for me?
As a mother, had I been good or bad? Myself, I cannot
say.

While in that milieu in Europe the emphasis had been

upon breaking a child's will, in America, where in turn my son was to acquire his sea legs, the emphasis was all on fostering it. It was not submission for its own sake nor for God's that must be cultivated, but that expression of the self which is free choice. If the child chose to obey, so much the better, or at least so much the more convenient. If it chose not to obey, that was best of all, for from the consequences of disobedience it would learn how useful it is to obey, and thus develop reason. But when this Pandora's box of freedom was opened to my son, he hid in fear from the multiplicity of choices that flew out in all directions and waited for someone else to pin one down for him. As from the authoritarianism that was to have proved my love for my daughter, so from the permissiveness that was to have proved my love for my son, my instinct told me to draw back. But in the case of my son, so uncertain was I of my instinct that I went against it. And the time was to come when I would see him flitting hither and yon at an age when the will should be driving him forward and I would be helpless to focus it for him. Had the quality of my love been wrong? Had I been a bad mother? Again, I cannot say.

But from such experience as I have had I can only conclude that love is not enough. It is not enough between wife and husband, between parent and child, between friend and friend, people and people, race and race, or between anyone and God. Granted that without heart one is not living. Still, one cannot live by heart alone. Love is not the panacea, the cure-all, the whitewash, the solvent it is said to be. It does not shape or mend or preserve. All love can do is to give impetus. But without impetus there can be no life, so in the end there can be no life without love.

* * *

ALTHOUGH FICTION IS PEOPLED WITH MEN AND WOMEN who have some one characteristic so marked that they can be tagged with it as dolls are tagged with a name or an adjective that describes their personalities, life is not often so *simpliste* and people, just when one has them labeled conclusively, show themselves to be the opposite of what they are at the same time as they are what they are, and thus reverse as well as uphold one's conclusion. But if I have known anyone who could be labeled by one word, it was you. Not that you were not complex, as complex as we all are, but whatever your complexities, seen or unseen, they were contained within, and colored by, your anxiety. You were the anxious doll.

So anxious were you about both past and future that the present existed for you only as a fragment of one or the other. You wore on your face and revealed in your bearing a sense of imminent doom. Indeed, you were so pregnant with it that, watching you, one felt that at any moment you might be delivered of a disaster. Yet if by disaster is meant an Act of God—that violence to our being over which we have no control— only such disasters struck you as strike everyone who lives as long as you did. Your country was not invaded nor your house pillaged; your ship was never wrecked; your bank never failed; your parents, who survived till you reached your fifties, never charged you with their care; my father, though he left you a widow for twenty years, also left you a living and died keeping his agony to himself. You did not suffer in the death of a child that knife in the back which cannot be drawn out. And although you carried on for years a flirtation with death that one could be forgiven for calling a love affair, when the day at last came for death to possess you, you were asleep. No one but you could have said you were not lucky. But among all the benefits you collected, the one you most stubbornly refused to recognize was luck. Darkened as your eyes were by your nameless anxiety, you could not see it.

I call your anxiety nameless because for the most part you could not yourself have given it a name. Yours were not common fears. You did not fear the water, though you could not swim. You were not afraid to miss trains and boats, though it was never by more than the margin of a second that you boarded them. You were not afraid to be driven by reckless chauffeurs. You took, at eighty, your first flight in a plane with as much *insouciance* as though you had taken a *fiacre*. When my father made his nightly round of checking lights and locking doors, you laughed at him; when he insisted, during my illness at the Farm, in having me carried down the narrow stairs that were a firetrap and installed on the ground floor, you thought the precaution absurd. Yet you shrank from his Airedale as though she were a tigress. You jumped at the sound of something falling or of a loud voice as though at a thunderclap. Your anxiety before each of your dinner parties was such that you brought the staff to tears and yourself to a pitch of nerves where you could not dress without help. Before any plan or decision, from a picnic to a marriage, you drew back as before the breath of doom. Any illness you heard about you were sure you had till a new one eclipsed it, and every pain in your body you diagnosed as cancer. The only anxiety from which you seemed never to suffer was anxiety about anxiety itself. But this, I could have told you had you been willing in the days when I most needed you to hear my troubles, is the most crippling of them all.

Before I had ceased to be a child, I was determined not to be like you. Because strawberries disagreed with you, they became my favorite food. When you campaigned for Votes for Women I sided, in my eleven-year-old wisdom, against them. When you fixed on a certain dress for me, it became the dress I disliked the most. Any young man you brought to the house I regarded a priori as a threat or a bore. Whatever you feared, even if by chance I also feared it, I made a point of braving. Nothing, I resolved, would show that you and I were kin.

That I had a dry mouth and wet hands before examinations or dances, that even the thought of heights griped my viscera, and that my every knock at your door was accompanied by a constriction of the throat and breathlessness, I did not call anxiety. Nor would I, looking back on these agitations today, concede them to be like yours. Born of the instinct for self-preservation, they were as necessary to me, and also as automatic, as that which drives the hare to cover or the bombed to cast themselves upon their faces at the first hint of an alien sound. The anxieties of my youth had their roots in fact.

Moreover, though I am here mainly concerned with a form of anxiety—yours all your life, mine for that part of my life spent in Poland—which undeniably rusts all it touches, I would never say that in itself anxiety is a corrosive. On the contrary, I would call it the leaven of life. If generation after generation has brought to maturity its young in the face of hunger, disease, injustice, and catastrophe, it is surely anxiety that has prompted, tutored, and egged us along the way. No great poem has ever been written, no revolution has

ever been undertaken, no faith has ever survived the continual encroachment of doubt upon it, except through
anxiety. It is anxiety that has led us to measure the stars,
to split the atom, to spot—in time—the mortal shadow
on a well-loved face. It is anxiety that teaches us both
life's demands upon us and how to meet them. If we are
to be saved, it will not be through peace of mind, but
through anxiety. It is only and always upon unrest
that we rest our claims.

But to return to that anxiety which is not seminal, one
can of course be so apprehensive about the self that one
is no longer capable of risking it, so apprehensive about
others that one no longer dares trust them to life. Yours
was that kind of anxiety. You became the skeleton that
everyone at the feast felt it a matter of life and death to
shun. And with the birth of my daughter, I too became a
skeleton at feasts and I too, quite properly, was shunned.

At first my anxiety was evenly divided between my
child and me, but it soon turned so far in on me that I
was on the way to thinking of her only as an intrusion
upon it when, by one of those Acts of God which I
cannot even pretend to forgive, she fell gravely ill.

It is hard enough to believe, in the face of even the
usual inequities, that God's eye is on the sparrow. In the
presence of a child in pain it is impossible. What sort
of God would send into such battle the smallest and
frailest of His creatures, unarmed, unsuspecting, not yet
communicable? If a father were to do so, we would cast
him out. Yet from our Father above, Who is said to be
All Merciful, we are asked to accept this unacceptabil-
ity as a sample of His mercy. We are asked and even
urged to prostrate ourselves before Him and plead, not
to say bargain, for the life of the child. If He proves
deaf to the plea or the offering, we are commanded to

love His very deafness, though at the same time we are assured that His hearing is intact. I have wondered whether it is because He fears that by accustoming us to His mercy we might acquire too sweet a tooth for it that He accords it so sparingly; or whether His mercy depends, as it did with you, upon His mood; or whether, again as it often seemed to be with you, it is on some particular tone or phrase (since all too clearly it is not on the urgency) of the prayer that the withholding or granting of His mercy depends. If He is so much more than human in His power, could He be so much less than human in His compassion? Is compassion then a sign of weakness and resistance to it one of strength? If so, why, since we are supposedly created in His image, can we not look upon the suffering of a child with His apparent equanimity? If He made us as we are, how is it that we have come to consider as lower than the beasts those who voluntarily hurt a child? And if He has so willed our judgment, are we not also justified in judging Him when He is merciless? Did He invent us to remind Him with our every heartbeat to be merciful? Or did we invent Him to help us to remind ourselves with our every heartbeat of the need for mercy? Perhaps it is no matter, so long as mercy does not die.

Since during the long weeks of my child's illness, neither my husband, who twice left his business and crossed Poland to see her but only then when the doctors said she would not survive, nor her Polish grandmother who went out of the country while she was still in danger, seemed to understand what it meant to be responsible, in a strange town and in a language one could not command and without a friend to turn to, for saving a child's life, there is no reason why I should have expected you, who were never alone with responsibility even at home, to put yourself in my place. Nevertheless

I did expect it, and have still not forgiven you any more than them. It is not that there could exist a price too high to pay for the child's survival. It is only that it left me as drained as it left her, and when she needed me most. My loss of trust was like a loss of marrow, except that the blood can re-create marrow while the heart cannot re-create trust. Henceforward, I had to meet each onslaught of anxiety disarmed. But I had learned what not to expect of others. I still had to learn what I could not, and yet must expect of myself.

MEANWHILE THERE SEEMED TO BE NOTHING IN MY LIFE in Poland that did not tend to foster my anxiety. Indeed, had I been less bottled in my concern for the pale, languid child whom I could now carry on the palm of my hand, had I closed my ears to the protests within my own body and opened them to those of the outside world, I would have been forced into some perspective. I would have had to realize how altogether insignificant and even specious (except to me) was my private fever in a country and on a continent where the political pulse had become so dicrotic as to suggest the beginning of the end. To be sure, however, I could not fail to hear the angry grumble of charge and countercharge, claim and counterclaim of which, then and now and always, the dialogues of history are composed. I could not fail to know, if not from the people around me who clung to their conviction that Hitler would keep the "Bolsheviki" out of Europe, then from the liberal American weekly I read in private in my room, that Germany was no catalyst but a threat, and that those who destroyed Jews could destroy Christians too. But this was not an argument to people who believed that only Christians should be saved. Moreover, since to them Christendom was

Catholic, and I was not a born but merely a naturalized Catholic, they did not count me quite Christian. No argument was therefore possible. The sighted do not ask the way of the one-eyed any more than of the blind.

Fearful of discussing politics with my husband lest we be further divided, I avoided them altogether, and in so doing doubtless shocked him more than by any argument. I had no special knowledge nor any experience to authorize what I believed. But I wonder it did not strike me sooner that even opinion born of knowledge and experience is sometimes no more authentic than that of intuition; I wonder I did not have in politics, as I had for example in motherhood, the courage of my ignorance. For it turned out to be not my ignorance but my stubborn indifference to politics that was my crime. Of all the mistakes I made with my Polish husband, perhaps the most foolish was the attempt to shut politics out. In the recesses of my mind to which I consigned what I could not cope with, I knew that outside our gates the tiger had began to prowl. Yet, contracted as I was within my own and my national parochialism, I found it easy to dig my head into the sand where I could not hear its restless padding or see its lashing tail.

At that time, too, my mind was bracketed between birth and death. The price of birth has been death since primeval slime. It is the most common of our commonplaces. Yet the shock of payment never dulls. As when my daughter was born, her father's father had died, so while my son was still kicking against the maternal walls, my own father's end began. The yellowed leaves of a generation were falling to give place to the green of succession. It was not only inevitable but fitting, as I had reminded my husband with that ready philosophy with which we meet all griefs save our own. From behind the carefully unspecific and insistently hopeful words in which you informed me, just before we sailed with our daughter and her nurse to establish them for the summer at the Farm, that my father was in the hospital, the truth jumped out at me. Here was the only eventuality which had ever weighed in the scales against my going to Poland, an eventuality which, had it not been for the greater weight of my fear of you and my longing to escape you, might have so much more than counterbalanced my hope of happiness as to keep me at home. Each time I had seen him, I had asked myself if it were to be the last. This time, there would be no need to ask.

I was there when the attendant wheeled him back into his room. His face was still hectic pink and his eyes still too bright from cocaine. "How is Algy today?" he asked, referring to my unborn child by the ludicrous nickname we gave it and smiling his characteristic half-smile which was somehow so much more gleeful than any grin. He closed his eyes then and lay quiet. When he opened them, the smile was gone. He turned toward the window and with a sudden rasp in his voice, he said: "Don't tell your mother but in a year I shall be dead."

That same night my husband and I went with friends to a nightclub and as I sat by the host and watched my husband waltz smoothly around the room which was completely dark except for the tiny bulbs embedded in the columns that decorated it, my companion, draining his latest whiskey, leaned toward me confidentially. "Those lights," he said, pointing to the column nearest us, "are the radium seeds in your father's neck." When my husband came back to our table, I asked him to take me home. In the taxi, I told him why. "Nonsense!" he said, and gave me the kind of pat men give a fussy woman or child and from which only a pachyderm would not recoil. He left me at my door. It was daylight when he came back. By then I had resolved that as my father could face his death, so I could face my life, alone. Though this resolution lasted no longer than any of my brave resolutions, it carried me over going back to Europe when I had to go. "You will do," my father said as I left him for what both he and I knew was the last time. Two months later, as I was being carried upstairs after my boy's delivery, my husband said: "Well done." These small words from the one and the other of the two men I most admired have been, and are, and will remain my accolade.

IF IT IS NOT IPSO FACTO AND NECESSARILY BETTER IN EUrope or America to be a boy than a girl, it is certainly better in Europe to give birth to a boy. My bed in the Warsaw hospital was strewn with telegrams and visiting cards and notes from people I did not even know and the nurse who took for granted her twenty-two hours of duty out of twenty-four almost wept at the task of taking away and bringing back again the flowers. Upon my daughter's birth, I had not received such attentions. Now I was flooded with advice about how to nourish and how to bring up the new Polish peer, and at the same time exhorted to begin again in order to cover the first one with a second. The point to my existence was made quite clear. I was to ensure the name.

Was it merely proof of egocentricity that, with birth and death to contemplate, I forgot to contemplate war? Admittedly, it showed in me a most singular, first person perspective. But if men must forever be forgetting the bloom and blight of individual trees in the frenzy

of their quarrels over the forests, is it not all the more
imperative for women to keep vigil around the felled
trunks and the seedlings? The singular is lost in plurality.
Yet it is the singular within the plural that gives the
plural significance. The plural is no more than the sum
of the singulars that go into it. So in the end it is the
singular that counts. Wherefore I was perhaps not so
strange in my first person singularity as I was made to
feel. Mine was in part at least the safeguarding instinct
of womankind which has always refused to be distracted
by men's battles into forgetting its generic appointment
with the dying as well as with those being born.

No woman marrying into a society foreign to her
own is at such a disadvantage as an American marrying
in Europe, unless of course she has a fortune. European
society (society, that is, in its narrowest sense) automatically assumes its superiority to Americans whether they
have money or not, but money tends to blur the sharp-
ness of the distinction. American women, on the other
hand, if they belong to what Americans call society,
feel as equal without money as with it to any society they
enter. Coming as I did from a milieu which, for all it
was a segment of American society, nevertheless put a
premium on intellect, and entering a milieu which, for
all it was the quintessence of European society, put
descendance, piety, patriotism, and sportsmanship ahead
of intellect, I found myself as out of place among Polish
aristocrats as I would have been in the bridge-playing
suburb of an American town. Moreover, having been
brought up to believe that intellectual brilliance was the
distinguishing mark of European society, I was too
startled by the lack even of interest in it to attempt to
measure the values they put in its place. If to the Poles
I knew I was as a Gaul among Romans, to myself I

was the Roman and they the Gauls. Though I learned their language, practiced their religion, and took on such of their habits as I had to, I viewed them as they viewed me with a mixture of curiosity, incredulity, and —I fear I must admit it—impatience and some contempt. I saw in them a provincialism, a *Kleinstädtigkeit*, of which I failed to see that I too in my way was equally a victim. Born as I had been in a land of unbounded resources, a land which none dared to covet much less to invade; come of age among people who took for granted the pursuit of happiness as a goal as much as a right and between whom the social frontiers were crossed and recrossed so continually that the lines of demarcation had been all but trod out of sight—I lacked the imagination to put myself in the place of a people impoverished by centuries of warfare, a people whose teeth had been so set on edge by the gall of circumstance and whose nerves had been so stretched to meet the challenge of survival that they had had to band their imaginations with hoops of steel and conserve their energies by eschewing rather than by cultivating material and psychological ease. Considering my inherited advantage, I was narrower in my refusal to look through their eyes than they were in their inability to see through mine.

It did not occur to me (and I am not unaware how often this phrase recurs in my narrative and how inevitably it bespeaks a certain pigheadedness both personal and national) that I represented, however accidentally and unofficially, America, and that I therefore had a mission, no less definite for being private, to represent it at its best. Almost as soon as I began living in Europe as a European, I shed the illusion that I was as European as I was American. Reacting almost violently against the tacit assumption on the part of those Euro-

peans who felt obliged to accept me that I would
change my spots to match theirs, I felt more American
than I had ever felt before. But, like the Poles yet without their excuse, I took up a posture of self-defense.
Their beliefs I regarded as superstitions, their patriotism
as chauvinism, their class consciousness as feudalism,
their poverty as social injustice, their arts as too national-
istic to be universal, their grievances as chips on a para-
noidal shoulder. If I was partly right, I was in general
wrong, since it is always wrong (though overwhelmingly tempting) to lift particulars out of context and
turn them into all-embracing conclusions. It was in the
context of their history that I failed to see them.

Even after it was all over, in the aftermath of the
débâcle which brought about so abrupt an obliteration
of that entire way of life, I still viewed it not from the
standpoint of the Poles I had known but from my own.
When, with the offer from an American publisher of
a contract for a book about my six and a half years in
Poland, I was surprised into writing it, I sat down to
the task with the conscious intent to report impersonally,
but unconsciously bent on self-defense. It was to establish from the start that I knew the picture was one-
sided and hence oversimplified that I called it *Polish Profile*. I was as shocked at its reception by the Poles, and
especially by the American Poles who had never been
to Poland, as they were by the implied social criticism
which they felt to be unjustified in any circumstance,
but unpardonable in the circumstance of Poland's raw
wounds and fresh defeat. I had told neither lies nor
secrets. I had described nothing I had not seen. And
when my husband, shaken by the storm of voices demanding, "How could you let her do it?," asked me in
turn, "How could you have done it?," I was not afraid

to remind him that, before publication, he himself had passed on every word. It was the long shadow of his own and Poland's tragedy that had fallen athwart the book.

However, having said this much out of that compulsion to justify myself which you always despised in me yet never helped to obviate—or at least never until that last moment when you commented on the book sympathetically but far too late—and having underscored, as I insist still upon underscoring, that if I were to write *Polish Profile* again today it would probably be little different, I will now concede that I wholeheartedly wish this were not so. I wish, and no one could surmise how much I wish it, that I had been, that I were, another kind of person, the person with vision, with a self that learns to scotch itself, with a greater concern for loving than being loved. A person so exactly matching this description as to take my breath away I found between the pages of the book an American woman wrote about her experience as the wife of a Japanese diplomat before and during the time when America and Japan were at war. Here was the woman I would have wanted to be, forging, in a fire the dangerous heat of which I could not even imagine, the kind of marriage I had dreamed of forging, bridging unbridgeable differences, looking steadfastly past the hostility in alien eyes to the common humanity behind it, making of love a splendidly encompassing and indestructible edifice. This is what I would admire to have been, admire to have done. What I am and what I did, I admire no more than you admired it. On the other hand, neither from you nor from anyone else has it been admiration that I sought. I wanted to be acknowledged right when I was right. I wanted justice. But what I wanted most was for you to try to understand.

* * *

ONE OF THE MOST SEDUCTIVE IDEAS ABOUT THE NATURE OF
the self now set afloat by the ego scientists on the
stream of modern consciousness is that to love another
one must first love oneself. Philosophically, it may be
true that the capacity to love is all of one piece and
that any part of it that does not function impairs the
functioning of the whole. Emotionally, however, love
is not an in-turning but an out-flowing, a conscious
and unconscious impulse away from the self, which ex-
plains why the self seeks its reflection in other eyes than
its own. But I am not convinced that in order to love,
the self needs to love itself even in reflection. If one is
to judge by what most elates it, the self seems to need
not to love itself but to lose itself altogether. If one
observes those who, having found what they believe to
be a scientific and hence irrefutable justification for self-
love, uncorset it and allow it to swell as it will, one finds
that their love for others diminishes proportionately. I
do not believe this to be a *non sequitur*. Taken at its most
literal, in the flesh, self-love as we all know neither satis-
fies nor fulfills. Being true of the body, must it not
therefore be also true of the soul?

However, if no self can be realized through self-
seeking and if the ideally realized self would seek nothing for itself at all, to understand and achieve this is a
task for saints and martyrs, but not for that *homme
moyen sensuel* who is everyone else. And it seems to me
that of all the forms of self-seeking, the most under-
standable (though here again I may be catching my
foot in my particular trap of self-rationalization) is
our need and demand to be understood. Sceptical as I
am of the prevailing doctrine that a child whose mother

does not love it must necessarily grow up to be both unloving and unloved, I am persuaded that one cannot easily give understanding if one has not been understood. Since I have after all both a mind and the capacity to use it, this is the only explanation I can find for my habitual ineptitude (I will not call it lifelong ineptitude and thus jeopardize this present effort) at putting myself in another's place.

I was never able, and am not even able now that I have become willing to try, to put myself in yours, nor in that of my sister nor years later of my best friend when they turned against me, and only briefly, and at critical moments, was I able to see in sudden, unbidden flashes how things must have looked to my father and how he must have felt about them from where he stood. The configurations of some other viewpoint than my own are as undemonstrable to me as were, in my youth, the configurations of the parallelograms and cubes in geometry. Small wonder, therefore, that with an imagination so in disuse I could not stretch it enough to identify myself either with the people in Poland who were strangers to me or with my husband who, though no stranger, became for me always more rather than less strange. I was seeking not to give but to get understanding. I did not make the discovery until the time for its fruition had gone past that giving and getting are as inseparable in the act of understanding as in the act of love.

Everyone is of course *sui generis,* and although some of us—the bearded, the festooned, the mannered, not to speak of the other-colored—appear to be more *sui generis* than the rest, there is a high degree of probability that beneath the beards, the festoonery, the manner and the other colors, they are just as, but no more,

different from us than we are from each other. I am
not trying to say we are equal, since this would be flying
in the face of the too obvious fact that some are so much
more equal than others. But we are all both peculiar and
commonplace, both specific and general, both ourselves
and everyone. We vary as do the leaves of one tree from
those of another or, with less definable variation, as does
each leaf from the other on the same tree, yet still we
are all leaves, and as such caught and held in the selfsame
cycle.

But there is a greater tendency, I believe, on the part
of Americans (all the more ironic for the fact that they
are more composed of everyone than anyone else) to
see themselves as *sui generis*. The capacity to set aside
one's own skin long enough to try on the skin of someone else demands a flexibility as rare as it is valuable,
and although most of us are forced to at least attempt
it within our own families, few seem to attempt it in the
outside world, and of those few the fewest are Americans.

By the very nature of our history, we Americans have
come to expect, not to have to get into other skins
than our own, but to have all others exchange, upon
arrival on our shores, whatever shape or size or color
or texture of skin they start with for ours. We have long
since somehow persuaded ourselves that ours is the skin
of skins. We forget that as a composite of all the skins
there are, ours is made up not only of those of the lion
and the lamb, but of the shark and the hyena. Moreover, though we loudly protest our own vulnerability
and cry out against every real or fancied pinprick, we
tend to consider all other skins invulnerable. Frankly
amazed when they cry out at being pierced by us, we
are injured by their sense of injury, offended when

they criticize our criticism, stricken if we suspect them of not being as grateful for our suggestions as to how they should handle themselves as we demand them to be in return for our help. We not only do not put ourselves in the place of other nations; we do not even think, as the self-appointed asylum of the world, that we should. And when we go forth east, west, south, and north to visit them, we go as to a zoo or an aquarium, gazing with a certain awe at the mystery of the alien life inside, but seldom tempted to take up our abode with it.

If there has always existed and still exists in intellectual America (which, contrary to all rumor, does itself still exist) a traditional reverence for European art and learning and a traditional acceptance of our inferiority in them, there has also and simultaneously always existed and still exists in that conspicuously larger America that is not intellectual, and perhaps more stubbornly than ever now as an aftermath of the wars, a traditional belief in the superiority of our system and our institutions to any other system or institutions in the world. Just as it confounds us to hear little children speaking French in France or Chinese in China, we are confounded by the fact that, without our foods and juices, our doctors and medicines, our heating and refrigeration, our roads, schools, vehicles, and vestments, other peoples still manage to survive. If there have been a few Americans who wanted to become Europeans, and some among these who have actually become so, most Americans, I think it is safe to say, would view ceasing to be American as a kind of death.

Although there was a time when I counted myself one of those Americans whose eyes were fixed on Europe, it took only the jolt of living there as a European lives to turn my gaze right back toward whence I had come. In all fairness to myself (and no one could be fairer to me, I admit, than I am being), most Europeans, when they start living in America as Americans, have a like experience. Even those who become American—not to speak, for the moment, of those who have come here in our time only because they had nowhere else left to go —clutch with the grip of the drowning to what they brought from home. But none has held with more tenacity to the prejudices, if not always to the principles of his heritage, than, when I chose Europe, I held to mine.

At first, my nostalgia was of the senses. It was not that I was not comfortable, for I had a more cushioned comfort than I had ever had before, since the undeniable comforts of your house had quite naturally been designed for you while now I could collect all the comforts for myself. It was rather a question of that unease to which most of humanity seems to be prone when forced to adapt itself to other rooms, other foods, other conveniences or lacks of them, and other customs than those it has learned to take for granted. I could not know until I lived with them how little I fancied potted palms and Crucifixions as decoration, bed quilts buttoned into sheets that did not tuck in, vegetables bathed in crumbs, white asparagus, venison so high that one smelled it before one saw it, and flowers arranged as though to lay on coffins. I could not know until I saw them that I hated the pillows into which infants were tied to carry them more safely; the outdated, shabby clothes worn by all but a handful of society women; the operatic arrogance of doctors; the pomposity of all men still uncertain of their prestige; the coldly understated manners of aristocrats, the self-conscious bridling of the classes just below on the social slide rule, and the sly obsequiousness of servant and peasant with their insistent kissing of one's hand. I could not know until I had to exchange such dull currency with other matrons how little I cared to tell or hear about the weather, health, and household trivia that provided us with our only common ground. I could not know until I discovered that as a woman I had a defined and unbreachable role to play, that I did not want to be merely someone's wife, someone's daughter-in-law, someone's mother, someone's keeper of the keys, someone's image of piety, propriety and fertility, or someone's idea of the bearer of a name. I could not know until I found it to be assumed, and then I found I could not accept the assumption, that I was a member of a sex which—however invaluable as conserver of hearth and ethic—came second in the human order. I had crashed headlong into a conformity so rock-ribbed that to defy it was to invite nothing less than estrangement and isolation, a conformity both moral and social and even domestic which makes the American conformities now being attacked on all sides with such gusto look like rebellion by comparison. I only discovered when conforming was inescapable that I hated even to do what I wanted to do if by so doing it meant that I conformed.

The idea of conformity was of course not new to me. You yourself had made quite an elaborate game of it. Indeed, it was the only game, except the game of cat-and-mouse with your employees and your children, that I ever knew you to play. While conforming to the conformities with ritualistic precision in matters of appearance and conduct, as also in those of aesthetic and intellectual appreciation, you conformed only to non-conformists in religion and politics, waving aside ortho-

doxy as one who had put away childish things, refusing
to enter a church except for the sake of its structure and
embellishments, refusing to vote Republican or Demo-
crat if there was a Socialist candidate, standing against
God on the one hand but for reform on the other, and
thus able to have the cake of conformity and eat it too.
But my father, who gave not a fig for appearances, went
through life appearing to conform. "Why fuss?" he said,
with a quizzical look, when he saw me rebelling. "After
all, you can think what you please." But it was not until
long after I had left Poland that I finally digested this
hors d'oeuvre from Polonius's table.

After the first two or three years, however, the alien
sights and sounds and tastes and smells became inevitably less alien and even familiar, and would, I daresay,
have become as automatically acceptable as those of my
youth, had not a sharper sense of difference fastened
on me and, funguslike, begun to grow. Like most fatali-
ties, it bore none of the earmarks of importance at the
start, though the fact that so many small fingers pointed
in the same direction ought to have made me recognize it
sooner than I did. When I ordered a bath to be heated
for me every day, my husband's mother suggested that
I might do well to pay less heed to my body and more
to my soul. When a peasant woman came weeping to
tell me that her baby had died and I said she should
have nursed it more regularly, she buried her face in her
kerchief and said: "The will of God." When a cousin at
the peak of his manhood fell mortally ill and I asked if a
specialist had seen him, I was told that God would decide. When my own child had to endure her long as-
sault of pain, I was informed that it was because I had
not prayed enough. Whatever the question—hysteria or
cancer, hunger or fear, theft, murder, or mere nameless

misery—the answer was always the same. But to me, it was not an answer. Their house was founded upon certainty; mine rested on the air. The track on which their minds ran had been laid down for them at the start. I had to make a track of my own through the waste land. What they could not understand they accepted; before I could accept, I had to understand.

One of your favorite anecdotes which I remember from almost as far back as I remember anything was about the little French girl brought to play with my sister who announced as she entered the house that she was Catholic, and when my sister failed to reply in kind, looked at her solemnly and inquired: *"Es tu Juive ou Libre Penseur?"* My sister being unable to answer, you explained for her in your painstaking French that she was not yet old enough to decide her religion.

By the time I had gone to Poland, I was old enough, I thought, to decide mine. I had decided to be a Catholic. But to be or not to be a Catholic is not at any age a matter to decide as one decides to leave or stay, to sleep or wake, to marry or not marry. To become a Catholic is to profess a faith, but to be a Catholic is not a profession (though of course there are professional Catholics). One can study to be a Catholic, but to be one cannot be learned. Like science, it is a discipline, but unlike science, the discipline is only the form by which something inexpressible is expressed. To write a poem or compose a symphony is also a discipline, yet the discipline does not constitute the poem or the music. Still less, indeed immeasurably less, does the discipline of a belief constitute the belief itself. As I grew more and more aware of this discrepancy, I began to realize that I was not only not a Catholic but could not be one, that by nature and by conviction I was a

"*Libre Penseur.*"

To you who considered yourself a refugee from orthodoxy and who lived, all your grown years at least, in
a society that did not require you to print on your card
of identity any religion, what you believed or did not
believe would have seemed, had you found yourself in
my place, indisputably your own affair, provided you
genuflected and crossed yourself and knelt at wayside
images and walked in Holy Day processions and attended funerals and prayed aloud in unison as was
expected. Wanting to be of that world, you would
likely have allowed your right and left hands to go
their separate ways, and by so doing sought to put
others, and keep yourself, at rest. I knew of course
that this was what it behooved me to do, and I tried to
do it, but no one else, any more than I, was fooled. A
libre penseur can no more be concealed in a religious
society than a torn hem or trailing petticoat on a ballroom floor. Technically, the term *libre penseur* marks
only religious status or rather the lack of it, and to be
so marked in the milieu in which I lived was anathema.
Everything despised and feared, from Communism to
economic socialism, was blamed on the Masons, the
Jews, and the "*Libres Penseurs.*" The only difference
between being a *libre penseur* in a Catholic society and
a witch in a Puritan society was a difference in treatment accorded. Witches were burned or drowned,
whereas I, a sheep strayed into a Christian society, was
nuzzled toward the fold with Christian patience.

But when I say that I was and am a *libre penseur*, I do
not confine myself to the technical significance of the
term. To be a free thinker, as I see it, means to be a
wanderer at random from field to field, a hopper over
fences, a plucker of fruit from any man's garden, a

sleeper in strange barns, an uninvited yet welcome guest at chance tables, a hobo at large among ideas. A free thinker may be as arrogant in defense of what he thinks as one who has surrendered his freedom to think; he may also abstain as freely from free thinking as one who has abjured freedom of thought. But the thinker who is not free does not concede the right of the free thinker to think freely, while the free thinker will defend with his life the right of the thinker who is not free not to think freely. Yet the two are not so far apart in their thinking as we tend to think they are. One is looking for, the other thinks he has found, the truth.

To me anyway, the term *libre penseur* evokes with the next breath an American. Every American, no matter how orthodox in religion, is in the non-technical sense in which I mean it and to the extent that he is a *penseur* at all, a *libre penseur*. This is not to say that Americans are not as pigheaded, myopic, and temperamentally cussed as other peoples. It is merely to suggest that to be an American entails, ipso facto, never being altogether certain that what is true is the only truth. Americans, no matter how small, have somewhere behind their eyes the potentiality for largeness. They have at least been designed, if they are not educated, to be commensurate with their heritage. They cannot take credit for it, though for ignoring it as often as they do they deserve the blame. But this largeness is of course not always an advantage. Largeness can become so slack that it offers no support; it can be so stretched that it breaks and one falls through it. It can be even more fatal than smallness, for in smallness there is after all a certain centripetal strength while in largeness the strength can be so centrifugal that it peters away. But largeness and smallness are no Scylla and Charybdis, at least not to me. I would rather be large and perish than small and survive.

If I say that I regret being a *libre penseur* in the specifically religious sense of the term, in my own non-technical sense, I do not regret it. Where I erred, it seems to me now that I look back on the anxiety which beset me in Poland, was not in being *libre*, but in not being *libre* enough. I was not the large, but the small, the narrow American. I was not *libre* enough to see the magnitude in the effort to preserve a continuum of custom and belief from generation to generation. I was not *libre* enough to see in this continuum the value of continuity itself. I was *libre* only in according myself the right to think freely, and therefore I was no more *libre* than those who denied the right to be *libre*, or at any rate I was no more of a *penseur*. My attitude, shaped in great part by what I had unconsciously taken and what I had consciously refused to take from you, and in very small part by what I had learned from my own experience, was as deeply ingrained in me as their attitude, carved into their unconsciousnesses before their fathers or even their fathers' fathers had been born, was ingrained in them. From which I conclude that it does not take much history to set the American mold.

Now that there is no one likely to trouble to denounce me, I could avoid self-incrimination with regard to my life in Poland altogether. But I do not wish to take refuge behind this fact any more than I wish to take refuge behind the fact that you are no longer here to judge me. On the contrary, I am deliberately writing my narrative as though you were judging me. Yet this does not mean that I should lean so far forward in the proliferation of *meae culpae* that I fall over on my face. It seems therefore only fair to say that in my early thirties I was not yet petrified; my clay was still somewhat malleable, or would have been found to be, had anyone taken off the wrappings to have a look. I could not be, I never would be manoeuvered. But if love had been added to patience, I might have been shaped to fit. However, though one can command patience from others as also from oneself, from neither can one command love. Love comes and goes as willy-nilly as the wind and like the wind, it does not suffer harness. Of all that is free, love is the freest. And when it is gone, it is gone for good. Whatever semblance replaces it even the sightless can see for the simulacrum that it is.

CONSIDERING HOW SORELY I WANTED MY POLE'S LOVE AND how dependent for my very oxygen I was upon it, I gaze back now in astonishment upon the automatic efficiency with which I whittled it away. "Where are you going?" "What time will you be back?" "Take me with you." "Don't leave me." "How long must you be gone?" "What day are you coming home?" "When can we be together?" "Why can't we have a little house alone?" "Must you ski (golf, play tennis, ride, shoot, etc., etc.)? Am I then not enough?" And when he did come home, or take me along, or give up his pleasure for mine, I did not think to conceal that I had a pain or a worry, or felt left out, or was bored, or hated the gloom from which he, but not I, could escape. That these were bona fide complaints seemed to me reason enough for uttering them and even when I realized that each was another nail in my coffin I still thought that by their utterance I would bring about the changes for which I longed. But the only change I brought about was the one I never sought.

The question is, was that change in fact a change? Frankly, the uncertainty dogs me still. It would be senseless to imagine that a Polish student, in no position to marry, would have proposed marriage to a penniless American and thus subjected himself to the ignominy of parental disapproval, the misery of separation, and the embarrassment of having to put off the union from year to year, had he not been in love. But that had been nine years before we were finally married, and however far-fetched it may sound, I cannot call it beyond question that when he asked me for the last time to marry him, it was from a sense of duty.

I can see the disbelief on your face, had you read these words. You would have been no less disbelieving than the members of his own family. To you, no one in his right mind would have undertaken to espouse me unless stricken with an aberration of love. To them, somewhat madcap though they believed him to be, he could not possibly have construed as a duty that which was so clearly the essence of his duty to eschew. Indeed, on the face of it, there was no reason for a man by that time so eminently marriageable, bearer of a legendary Catholic not to speak of historic name, to go to such pains to obtain a wife who had become a Catholic only to abandon Catholicism, who had not waited for him, who had indeed made a marriage which, though outside the Church and hence invalid to Catholics, was all the same valid in the eyes of the world, and hence valid enough to disqualify her.

One would have had to know my Pole as I knew him and to have known me as he knew me to give any serious consideration to the idea that in the end he had married me from a sense of duty. But given the quixotry which so often acted as a yeast upon his worldliness, lifting it out of itself and transmuting it into an idealism he was not even aware he had; given his memory of the innocence which—despite my budding pretensions to the contrary—was still mine when first we met and his knowledge of exactly what had become of that innocence between our first parting and the last before we married, it is not only no effort for me to imagine but an effort for me not to imagine him persuading himself that he must assume responsibility for what I had done; for what, if he did not undertake to prevent me from doing, I might still do; and above all for shepherding me back into the Church to which he had first led me. During the brief retreat he made in a monastery before reopening the subject of our marriage, he may well have prayed, not for forgiveness for taking what he wanted though it was wrong, but for strength to take what he did not want because it was right. Even as I gave his rhetorical question the inevitable answer, I thought this a possibility. For a time, it festered. But I could not dig it out, and after a while it embedded itself so firmly in my tissue that it ceased to hurt. Occasionally, brushing against it by accident, I was reminded that, foreign body or not, it was still there. Then I forgot it.

Evidently I was not cast for a Mary Magdalene, since I was neither overwhelmed by a sense of sin nor by gratitude for my salvation. Quick as I had been among my own kind to recognize my inadequacy in comparison with those more adequate, in Poland I was what I would now call ridiculously sure that, if I appeared inadequate, it was because those around me were blind. That I could be blind did not occur to me. I wonder if, in this loss of capacity to take the measure of both others and myself, I was not closer than even you ever imagined to losing my right mind. I say this with the natural reluctance of any ego to expose its most dreaded flaw, but also in defiance of what is today the generally accepted doctrine that self-doubt is a sickness, that to admit inferiority to anyone (no matter how obviously superior) bespeaks a disturbance of personality. I believe this to be one of the most outrageous fallacies currently in fashion. I am certain, and in this my father upheld me out of his fifty years of experience with insanity, that it is those who have no self-doubts, those who are unable to suspect themselves of inadequacy, those who see no one to whom they feel inferior who are, in fact, the insane. If it is a sign of a certain distortion and of an excessive preoccupation with the self to see everyone else as superior, I submit that it is not a lesser but a dangerously greater distortion to see oneself as superior to, or even as equal to, everyone else (except, in the latter case, in the eye of God), since wherever one may be there is always someone either superior or at the very least more than equal. To recognize this requires less humility than judgment. And it is by our judgment that our sanity is judged.

With the birth of my son who, as the *Stammhalter*, made me all unknowingly the additional gift of an almost Chinese prestige in a family to which continuity came second only to piety and honor, the imbalance between me and my husband (which was of course the root of the imbalance between me and his world) might have been rectified. Both of us were pleased. His pleasure sprang more from the fact that the child was a boy than from the incommunicable, yowling bundle of the boy himself; mine was twofold in its satisfaction at the accomplishment of duty and its joy at the prospect of watching a creature as mysterious to me as is the male unfold.

Here was my second chance, that chance for which everyone finds himself praying, a chance that would have to be described by the most unbelieving of unbelievers as God-given, a chance to mend, refurbish, renew, to reinfuse with joy a tattered relationship out of which joy had all but emptied. Unlike so many second chances which come and go unrecognized by those who so ardently seek them, this one was too obvious to miss. I recognized it. Whether my husband also recognized it, I cannot say, since he was at no time willing to discuss our relationship either in part or as a whole. "If you talk about a thing," he once told me, "it becomes real. If you don't, it is as if it did not exist." While I am as disinclined to apply this ostrichlike principle to close relationships as I am suspicious of the opposite principle that talk in itself—if it goes on long enough—will prove a solvent, I have nevertheless upon occasion tested it out and not been as dissatisfied with the results of what can only be called burying alive as I expected. That is what I did with the suspicion that my Pole had married me from a sense of duty. It lay for years below my consciousness as good as dead. Only when I entered into colloquy with death did it prove after all to be alive. But then, death, whether or not one has made one's own appointment with it, raises even the dead for a last encounter with memory before engulfing memory itself.

My second chance, its face wreathed in hope, held out both hands. All it demanded from me was to wear my maternity cheerfully, to accept with a sweetness assumed if I could not feel it the advice and suggestions about the baby and the quotidian concern of everyone in the household (except my husband) over whether, as the most important of the cows, I furnished the desired quantity and quality of milk; to outwait with a patience

so cleverly concealed that he would not guess my need
for it my husband's embarrassed disgust at my new function; and to be ready for him when he turned again my
way.

But as the still warm autumn days went by, each
somehow longer to me though shorter to the sun than
its predecessor and except for the "good mornings" and
"good nights" and brief inquiries about the children
which it would have been hard to avoid and yet be as
fine-mannered as he was, my husband showed less need
than ever to spend with me more than the half hours
after meals when the family sat together and remained
if anything still longer in the little chancellery across
from the big house which served as an office for the
affairs of the estate and the very name of which I now
hated to hear, that best foot of mine which I had resolved never again to fail to put forward began once
more to drag. The ghost of my second chance merged
with those of all lost chances and vanished out of sight.

Would anyone else have so failed, I wonder, in my
place? Enveloped in comfort; removed so seemingly far
from those first sea pusses in which neighboring nations
were beginning to be sucked down; collecting daily the
munificent and unearned increment of the two children
who had come in answer to my call; living (even if only
in a manner of speaking) with a man whom I loved as
unquestionably as he deserved loving—I yet dared not
be content. Comparing my anxiety with the miseries to
which women of every age and class and climate have
put up so brave a front, I find it now almost incredible
that I did not veil my frowns and put a *sourdine* on my
sighs. Was I then, for all you had not exactly spoiled me
and for all my contempt of spoiling, even more spoiled
than you?

One of the few Poles whom I looked on as a friend was a child specialist. Early that winter he had driven out the fifty miles to our house on a bitter rainswept night to inspect the children. When he had finished his check of their neat little bodies, he turned to me. "And what's the matter with you?" he asked. "Nothing," I answered. "Or at least I don't know." "Well, if you don't I do. You're getting to be a Pole." He beamed at his own malice. "Polish women are all martyrs. You'd better look out. It's catching." He swept from the room. I followed him downstairs to see him off. As, with a flourish, he bent to kiss my hand, he murmured: "For God's sake, be an American. Have some fun."

It was with the idea of having fun that I went with my husband to Vienna and attended the Opera Ball which the diplomat who had brought us said—and how rightly we were to see all too soon—would be the last. It was with the idea of fun that I let my husband pick for me a pink lamé, long-trained evening dress to go with the diamond necklace his mother had given into my keeping upon the birth of my son. It was with the idea of fun that I followed my husband to Warsaw on his next business trips and went to the dinners and called on the hostesses and ran the gamut of the amiabilities. It was with the idea of fun that with whoever had the reputation of being a wolf I played wolf in sheep's clothing. It was with the idea of fun that I insisted on making my husband share double-acrostic puzzles with me when he could spare the time. It was with the idea of fun that I bought a peculiarly demure gray chiffon nightgown. Tooth and nail, I went at the idea of fun. I have always thought there was more sense in pursuing fun than happiness. But if I am to be honest, fun, like happiness, seems to be lost in the pursuit.

*   *   *

UNTIL NOW WHAT I HAVE BEEN LARGELY CONCERNED WITH in this narrative which you would have been so very unlikely to read and yet which I persist in imagining you as reading now that it is safe for me to give my imagination such an intoxicant, is, or seems to me to be, the problem of innocence and the lack or the loss of it in relationships where love either should have been or was at the heart. I do not deny that concern with the heart alone is a kind of parochialism, any more than I deny that none can afford the luxury of remaining parochial in this or any other sense at a time when, and in a world where, the sky has ceased to be the limit. But I cannot pretend to have been any less parochial than I was and still cling to that pretension of honesty by which, as by a single yet tenacious thread, my narrative is suspended. I was and would have remained, had I not been wrenched out of it, as parochial as though I had inhabited an egg. My eggshell was so tough in its fragility that it did not shatter till it met with the violence that was to destroy for evermore and for everyone the possibility of such a habitat.

However, the first crack in the smooth surface appeared some time before its smashing. In the spring following my son's birth and only some two months after the Opera Ball my husband and I had attended, I was sent back again to Vienna by myself to consult a diagnostician known as a *coryphée* because he had succeeded in curing some ailment of Mussolini's. While for my ignorance of what was about to transpire in Vienna on that fatal weekend I can offer no real explanation, it may perhaps help to make this ignorance somewhat less incredible if I point out that my husband, who was as anxious as I was not about political developments, would scarcely have insisted on my making this journey had he not, despite all his newspaper reading and all the information gathered from his supposedly informed connections, been as unaware as I that I would step out of the train into revolution.

Arriving late for my appointment, I kept the taxi which had sped me through strangely emptied streets to the modest hotel where all but the richest and most worldly aristocrats put up, and drove on out to the edge of the city. Around the doctor's villa was a high wire fence aflutter with dozens of red *Hakenkreuz*-stamped pennants, and from behind it, as I approached to ring at the gate, a battalion of dogs of all shapes and sizes bounded toward me. The doctor himself came out to beat a safe path for me through the clamor. After a few questions and a jab at my stomach he gravely pronounced that I had an appendix, that to go back to Poland with it would be to take my life in my hands (what else can one do with one's life anyway, I have always wondered, and how much better than to leave it in the hands of another), and that he would arrange to operate on Monday. Cuffing and shouting down the dogs who snarled at my heels, he led me back to the gate. "I take it," he said as he locked it behind me, "that Excellency can make up her own mind."

At that moment I was no more making up my own mind than beef makes up its own mind to be shipped for slaughter. Had I not been afraid of being a worse sport than ever, of having spent more money on doctors fruitlessly, of being met with still more exasperated politeness if I hastened back to my husband in the same shape in which he had despatched me for possible repairs, I would have left Vienna at once. When I got to the room

assigned me the man who brought up my bags asked
quietly if I would not prefer a room on the other side
of the hotel. I told him this one would do. It was only
when he had left and I went to open the window that I
realized that by chance I had acquired a front-row balcony seat on history. The curtain had gone up. The
scene in the street below my window was black with
two opposing crowds, shuffling, shifting, ceaselessly moving yet somehow, since they neither joined nor parted,
motionless. All that afternoon and night I listened to the
hoarse antiphonal of their allegiance. But when, the next
morning, with a louder drone than had yet been heard
in any sky, a hundred bombers flew over the city, the
deep-mouthed heavy bay of the crowds began to resound in unison. I thought it was the end of the play. I
did not realize that this was merely a prelude to a drama
that required so large a cast that it was to call up on the
stage every last member of every audience from Narvik
to Tobruk before the final curtain.

If I must blame myself for not having recognized the
fall of Austria for the curtain raiser that it was, I am also
tempted to blame those I knew who only a few months
before were exchanging courtesies with the leading villains of the piece and sedulously keeping their eyes closed
to perfidy until they themselves became its victims.
Now, however, with all the ghastly miscalculations, mis-
interpretations, and missed opportunities silhouetted in
the glare of hindsight, we have had to learn not only that
no one is without blame but that blame itself is a boom-
erang with which we cannot be trusted. We have seen
blame more liberally distributed in our time than ever
before to pay off old grudges, undermine potential rival-
ries, and enhance the prestige and fortunes of the blamer.
If the word of blame is well dropped, it will not sink

till it has sunk the blamed, but the time is certain to come when the blamer in turn is sunk. Our houses are all made of glass; when the stones start flying, none can escape breakage. I shall say only therefore that I do not understand why the politically aware among whom I lived and to whom my political unawareness seemed so shocking should have been no better prepared for what came than I. Perhaps it is the expediency in the political eye that blinds it.

Someone has said that it is not the answers that we do not know but the questions. Like all paradoxes, this one has a siren sound; yet like most of them, it suffers from closer inspection. I, for one, am ready to risk what intellectual status I fancy I have to challenge it. Looking back across the last years and up to the last minute before the Nazi war began, the mind positively bristles with unanswered questions.

Why, for example, did the readers of *Mein Kampf* take it less seriously than they took *Gone with the Wind?* Why did the travelers on the newly constructed *Autobahnen* silence the apprehension that stuck in their throats and gave them gooseflesh as they passed green-tarpaulined military camion after camion almost before each camion was out of sight? Why did those of us who saw a Jew caught at the scruff of his neck by a frontier policeman and heard his screams accept the violence without protest and sleep without seeing the deed or hearing the screams again in dreams? Why did no one of us who saw at the entrance to nestling German villages the sign saying *"Jüden sind nicht erlaubt"* stop the car and tear it down? Why did I, for instance, bearing an American passport, submit to being stripped by a female customs official to my skin and to having not just the linings of my shoes and hat but my body itself ransacked for contraband, as two thousand years before slaves had to submit, for survival, to their captors' scrutiny? Why during that last summer did the Poles, whose long history of being hunted now told them that the hunters were again closing in, set about storing provisions, burying silver, and barricading doors as though they had never heard of bombers or seen a picture of a tank or learned the word motorization? And why, if I question the fantastic unreality of Poles preparing to throw gleaming horseflesh and Polish bone and gut against machinery, do I not also question how it was possible, when on the third day after the Germans had invaded Poland a plane flew low over our house and I rushed out to stare at its sunstruck brilliance, for me not to recognize the black dot it expelled from its viscera till a distant thunder told me what it was? And why, after the almost two weeks of war during which I had ample time to see on the faces and hear in the voices of those who had already been driven from their homes their hopelessness, did I insist till the hour before I was made to leave that it was my duty as well as my overwhelming desire to remain? Why had I failed even to consider the future of my two small children till my husband appeared in uniform late one night and bade me take them up and go? And how, after what he had already seen, could he still expect to wrest even a respite, much less victory from ruin? And how was it that I managed to stop imagining, after he had vanished into the half-glow of the burning town where we parted, that I might not see him again?

These questions are as impersonal as they are personal. In some form they have harried every generation. The interrogation began with our beginning; it will end only with our end. On trial is history, but since we have always been and always will be at once the culprit, the prosecutor, the defense, the judge, the jury, how can the trial be brought to a close? But why must history be tried? Did we ordain it thus or was it ordained for us? Did the idea of right and wrong evolve in us with our shape and substance and capacity, or were right and wrong here before we came? Were we created to be their protagonists, or did we invent them out of the need to have something against which to be pitted and to pit? Did we emerge from chaos only to ensure the continuation of chaos so that we could keep on emerging from it forever? Or is there an end to chaos that we are not yet evolved enough to see? How could we have come by the idea of peace, if warring is our destiny? And if peace is what we are intended for, why does generation after generation go to war? But beyond these questions is the question of questions: why are we as we are?

The answer would give us the key to all other answers. Yet even those who are certain they know Who made us have no other answer to the why than that we are born to die. This does not explain our killing of each other. Fish, bird, bug, and beast must kill to live, but we do not need to eat the flesh or drink the blood of our brothers to keep ourselves alive. Our wars have no excuse in the natural order. Nor, therefore, can they have any excuse in God, for if He exists, the natural order is part of Him. The only conclusion is that our wars, and hence our history itself are, by our own principles, inexcusable. Yet for every war the launchers and the launched-upon find excuse in principle. The trial goes on. The questions vary so little that by now—whoever says that we do not know them—I say that we know them all by heart. And so far, at least, they prove unanswerable.

*   *   *

THROUGHOUT THAT SUMMER OF 1939 WHICH WAS TO BE, for more people than have yet been counted or indeed, since so many have vanished without leaving even a lock of hair or the filling from a tooth to count, for more people than ever can be counted, the last of the summers like other summers on which until then they had thought they could always count, I was busy trying to seal over the crack in my eggshell, to pretend that the egg of my ego-centered existence could not have been and was not cracked. Ignoring the newspapers upon which, when they reached us at noon, those around me seized with such anxiety and closing my ears alike to the self-righteous harangues from Rome and Berlin and to the self-doubting analyses from London coming over the radio at any hour of day or night, I plotted how to inveigle my husband into installing for me a new green-and-white tiled bathroom; how to replace the neurotic nanny in charge of my son; how to have a tweed suit built for me by my husband's tailor; how to lighten the big, dark double guest room with pretty chintzes; how to acquire German reproductions of Cézanne and Matisse to counterbalance the holy pictures on my children's walls; and how, without jettisoning all my pride, to reinstate myself as a not impossible pleasure to my husband. If I was fiddling while the fires that would burn Rome were being ignited, it was because I had managed to convince myself that in our day and time Rome must after all turn out to be fireproof.

Nor was mine the only fiddle played. In Hungary, where my husband and I drove for the last vacation we took together, the talk in the castle where we stayed was of tennis, iced soups, and internecine flirts. At the pageant we saw on an outdoor stage in Budapest, the riders, as blooded as their mounts, dressed as their families had been since medieval times, manifested such a continuity of privilege that a break in it seemed inconceivable. When the snowy-haired, petal-skinned, immaculate honorary "Aunt," whom we visited in her village mansion toward the end of the trip, spoke trustingly, as she spoke of all save "perfidious Albion" and the "Bolsheviki," of *"unser guter, lieber Adolf,"* it was suddenly hard to remember the innocents whom the *"lieber Adolf"* had already despatched into exile or oblivion, the ceaseless rumble of camions on his great, wide roads, the drone of the giant bee-cloud of his bombers over Vienna, or the exact timbre of the snarl, the whine, the menace in his voice.

Fiddles were indeed still being played even in Poland that August, and only a few miles from where, just west of the western frontier, the soldiers of *"lieber Adolf"* were doubtless already bivouacked. Having sent our daughter with her governess for her first stay in a friend's house, we had gone there to fetch her home and were playing ping-pong in a huge, fragrant room on the garden when someone broke up the game with the news of the Russo-German pact. It was then that the fiddles, in that part of Europe at least, were put away for good.

Less than six weeks later, I was sitting with the uncontrollable tears rolling down my face and onto the foolscap in front of me, writing, with no other thought at that time than the absolute necessity I felt to write it, what I had seen happen to my children, my husband, his family, his land, and his country since the day I had brought my daughter home from her visit.

I was back in Hungary, back with the honorary "Aunt." Again, I was her guest, this time without my husband whose whereabouts I did not know. My children, the governess, and my maid were with me, crowding the house to its limits. But to this visit no limit had been set. We had neither clothes nor money nor plans. And still, with my world opened up and yawning beneath my feet, I did not understand. "I expect," I said to our hostess, "that it will be some time before we can go back." "My child," she answered, "I have lived three times through a war, and I am still here. You will see. One gets used to it."

Months later, when what I had written in her house appeared in print in New York, I was ashamed of how brave it sounded, for although I had been as brave as I could at the time, I had since seen and heard of courage such as I knew I could not have mustered, had seen and heard of dangers escaped or not escaped that made our own escape seem by comparison an embarrassingly swift transition from horror to tranquillity, a too easy leap out of pain and fright into warmth and safety. But for my children's sake, I cannot after all be sorry. They had not asked as I had asked at least subconsciously by marrying whom I married, to risk meeting history at the flood.

I have said before that it is from the contrast of negative with positive, of black with white, of everything with its opposite that I can recognize each for what it is. The subtle may learn from the essence of a thing, from the *Ding an sich*, but for such as I there must be contrast, and the contrast must apparently be violent. Fresh from the jammed, gutted roads and burning towns of Poland, the lazy street and cool housefronts of the Hungarian village where we found haven were not merely sweet, as I had remembered them from early summer, but priceless beyond speaking. Newly despoiled as we were not only of such irreplaceables as house and land and very footing, but of those kerchiefs, powder puffs, and toys the familiarity of which seems to be what makes home home, the small presents left for us at the door by neighbors who had doubtless watched our arrival from behind discreetly shuttered windows were like a laying on of hands. My five-year-old daughter had stood for a long time staring at a red-and-white spotted oilcloth giraffe displayed in the window of a shop, but when I said I would go in and ask its price she had pulled me away, saying firmly: "I do not need a giraffe." Someone must have seen or heard us, for the next day the giraffe appeared. Absurd, hideous if you will, and doomed from clutching and hugging to premature disintegration, it was not too insignificant a thing to weigh against inhumanity. Never again have I heard without a tremor the sound of the word kind.

As time goes, there was not much of it from the night my husband and I were so abruptly parted until the night I had not dared to hope for when, some three weeks later, in oddly assorted civilian clothes and with a face as ridged and grooved as a contour map, he stepped out of his dust-caked car and hurried into the house. Yet a country, a past, and an era lay dead between.

A man had gone to war, fought well, been defeated, lost all but his wife and children, and now these he had found. It sounds like the narrative of a ballad. If by a ballad is meant a poem in which the bitterness of misunderstanding has been so distilled as to preserve its taste for generations, then this one was a classic. No balladist could have invented misunderstanding more complete.

For once, for less than an hour, for the part of the night before he slept, I knew enough not to be me. To him, I was a soldier's girl, nameless, impersonal, generic, one with my species and my kind. To me, he was not my husband nor the father of my children; he was not more, but less than a man. I did not sleep. How could I, when questions tramped by with such relentless regularity? But in the morning, he spoke first. "You must take the children to your mother in America," he said. "I will find you again when the war ends." Sweat formed on my forehead. Blood drained out of my head. "And you?" I asked him. "What will you do?" "They have requested Hungary to intern Polish officers. I must start for Paris tomorrow. After that, I do not know."

I left him with the children and went into the garden at the back of the house. It was there that the "Aunt" found me. She sat down beside me. For a long time, neither of us spoke. "Do you want to keep him?" she asked, at last. I nodded. "Does he want to keep you?" I shook my head. Again we sat in silence. Then she stood up and put her hand on my shoulder. "He does not know what he wants," she said. "How could he? You must go wherever he goes. I will keep your children. I will keep them as long as you want me to. And if you do not come back," she went on steadily, "I will leave them what I have left."

If I were never to hear again, as I never before had heard, the music of absolute understanding, that one time will have been enough. The dominant chord which had crashed upon my ears that morning, pulling tight every nerve in my body and drawing the very breath from my lungs, had been resolved. Not a mother, nor a friend, nor a lover, nor a husband had resolved it, but the snowy-haired Hungarian lady who owed me nothing, but to whom, then, I owed my life.

I did not tell her that my fear of following my husband wherever he went, now that I knew how little he wanted me, was only less decisive than my fear of returning to you. I feel sure that, for once, you would have agreed that I was right. To tell, at such a moment, such a truth, seemed to me, no less than it would have seemed to you, insane.

III

A MATTER OF LIFE AND DEATH

Y OU AND I SPOKE LITTLE OF THE VALHALLA YOU envisioned as your eternal abode, not because you, but because I shied away from it. The image I suspected you of having was of a vast, celestial drawing room over which, seated behind a lace-covered tray laden with untarnishable tea things, and surrounded by the imperishable great of your choice, you would preside. Most widows of a lifetime of honorable marriage contemplate the next world, if they contemplate it at all, as the scene of their reunion with the departed. But not once did I hear you number my father among those you expected to find awaiting you. I do not mean to suggest by this, however, that you forgot or excluded him. There were simply to be no familiar faces. If your next world was to have all the comforts, it was to have none of the tedium of home. Out of your discontent, so much more earthbound than divine and yet not without a touch of divinity in the reach that so far exceeded the grasp, you were fashioning for yourself an afterlife in which what you had found unattainable would become attainable and what you had attained, since it so little resembled your dream of attainment, could be shed. When you referred to your afterlife, it was always as an adventure, and since you had ventured nowhere in your long life unaccompanied, except in your imagination, it was probably the daring of making so distant a journey for the first time alone that somehow pleased almost as much as it terrified you. You saw your own *"animula, vagula, blandula"* (to use the words you yourself particularly loved) lifted effortlessly out of its small, weary encasement, liberated forever from the imperfections of husband, children, servants, and inanimate objects which you were so helpless to perfect, free at last in time and space to select only that which you considered perfect, and that which would seem to you perfect had to be what you had not known, for with reality you had never made your peace.

If I still begrudge you your hypersensitivity to imperfection which I aggravated more than anyone, I no longer begrudge you the daydream of escape from it which seemed to me while you were alive absurd alike in its vagueness and its precision, but in which I now recognize all the same a stature not common to most dreams of escape. And if you have found a Valhalla where neither love nor effort is wasted, where pettiness does not exist, where cooks never fly into tempers nor weeds suffocate a garden, where all voices are magic flutes and all words poems, I wish you well of it. But this is not to say that I am not glad for your sake and for mine that you are gone.

You are dead and gone, gone from the eye and the ear and the touch, gone from your anxieties and fears, from how to pay the income tax, whether to call the doctor, how to force the city to keep the block you lived on clean, what to do with the days when you had no more strength or money to go shopping and with the nights when you had no more sight to read yourself to sleep, gone from the relentless encroachment on your thoughts of your inevitable going. You are as gone as are all the dead embalmed in glass coffins, in the pages of history, in the lines of a sonnet and the themes of a symphony, in the bridge named after them, in the statue commemorating them, in the laws they codified, in the hearts of the descendants of those they murdered; as gone as those who have only a name on a stone and as those who died nameless. But how gone is gone?

Just the other day, nearly twenty years since, in a burst of petulance at the wartime restrictions which were depriving you of the gardener and gasoline and guests as necessary to you as the roof over your head, you sold the Farm from under the still uncertain feet of my children, my husband, and me whose only refuge it had been when we arrived as refugees in America, I went back with my now grown son to see again that hill at the confluence of rivers that my father had so loved, to see the houses—main house, guest house, playhouse, farmer's house, garage, and barns—which enclose some of the worst and best of my memories and, taken together, embody my son's only memory, too young as he was when he left the house in Poland to remember it, of a house of his own. No one lives there now. Still as splendid in its isolation from the whine and cough and sputter and whir of this day as it was from the put-puts of all but the intrepid Model Ts when my father bought it, the Farm stands beneath the great elms, white and green-shuttered and green and white-shuttered, empty, a cenotaph to my father who had fought to keep the wildness of its surroundings and to you who had fought to tame them. "Look! Look!" my son said, his face paling under its summer color as he pointed to the shaggy lawns, the all but vanished sunken garden, the weather-stained paint, the old broom leaning against the front door in sorry desuetude. "What would Granny have said?" And all at once I knew you were not gone. You were not merely not gone from the Farm which you had loved only to the extent you could manicure it; you were not gone anyway because you cannot be gone while I am still here. You were not gone, and never would be altogether gone. You were in the dismay in my son's eyes and the disgust in his voice as he gazed at the ruin of what you had created, and you will be in his eyes and his voice when he comes to create something of his own, and from that something of which you will be a part his children and children's children will still, however unwittingly, keep you from being gone. Like everyone who has ever lived, you are gone and not gone at one and the same time.

But you were gone neither in flesh nor in spirit, neither in willfulness, temper, or tenacity of demand, neither in your *voulu* charm nor in your equally *voulu* lack of it, when we disembarked, shabby except for my husband's custom-made dark suit and my Paris hat with its bow of watermelon pink, from the last American passenger ship to leave Genoa in the dark May of 1940. It was on the cash advance from the publisher of *Polish Profile* and, for the rest, on your bounty that we had come. My diamond necklace and a milky, flawed emerald brooch the size of half an egg constituted our capital. Had we had only ourselves to provide for, and not a daughter ready for schooling and a son whose pallor and frequent tears and nightmares cried out for special care, we could and would have stood alone. As it befell, however, I was, as I had foreseen that I would be, as much at your mercy as the day I was born.

Never before, it seemed to me, had the green been so green, the shimmer so shimmering, the peace so radiant as on that spring day when we drove up the hill from the river in your old black limousine with the children and the nurse I had found for them to the waiting Farm and you said, as they climbed out and stood dazed in the road: "Welcome home." The blossoming bushes, the bellying curtains at the windows, the new tricycle on the guest-house porch, the swept and burnished look both outside and in must surely have eased the tightness of young nerves braced for change after inexplicable change yet needing more than anything else that could be prescribed for them that tonic of tonics which is a sense of permanence.

For me too those first days were heady with relief. To find again my room, my fireplace, my bed, my hammock in the pine grove where once I had swung restless feet and battled with restless imagination and where now I wanted only to lie still and breathe that sweetness to the lungs which is native air, to let May's promise so fill my senses that the fears of the past months would be displaced, to give home a chance to wipe out the memory of homelessness, to give myself to a peace which only now that I had skirted war I could measure in its fullness.

How ironic, indeed how bitter peace must have seemed to my husband, it took me, alas, a long time to see, for I did not want to see it. I am still shocked to remember how from the moment we had reached Paris, whither I had so insisted upon accompanying him eight months before and where we had lived side by side through the freezing, ambiguous, dark first winter of the war, we were further apart than any dividing ocean could have rendered us, further apart than two strangers from the antipodes, since nothing so estranges as to have once been of one mind and then to become of two. My face was turned to the future, his to the past. I longed for escape and renewal, he for return and redress. I wanted him to forget; he wanted to remember. He wanted home and country; I wanted him.

On that first wartime Christmas Eve, after I had spent nearly every evening for the past two months alone in unheated hotel rooms waiting while he worked far into the night with the Polish general to whom he had attached himself, we were to have gone together to the warm flat of an American friend for a modest celebration. He came back late, holding out a letter, transmitted from hand to hand across the lines of enemy occupation, in which the old major-domo of our house in Poland had dictated, since he could not write, a description of what had happened to it. "If it please you, I must tell you that the glass is gone from the windows, the beds have been broken up and carried away, the doors bang in the wind, and no one goes in or out." I felt the gooseflesh prickle as I read. But all I said was: "It's time for dinner." Whatever he had been about to answer he held back. Closing the door into his room, he went to bed.

That had been my *maxima culpa*, the sin, not of failing, but of not wishing to understand. If there comes a time for the forgiveness of sins, that will be the hardest to forgive me (as perhaps you have now learned that your not having wished to understand me was hardest to forgive you). And what I have had to learn to understand in you, after first learning to understand it in myself, is that once one has battened down the door against any attempt to understand someone else, one forgets that the door was ever there, so easily does one become entrenched in habit, so easily does one glide from having had at first to refuse to understand to the point where of understanding there is no further question.

Throughout that winter of exile in Paris I kept pressing my husband, without putting myself for a moment in his place, to abandon the war and his exiled compatriots and accompany the children and me to America. When in the early spring not I, but a former American ambassador who was close to us both, succeeded in persuading him, against the bottom-most of his instincts, to leave Europe, I was so lightened by the decision that I gave no thought to how heavy it must have been for him. All I thought of, as I traveled back by train through Trieste to Hungary to prepare the children for the journey and bring them down to Genoa where he had agreed to meet us, was how to get over this latest separation, and all I could feel as the time approached for turning our backs on a fear-ridden Europe was my fear that in the end he would not come.

After my long absence from the children my daughter, who in the intervening months had become so unexpectedly sturdy and my son, who had become so alarmingly frail, were almost strangers to me, as was I to them. The train trip within the shadow of war frightened me as well as them. We reached Genoa with every visa on our passports canceled; there was no country left behind us to which we could return. We had to sail. My husband had not yet come. For a moment, then, I saw the dimension of his sacrifice. To the God I did not quite believe in and on my knees, for once because not custom but my heart demanded it, I swore that if he arrived in time, if I could only keep him with me, I would make sure that he did not regret it. Unannounced, and very late on that last European night, he came. The children, who had been asleep, raised their heads from

their pillows simultaneously. "Papa!" they called in unison. The joy he saw on their faces eased, for the time being at least, the set look on his, and I like to think, though
I shall never know it, that he has been able to warm himself at the blaze of that memory, as I have, ever since.

YET HE COULD NOT HAVE WATCHED THE PANOPLY OF THE
New England May with anything less than bitterness,
when at the very moment that we were settling into it,
the Europe he belonged to—whatever their animosities,
the nationals of any European country belong as much
to Europe as the citizens of any state in the United States
belong to America—was disintegrating, was indeed dis-
solving like the Graf Zeppelin before the camera eye of
the world, its fabric torn, its ribbing wrenched asunder,
its human cargo tossed out with the flaming parts or
leaping blindly into space to escape them. How would
you and I have felt had we sat, say, in a Locarno villa
or an English rectory and listened over the radio to the
fall of Massachusetts, Rhode Island, and Connecticut,
and heard the march of an enemy over the bridges into
New York? Would we have been able to view the view
with serenity or partake of tea and scones with undiminished appetite? No one who has not been safe when
his brother was in danger, helpless when his people
needed help, farthest when he wanted to be nearest,
severed when he felt most tied, can say.

But of course, the clarity with which I see it now
comes as usual from hindsight, good old democratic
hindsight, common to us all. Then, he was in the trough
of the wave and I on the crest, and the pound of the
waters drowned out communication. Long since, too,
he had begun to worry about money, while I was still

sure it would not be hard to find. He had no assurance
of work, while I had the lift of seeing my book (which
he was coming to hate) take a modest place on the best-
seller lists. He was not among his kind and had only acquaintances to turn to, while I was within reach again of
my friends and especially, at the Farm, of my best friend
who lived only a few short miles away and was still then,
or at least gave more than enough signs of being, abundantly on my side. He who had had a certain power was
now powerless, while I who had not had power anywhere and had been stripped in his milieu even of that
shred of power which had been my ability to charm was
suddenly being courted and listened to with a respect
which, in my naïveté, I took for myself instead of for
the appearance of success to which, in fact, it was being paid. Yet he bore himself as always with an unassum-
ing equability the cost of which no one knew. If it
seemed to him peculiarly ironic, as it must have, that the
disaster engulfing the rest of his family was actually lib-
erating his wife, he did not say so. And of all his for-
bearances at that time, perhaps the greatest was in for-
bearing to remind me that it was due rather more to the
accident of my sharing his name and his drama than to
the quality of my book itself that I was being thus suddenly decked out in prestige. It was to be some time before I discovered that finery is only fine when one owns
it outright.

So much more fortunate than most refugees, with the
exception of course of those who had seen the wave of
the future long enough ahead to arrange for the removal
of their capital before their own or conquering official-
dom could take it (and the Ritz and the Pavilion were
surprisingly full of such as these), my husband and I
nevertheless had to face what turned out to be as new a

world to me as it was to him. America, now that I
looked at it through his eyes, was not the America I had
thought it was, nor was it, even when I looked at it
only through my own, any more my America than his.
To see him welcomed effusively at the dinner tables of
men in positions of power but shunted, when it came
to asking them for a job, from one office to another
with expressions of regret behind which gleamed, implacable and unmistakable, their determination not to make
room for him in their own, was to behold the obverse
of our celebrated hospitality in all its bleak reality. To
stand by helpless, while month after month he followed,
uncomplaining, the trail of these smooth refusals to risk
even a pittance in the name of friendship, and to watch
him in the end and in the quietest of desperation go to
work wrapping cold-cream jars for a questionable cos-
metic firm and return to the shabby hotel rooms we kept
as our city stronghold with his carefully brushed clothes
impregnated by the sickly smell of a beauty product
obliged me to reappraise my kind.

Moreover, to see myself constituted an expert on war
after two weeks of greeting its backwash at my door,
one night under the canopy of the enemy-held sky, and
a few months in a black-curtained city to which war had
not yet come; to be asked to speak at lunches and dinners
and over the radio by people who, though as aware as
I that I had nothing to speak about, assumed that the
publicity would be as useful to me as the use of my
name was to them; to find myself in such sudden demand and yet to discover at the same time that I had no
cash value, that as soon as I brought up the need for a
livelihood their smiles froze and their jaws became rigid,
gave me my first incredulous look at the expediency
which carries on, behind our noble national façade, its

furtive affair with self-interest.

Yet, shaken as I was by what seemed to be happening to us in this home of the brave which, all the time I lived away from it, had shone beaconlike in my memory, I did not at once, or indeed until many incredulous looks later, begin to generalize. Each false cordiality, each false promise, each masquerade of benevolence I took for a single instance. It is in fact only now when the instances, stretching over twenty years, have reached indefensible proportions that I no longer attempt to defend the whole against the sum of its parts.

IT WAS NOT YOUR FAULT THAT, IN BRINGING ME UP, YOU gave me no inkling of the ways of the market place, since you never went nor did my father go, in that sense, to market. Whatever you and my father did not have in common, you shared conspicuously a lack of shrewdness. In the dream world he allowed you to inhabit undisturbed, your calculations, however small, were not concerned with loss or profit; and in my father's world, compounded as he had taught himself to compound it, of dream made real and reality made dream, there was not so much as an abacus. I do not hint at a reproach. On the contrary, I would not have had you otherwise in this any more than I would have had my father otherwise in anything. If, from the world's standpoint, your not having opened my eyes to calculation was a disservice, from my own standpoint it was a service greater than any other. Supposing I had to choose, as when fleeing an enemy one must often choose only one treasure from the past to pocket, liefer would I leave behind the tastes you gave me, the voice of cultivation which thanks to you I possess and without which

I would be stripped indeed, and even that passion for the written word which alone of my passions has been of unfailing solace, than to leave behind the lack of shrewdness which you passed on to me not as your heritage or mine alone, but as the real, the authentic American heritage. They were not calculators who threw all calculations to the wind save those of a haven or a heaven when setting their hopeful feet upon these shores. That among their descendants there are not a few who have learned to calculate the advantage of brotherhood itself dries any tears for their afflictions before those tears are shed.

To my husband, no less than to any other European exiled to America in the blackening months before Pearl Harbor, the rift between those for and those against going to war was far more shocking than the mores of the market place. He had seen market places elsewhere and accepted more philosophically than I the pound of flesh named by all who can set their price. I, on the other hand, could understand that the longing to keep clear of war should so throttle Americans that they refused to see the European quarrel as their own, and although at the time, with my eyes and ears filled by the injustice I had seen and heard, I spoke for war, I am not sure that today I would not—at least theoretically—prefer us to go down alone than to be committed to the eternally unsettled and seemingly unsettleable struggles of our friends and foes abroad. The propounders of isolationism were not all pigeon-livered, nor all guilty of self-interest, whereas a needle would be quicker to find in a sandpile than an instance of disinterest in the market place.

I say again, for I would have wanted you to know for certain, that I have never regretted the fact that in my family no one was shrewd, or "smart" (to use the word that of all words in our common currency most sets my teeth on edge). If to be patriotic I would have to honor the national sport of outwitmanship, then I would rather I were treasonable. Yet I will have to concede that we did not invent it, as also, however reluctantly, that it doubtless began among the amoeba and had reached the discipline of an art by the time we developed the hands with which to outsnatch each other. Meanness is threaded into the texture of history; all philosophers, all novelists —great, not so great, and small—have taken it into consideration. Meanness is in fact the subject of every argument, whether between thieves, gossips or lovers, or between the saints and God. I know that we are mean as a species and as individuals. I know that, as you were mean, so too am I. I know, but I am not resigned.

My fear of returning to you as a refugee alone with my children may have been irrational. But to imagine that I need not fear you as much if my husband were with me was no more rational. I should have foreseen that, even more in the presence of my husband than in his absence, you could put me in such a corner as to make what I said or did look like ingratitude and what you said and did like mercy. With more stamina you might have made an actress, with more patience a teacher; but to be a ruler (which means to divide and rule) you needed nothing with which you were not born. As innate as the warble to the warbler was your unpremeditated art of ruling. By your emphatic sympathy for my husband (as explicit for having married me as for having lost home and country), by your trembling concern for my children (as great for their having me for mother as for their ailments and flaws), and by the sorrowing looks with which you greeted what I said or decided, you managed, if not to endear yourself to my husband as much as you had hoped—since your sedulous attentions were as instrumental as my rebellions in driving him into the relaxed and undemanding company of those prettiest ladies of my acquaintance who were only too glad to make him feel at home—then at least to keep him under such heavy obligation to you that it would have been impossible, given his sense of *noblesse oblige*, for him to side with me. If, as I must suspect, the goal of these instinctive manoeuvers was to belittle and isolate me, no statesman could have wished for a more patent success. I had no other roof to put over my children's heads than yours, nor would I, as well you knew, give up either the duty or the joy of their charge. I was caught, caught as I had never even dreamed of being caught, by a trap from which money, and money alone, could free me. Yet for a time I went on hoping against all signs of hopelessness that between us might be found an easier *modus vivendi*. It was only when my doctor showed me a letter from you in which, in your unmistakably educated hand, you had written: "My daughter's husband and I are both convinced that she is insane" that, watching him set a match to it and drop the charred remains into his scrapbasket, I knew that no grounds for hope between you and me could exist again.

Until then money for me had never been a matter for serious consideration. I had spent it whether I had it or not with the *insouciance* that comes only from having started out by taking it for granted. Though I had from time to time in younger days heard my father groan over our family bills and had been held, after my sister's proven extravagances, on tighter rein at home than she, I had gone on supposing that when he said of her latest purchases or of yours, "At this rate, there will be noth-

ing left," he was merely using his prerogative to remind
us of who earned our daily bread and that the edge in
his voice when he quoted *"Un père, c'est un banquier
donné par la nature"* was a joke. Indeed, I had believed
till long after I was grown, seeing the liberality with
which you dispensed the money, that some of what went
for our houses, our clothes, our servants, and our journeys had come from your parents and was yours to
spend. I had never counted the cost of a room, a meal,
a doctor, any more than the cost of schools until after
my first marriage, and even then, not having had more
at my disposal than a monthly allowance, I considered
the stipend on which we were to live so munificent by
comparison that it took me some months to discover
why it did not appear to cover what I believed to be
our needs. More and more frequently, we had no money
at all and I, being the only one of the two who wanted it,
should have worried, but I could not, not with the
Farm in the offing and my father's office, which still
then I thought of as a cornucopia, only a few blocks
away. Nor, incredible as it now seems, did it ever occur
to me during that marriage (though I soon found that if
I wanted dresses I must earn them) that the money I
sporadically earned from book reviews and magazine
articles should be pooled for our common use, or that,
having no children and no duty beyond dusting, I should
have been earning a salary myself. Though I considered
(as is the wont of all daughters) that I was so much more
modern than you, I was actually well behind my own
times in assuming that I should be supported when that
assumption was already under suspicion, while when you
made the same assumption it had still been assumed by
all women, no matter how penurious, provided of course
that they belonged to what you called "a certain class."

I cannot therefore look down upon your extravagances in those days with any justice, since if I had happened to marry, as you did, a man with a large capacity to earn, I would have spent his earnings no less improvidently. The thousand dollars you were said to have spent on your drawing-room curtains in that day when a thousand dollars were relatively hard to spend were no more disproportionate to the whole tenor of your living than the hundred I spent upon my back.

Living in Europe, and especially living among people with centuries of inherited means who had had to learn after the first World War to climb back out of ruin by doing without what I who had never had real means yet held to be necessities, I ought to have acquired a respect for money that you as the daughter and wife of self-made men had never had, but I did not. Though I saw in our house in the forest, before it became my task to keep it, how sugar and tea and coffee and candles and soap were locked up as I had only seen people lock away their jewels and dispensed as cautiously day by day as if any day, any hour, the supply of them might cease; how when a hog was slaughtered its parts were adjudicated no less carefully than if we had been a desert tribe whose lives depended on such exactitude; how paper and string from packages were stored to be used again, envelopes turned inside out, old clothing dyed and remodeled, brown shoes painted black to save on mourning, oil lamps lighted only when the last paleness had so faded from wintry skies that one could no longer see to knit, and such an expense as a new coat discussed in conclave before being decided on, I noted in these economies only the pinch, and not the historicity. Coming out of an economy of abundance in which long before my time a certain amount of waste had been recognized as a prerequisite for its health, I felt only impatience with what seemed such pointless parsimony, played at it only when I had to, and took, in flying in its face, a certain pride.

Besides, my Polish husband was no less instinctively spendthrift than I, no doubt for a diametrically opposite reason. Not having been able to take money for granted in his wartime youth, he was determined, now that he could make it, to obtain the full *quid pro quo*. As much or even more than I, he considered luxury necessity, and when he counted, he counted not what he could save but what he could spend. Not once in Poland did I see a bill or a checkbook, and not once for what was counted out to me was I asked to account. On the night of my escape from war with the children, when my husband handed me, as we parted, some thousands of dollars in Polish currency, I was as little surprised to be holding what for me still today would represent a fortune as I was little disturbed to learn the next day at the frontier that, with Poland almost overrun, the bundle of bills was not worth fifty cents. I was unaware as we crossed into safety of the dangers of being penniless, and thanks to the help we received from friends when we reached Paris, I remained unaware of them throughout that first winter of the war. It was only at home again, and from you, that I learned the price of dependence. That was when money as such, naked and slippery, swam up out of its shark-infested subaqueous habitat and entered my ken for good. And it was then that I lost the last, not of my naïveté, but of my innocence.

Let me not, however, so underscore my innocence as to falsify it. One could not have grown up in America and gone to a school where only the rich could go; gone to a college where the color line between rich and less rich (or poor, if you will), between those with the right inflections and sweaters and those with the wrong ones, was as well marked and as hard to cross as that in any southern station waiting room, and gone to dances where rich girls of whatever shape or size never wanted for partners; one could not, as the wife of a poor man, have failed to detect at the few tables of the very rich to which one was invited the patronizing indulgence with which most of them bought, as they might buy the doggy in the window, one's capacity to entertain—and still be unconscious of the power of money in social, as well as in all other relations. Nor could one, having gone from America to live in Poland, in a house a mere stone's throw from people as immutably frozen in poverty as birds in the snow, fail to become conscious of the death-in-life that is all the life those without money can hope for. In America, in the wake of the depression, I had heard a rich man say that whoever could not find work did not deserve to find it since in God's country, as all knew, there was work for all. In Poland, I had heard a rich man say, as he drove his coach-and-eight down a road on which peasants leaped out of the way and bowed low as we passed, that nowhere had he seen such a shocking contrast between rich and poor as in Chicago. And in the eyes of the unemployed standing in lines or sprawled on park benches in New York, as too in the eyes of peasants bringing their blue-lipped children to my door in Poland, I had seen envy and hate.

It was not the fact that money was powerful or that the lack of it made one powerless that I had failed to grasp, but that money played a no less dominating role in the region between these two extremes which was the region I inhabited. Your having enough money and my not having enough enabled you to hold me with one hand and lash me with the other, and it was the indignity of this position that finally revealed to me both the treacherous advantage that is even a little money and the fatuous stupidity of ignoring money altogether. But if it was thus belatedly through you that my schooling in money began, it was in the world outside of home among friendships that shifted with each shift in my circumstances and of course in the market place itself that, a fortiori and *ad nauseam*, my grasp of this grasping subject was put to the test.

Never since have I had, as during the brief weeks of heyday that my book, *Polish Profile*, enjoyed and until everyone had read it who would ever read it, so many invitations. For one who had sat, as I had, year after year at your table in silence except when you gave me the cue to speak, and who, after the liberation of my first marriage which I had used to put my articulacy through all the pirouettes and can-cans I could think of, had sat for as many years again at my mother-in-law's or husband's Polish tables in an equally imposed silence, the public and private occasions at which I now found myself not only featured but listened to were a habit-forming drug. But whether in time I might have become so addicted that no one could escape the impalement of my tongue (such addictions are not uncommon among those we Americans elect to feature) I shall never know, for my vogue, like the vogue of my book, like all vogues by their very nature, petered out. The switchboard operator at our hotel who, in the first months of our stay, gave me each time I came in a little pile of messages together with a conspiratorial, toothy smile, discovered to me, as the messages dwindled, less and less of her teeth. Like the "What-are-you-up-to-now?" and the "Has-your-husband-got-a-job-yet?" of my new friends when, at cocktail parties, they happened to notice me, the lips that were closing upon the telephone operator's teeth were a dependable barometer.

There were also lessons to be learned from those friends whose adoption I had long since tried. As time went by and neither my husband nor I accomplished anything that they could call an accomplishment, since merely to survive could not be expected to seem to them as much of an accomplishment as it did to us, those who had been the most enthusiastic about how easily my husband would fit into any business and how much money my book was bound to earn began to manifest, behind their still manifest good will, a trace of doubt, of fear lest their cordiality be mistaken by us for more than the token payment of those who have to those who have had but have no longer. Among fellow refugees too, the few who had managed to outwit their fate grew visibly less cozy and more formally correct in manner in order to establish the line between their increasing and our decreasing status. As with the operator, so with my acquaintance, I could take, without looking at any bank account, my measure.

BUT MY BEST FRIEND WAS STILL MY BEST FRIEND. ON weekends, hurrying over the hills between your Farm and hers in the old station wagon with my daughter and the nurse chatting busily in the back and my son interpolating in his new, odd English whatever words he could find to describe the cars we passed, I felt as sure of her welcome as, should the shoe have been on the other foot, she could have been sure of mine. While the children played with the little wagon she provided that coasted so well down grassy slopes and pulled so easily

up them, I too could satisfy, in backgammon, double solitaire, and dart throwing, a thirst for play almost as unap-
peased as theirs. And when play palled, there was the
road of the past we had trod together to tread again
half in regret and half in laughter, the future of her almost grown and my small children to speculate about,
and so much of what I would have called (had I thought
at that time to define it) mutual trust for us to draw on
that I never left her without a feeling of replenish-
ment. It was only afterward, when she was no longer
my friend, that I remembered how one afternoon, as I
stressed the precariousness of my husband's and my position, she had said: "Why don't you move into one of
those housing projects in the suburbs and put the children in public school?" "But I want them to have what I
had. That's not where we belong," I answered. "You
belong," she said then, "where you can afford to belong."
"If that were so," I remember laughing, "we wouldn't
belong anywhere. And besides, how could I go on earning?" "You could take in washing," she had replied. Nor
had she smiled when she said it. Behind and at the root
of the curious expression on her face that afternoon,
she must already have been thinking, as I was to realize
in retrospect, of her money, not only of the money I
had borrowed from her long before to go to my Pole in
Europe and which she had written off as a wedding present when I married him, but of the money she had sent
us after my escape from Poland, money she was regret-
ting, not because she needed it but because, though at the
time she did not say so, it irked her that I was assuming
she would not expect it to be repaid. But in the reposeful
state of confidence in which I will never again allow myself to repose with anyone, I thought merely on that
summer afternoon that she underestimated me. I could

do better, I had to do better than drop the advantages of my education and abandon the expectations born of it. I would not, I told myself, let my children down. Now that I have done what I did and could do and have had time to consider the results, I am not as certain as I was on her sunlit terrace that to have built my children's future from rock bottom rather than to have put up its framework on a floor of hopes alone would not have given them a firmer footing. The American dream of ceaseless material progress from generation to generation to the contrary notwithstanding, it is at least conceivable that to give one's children less than one had oneself to start with might be in the end to give them more.

If among the sweetest of adversity's uses is the discovery of who are one's friends, another is to discover how much more one is endeared to them by a modicum of adversity than by a modicum of success. Moving up and down the ladder as I have moved, never coming within reach of the top rungs but also never slipping below those at the bottom, I have learned that whereas new friends grow more friendly when one is ascending, old friends prefer one to keep one's place. Perhaps they feel that the smile of fortune, however ambiguous and hypocritical, is smile enough. One's best friends seem to love one best when one is fighting with one's back neither far from, nor yet against, the wall. Were one to stop fighting or to win the battle outright, one would risk losing them, for in total defeat they would feel too necessary, in total victory not necessary at all. For the perfect enjoyment of friendship, therefore, one should appear to need and yet not need it, invite it but not care too deeply if it does not come, accept it, flirt with it, even woo it, but under none but the most drastic of circumstances put it to the test.

Tall indeed would be the demands of friendship, were one to allow oneself to make them. How tall, one has only to take one's own measure as a friend to find out. Which of us is willingly wakened by a friend in pain or fright, sits gladly for an afternoon with his sick child, risks job or reputation to defend him, gives up an advantageous relationship with someone who maligns him, or even cancels an important engagement to keep him company? It seems somehow easier (at least in theory) to lay down one's life for a friend than to give up a week of it. All too frequently we remember best a friend's needs when attending his wake.

It is not because I have not heard of Damon and Pythias, however, nor because I am unaware of instances of like friendship in every age and climate no less luminous for having gone unrecorded, that I call it too frail a reed to lean on more than as lightly as one can lean. It is because in my time, in my city, in my society, there are no longer hoops of steel with which to bind friend to friend. Rather, friend feels compelled to beware of friend, lest the bonds prove too confining. In my time, in my city, my society has changed.

IF MY SOCIETY, BY WHICH I MEAN THE SOCIETY IN WHICH you placed me, was not the New York society, it was a New York society, and one which, though respectful of money (as which society is not?), did not judge by it. Money, like plumbing, was a necessity, used and appreciated but seldom mentioned. It was a convenience, not a criterion. It was a welcome by-product of skills and achievements and honors, but the skills, achievements and honors—and not the money—were the goal.

Money was considered too flashy to be trusted in itself; the possession of it did not open doors until it had been refined and transmuted by the alchemy of culture.

The society you and my father frequented was neither that of inherited fortunes nor of fortunes being made. Yours was a professional society composed of men who, like my father, often served the very rich in one or another distinguished capacity—building their houses, sculpting the statues in their private gardens and public squares, painting their portraits, educating their children, operating on their ailing tissues or healing their wounded nerves, publishing or writing the books they collected, heading the foundations they established, settling their estates and their disputes, creating both in theory and practice the climate of their time and place, but seldom overlapping with them socially except as parents in the schools the children of both attended or in the fund raising in which you and your like called upon them for such contributions as yourselves you could not have made.

Your pleasures were not theirs. None of you kept horses, few played bridge. When you traveled, it was not to resorts or dressmakers or beaches, but to historic or cultural shrines. Your names were not listed as box holders at the opera nor did your pictures appear in the rotogravure sections of the newspapers the day after an opening night. You were mentioned in social columns only on the occasion of your daughters' debuts and marriages and in the long, leading obituaries given your husbands when they died. You were not attenders of balls, or indeed of many purely social events. Rather, when you gathered in force, it was to spend the evening sitting very straight and quiet on the little gilt chairs rented to fill your drawing rooms to hear a talk by some expert

on art, archeology, poetry, revolution, the position of
women, Mother India, comparative religion, or the future of the world. You had your clubs where wit and
talent constituted the price of admission. You had your
dinners at which, though food and service were by no
means neglected, conversation was prized more and
maintained, if not always on mind and matter ("What
is mind? Never matter. What is matter? Never mind."),
then at least always above the acrimonious, the scandal-
ous, and the trivial.

Rare as were the occasions when I was invited to your
table when you had guests, I remember clearly enough,
not being tone-deaf, the key in which they were held.
At a comparable dinner party of my contemporaries
where I recently sat between two doctors now holding
the positions of eminence my father and his friends once
held, I was laughing at their reminiscences of nurses embraced behind hospital screens and fatally mistaken diag-
noses when suddenly my laughter stuck in my throat. It
was not because I did not find their stories funny; it was
because I did. It had swept over me that my father, to
whom nothing human was alien, would also have been
laughing, but not at what they said. He would have
laughed at them for saying it. Is theirs, I wonder, just another key adapted to changed *tempora* and *mores*, or are
they off pitch altogether? Is their cynicism a dinner-
party façade or an essential philosophy? Might they too,
as young medical school graduates, have asked themselves as did my father in the diary he kept at twenty-
one: "Will I ever be a good man?" and added: "Notl -
ing less is good enough"? Did they start with the same
dream as the generation before them and lose it along
the way, as my father did not lose it? Or are they, are
we, a lesser breed? I do not know.

A few of your and my father's contemporaries still walk among us. In the lines and folds of their faces there is still an innocence long effaced from ours, as too there is a certain grandeur which, if ours are ever to reveal it, should by this time begin to show. They greet us kindly, but the distance between us and them is such that at best all we can communicate is recognition, all we can call is each other's names. The lapse of time between them and us is too small, *sub specie aeternitatis*, to measure. Yet in that fragment of time an age has passed. It is not their decorous manner or outmoded hats, not their absent-mindedness, their reserve, their resignation that divide us. Theirs is another stamp. Soon, now, the footprints they have made will be merged with those of the dinosaurs.

TO TRY TO REACH FROM THE SEQUESTERED GARDEN TO THE market place where I now have to live is like trying to perform the *grand écart* of a prima ballerina without having learned to dance. What I have done either because I wanted to do it, as in the case of love, or because I have had to do it, as in the case of work, has closed me out from my inherited corner, yet it has not won me a place of my own among the hawkers and buyers of today's wares. If by conduct I do not belong where I came from, I can still be traced back to it by speech and manner and appearance. Indeed, it is this very speech, manner, and appearance which arouse, at literary parties, in television studios, and in the offices where I have always been at the behest of people younger than I and of another ilk, the suspicion that there too I do not belong. Buttoned up as it seems to me only fitting at my age to be buttoned; unable to slip easily into easy familiarity; unequipped with the ambivalent quips that constitute the small coinage of current communication; unwilling to taste much less digest and regurgitate the celebrity gossip that cuts across all distinctions of age and class and region to provide national common ground; as ignorant still today of the techniques of advancement and advantage as when I first found that they exist; still inclined, or anyway too inclined for safety, to assume innocence of motives till their guilt has been proved; instinctively emphatic and prone not just to blurt out but to overpitch what I think, yet at the same time ambitious as I was neither supposed nor encouraged to be at the start, I am from any standpoint a junk dealer's item. I cannot pass for white in either world.

But I could pass, pass without hypocrisy on the one hand and without humiliation on the other, if I had the price. In my society money would buy off today (as yesterday it could not) what I have done that I ought not to have done. And what I ought to have done and did do, had I been able to command the money for it, would have counted, which it does not, as done. By my price I am known as, had I had possessions, I would have been known by them, and the price is too low. To haggle over it would be fruitless. My muscles have been palped, my teeth scrutinized, my capacity estimated by weight and height and girth. All save one of my measures have been taken. Having no cardiograph, they could not gauge my heart.

How much sheer heart it takes to venture even into the outskirts of the market place from which one might still, at the first warning prickle, turn tail and run, you who preferred, and could afford to prefer, to tangle with the other world rather than with this one could not have been expected to understand. Nor did I, who had earlier skirted it, begin to understand until necessity drove me to forage in it. If to compare the market place to the jungle is obvious distortion, it is all the same only distortion and not calumny. As when in his kingdom a lion kills an antelope and there forms around him first a ring of hyenas to snatch discarded morsels and then outside the hyenas a ring of jackals to snap up what the hyenas chance to drop and then outside the jackals a ring of vultures waiting for the bones, so too on the market place the devouring, though not bloody, is no less hierarchic, and whoever cannot either attack or live off the attackers will be devoured. The only conclusion is that some of us must have been designed especially as provender.

Time was when I believed that to divide the world into devourers and devoured had become anachronistic, that such division belonged to the now yellowed pages of history, that if it could still be said to apply at all it applied only to those conventional bugaboos of my upbringing—profiteers, tyrants, and gangsters. Time was when I believed that the predatory instinct was checked at the door of the arts and humanities as automatically as an umbrella or a hat. Time was when I did not know that ideas were merchandised, not because they are in themselves fertilizing, but because fertilizer happens to be marketable. Time was when I assumed that the work of the mind was sanctified and called unto it only those who by nature or choice were dedicated. Time was when I would not have dreamed of questioning, for instance, that those who write books as also those who edit and publish them were by these very acts signing a pact with the public in which, in exchange for respect and honors, they were to give and give always the best they had. I suppose this was never true. But if it is true that it was never true, it was all the same truer once than it is now, for now it is only as true as, and no truer than, it is of any other merchandise. The arts and humanities are not specially peopled, as I had thought, with herbivorous grazers upon the meadows of their own and each other's imaginations. They too are of the market place, and hence must devour or be devoured.

You, whose devouring was done so decorously at home and with such variable and fastidious appetite, were of course unaware that nature had nonetheless cast you, or if not nature alone than nature together with circumstances, for a praying mantis. You, being you, would never have been devoured. Yet you saw not yourself but me as wild, intent, and hungry. "She is the kind," you once said of me, "who would get on a horse and ride anywhere." But if you had known me as I hope I know my children, you would have known that any horse I rode had his will of me and that whenever I have given rein I have always landed on my head. It would not have been possible, however, even if I had succumbed to the temptation I sometimes felt so strongly to tell you of my defeats, for you to see them except as the inevitable logic of what you called my wildness. When the time came, therefore, for these defeats to so multiply and to draw so tight a cordon around me that I could see only one, only a final escape, the temptation did not even flicker across my mind to turn to you. Indeed, on my long list of whom not to turn to, your name was at the top.

NOW THAT BOTH MY CHILDREN ARE GONE FORTH INTO THE market place, less trusting perhaps than I but for all that still more trusting than they should be since to gain a toehold in it one should cling to mistrust till every undercurrent has been learned, I keep wondering how best I might have armed them (if one can arm one's children with anything but money), not against the defeats of their own limitations through which alone they learn who they are and what they can do, but against the defeats brought on them by the limitations (not to say outright the meannesses) of others. What they should have been told above all, of course, is that they cannot, must never expect justice. But is it possible to learn not to expect justice from others and at the same time to go on expecting it from oneself? It was possible once for One Man. But is it not exactly as unreasonable to demand of one's children so complex and lofty an attainment as it would be to demand of them to write a masterpiece or build a traveling star? Yet one is left with alternatives almost too bitter for a mother's tongue, an either and an or of which the one is as corrosive as the other. For if one were to make clear that justice does not exist except as a figment, indeed an overwrought figment of the imagination, one would incur the risk of turning one's children into serpents. But if, on the other hand, one lets them believe in justice, one is incurring for them the risk, not perhaps of crucifixion, but most certainly of a chronic sting and burn of the viscera which not everyone can endure. To believe in God's justice, if one can, is heroic enough. But to have attempted, as we have been attempting for the last two thousand years, to create a justice in men that men can then believe in is by all odds the most heroic, if it is also the most foolhardy, of our undertakings. To compute the galaxies is no more than kindergarten handiwork by comparison.

In the fall of the year my daughter found her first job

as little better than an errand girl in the city garment district, I said to a very rich lady with whom I happened to be lunching that if there were anything I had wished to spare the child, it would have been the market place. "How foolish!" the lady chided me. "She will learn the lessons of life." That the lessons of the market place are lessons of life I can hardly dispute. But that they are worth learning, I will dispute to the end of time. If there existed a way to avoid them, if there existed an island of innocence on which to take refuge or even to be stranded in order to avoid them, I would ship whomever I love or honor to that place. It is curious that those most eager to protect a young girl with all the means at their disposal from the knowledge of calculated perfidy will in the next breath recommend that she spend her days in offices which provide natural breeding grounds, behind the appearance of harmony and respectability, for perfidious calculation. In offices, too, each is out for himself and himself alone.

With what you would have had to admit is a noteworthy restraint, considering both the lack of restraint that marks this narrative (indeed, that characterizes it) and considering too my peculiar ability to collect and arrange and display my grievances, I propose to spare you the lesser items of the collection, dusted, polished, and carefully preserved in my memory as still they are. If I am to be honest, however, I will say that I do not spare you so much out of a sudden, unwonted consideration as out of the fear that, like the pebbles gathered at the sea's rim and laid out to dry on the window sill, they might, once aired, lose their distinctive gleam. I will therefore forbear to exhibit the snubs, the bland evasions of agreement, the crafty underpayments, the dagger points stuck so playfully, so all in fun, between my ribs.

I will not speak of the bottom rungs to which I clung when I had to cling to them to pay the grocer, for what happens on the bottom rungs is such common knowledge that even I in my naïveté and you in your indifference knew, however vaguely, that any treatment one got there was to be expected. Rather, I will speak of what can happen higher up the ladder, high enough for those above to see the grip of one's hand beneath them and for those below to grasp at one's heel. To such a vantage point I could not have aspired, let me hasten to add, in any office, since for a woman to reach it among men requires her to be something more of a woman than most women and much more of a man than any man. But by myself, and as what I will call a performer, since what else is a public speaker whether on platform or on the air, I reached it.

I STARTED, AS YOU WOULD HAVE BEEN THE FIRST TO RE-mind me, not only with my husband to thank for the name which endowed me with an identity quite independent of what I was, but also with you to thank who had unwittingly transmitted to me your instinct to perform and wittingly equipped me with the speech and manner to substantiate it. As it has turned out, it was not for nothing that you spent—so capriciously, it seemed at the time—the money to have me taught by a great *diseuse* (then in her decline and therefore grateful for such increment) to recite the "Ballad of Barbara Allen" with inflections and gestures not unfitted to the Phèdre; to have me apprenticed to a Russian school of the drama in a New York suburb where I passed a whole summer extracting the pith from a Shakespeare sonnet. Nor was it for nothing, come to think of it, that I competed for leading parts in plays at school and college, though that I won them was undoubtedly due more to the articulation you had forced upon me than to what I then fancied, as girls are wont to fancy during their sexual awakening, to be my histrionic temperament. Amateurish as it had been, none of it was for nothing. Invited to an interview with a speakers' agent who was calculating that there might be some profit in a tour of the women's clubs by an American with a title and a best seller, I had not walked the calculated distance from the door of his private office to the desk from behind which he sat watching me before he made up his mind that, whether or not I had anything to say, he could get money from people to hear me say it. But that now, twenty years later, and without the title (though with the articulation), I am still a pack horse in his stable is neither of his, nor of your doing, but strictly and wholly of my own.

However, it is not upon the performance of lectures (though let no one imagine that to lecture does not include all the nuances contained in the word performance, not omitting that subtlest nuance which is to act the part of someone who is not acting a part) that I wish to rest my case against the market place. On the platform, after all, if there is no buttress save one's nerve, there is also no betrayal save as one may betray oneself. One sails alone. One is both navigator and crew. In its freedom as also in its full responsibility, the platform has, giggle or smirk who will, a stature of which only those lecturers who lecture with contempt can rob it. In any case, lecturing preempts merely an odd corner of the market place. There, too, of course, one wears a price tag for all to see. Indeed the price tag is perhaps even more irrelevant than elsewhere since it is fixed by the weight of the lecturer's name rather than by that of the lecture subject, and a name will be paid for describing how to set a table or for telling a not quite tellable joke five times as much as a non-name receives for the distilled essence of years of learning. Nevertheless, there is a certain innocence about it as a trade, if only because the motives of agent, lecturer, and audience are equally and comfortably obvious. Though lecturing is a member of the communications family, it commands about the same regard as an aging and impecunious aunt allowed to hang on in the wing of the palatial residence of radio and television.

How well I remember the tinny little box my father brought home under his arm one evening and installed, with a somewhat shamefaced smile, on the table by his bed. "Your mother wouldn't like it," he said. "All it can do," he grinned at me as he turned its buttons, "is to sing about Sweet Little Rowsy-Powsy. We're a nation of morons, and I suppose I'm one of them. Anyway, it will put me to sleep."

Who knows whether, had he lived to hear my voice when he switched the button, he would have found the swashbuckling debates I was either to engage in or to arbitrate as moronic as "Rowsy-Powsy"? In private, far less contentious than you, seldom contentious at all in fact except when gnawing on the Freudian bone, my father was nevertheless not embarrassed by public contention as you were, and would not, I fancy, have wakened in the night as you told me you often wakened to worry about the unladylike edge in my radio voice. But who knows how he would have measured anything I have done? Although I have always been conscious of standing on his shoulders, as we all stand on the shoulders of our predecessors when they

have shoulders to stand on and if we can stand at all, I
have been conscious at the same time that it was not for
the kind of thing I do (least, oh least of all, for a narrative such as this) that he gave me his shoulders on
which to stand. Yet he, I believe, would have recognized
my effort and approved of it as such. Whereas it was
only the results and the recognition of them about
which you cared. In any case, he would, I know, have
understood as I failed to make you understand how immeasurably shaken I was by the squall that blew up
around me just as I reached what was to be my highest
rung. He would have understood what it meant to me
to find myself both betrayed and impotent. He would
have known not only why but also how I suffered
when, in stumbling upon my so-called moment of truth,
I failed to recognize and live up to it.

It happened during that most divisive period when
Americans, tasting the ashes of Pyrrhic victory, turned
in the rage of dismay to clawing at each other's throats.
Lips that had never framed the word treason, tongues
that had never pronounced it, now rolled it out with
the truculence that is the other half of fear. There had
not been in my lifetime so urgent a call upon men of
good will to stand and be counted; there was no mis-
taking that the condition of good will itself was desperate. Unpolitical, untutored, and ill-fitted as I was to
speak, since my only basis for speaking was a sense of
justice and it was this same sense of justice that both
sides claimed, I found myself in a position where I
could and yet could not speak my mind. Appearing
every week on television as moderator of a debate in
which the debating was often political and the debators
deliberately chosen for their opposing politics and their
natural pugnacity, I had at one and the same time an

extraordinary opportunity to show my own leaning and the categorical obligation, in my neutral role, to forbear to lean.

That I occupied this lofty seat was, it should be understood, an accident. Long before, still during the war, when the program had been no more than a half-serious, half-mocking radio battle over current fiction, I had been invited to participate in a discussion of my second book, *Beyond This Shore*, and having endeared myself on that occasion both to the owner of the program and to my critics by agreeing that I was no novelist (it has never been the fiction of the truth but the truth of fiction that concerns me), I had thereafter served as critic on that program time after time, acquiring with its expanding audience—if only for my willingness to assail eminencies whom the shrewd considered unassailable—a certain reputation of my own. When the program went on television, I was discovered to have the added advantage, from the viewpoint of the market place, of a severity of appearance more fitted to the accepted image of a literary critic than the inviting display of professional actresses. All the same, however, it had been by the back door, and by default of a glamorous predecessor, but primarily because, as a relative nobody, I was a financial bargain, that I was allowed to become first temporary, and then, with public commendation, permanent moderator of the show.

They must exist whose picture of themselves cannot be softened or enhanced by adulation. But for me to claim so rock-bound a coast would be absurd. Unaccustomed as I had been to private blandishment and aware as I had become that the public blandishment I enjoyed so briefly as an author was more for my name than my book, I found the recognition for myself as

me both new and sweet. To be recognized by passers-
by on the street, to be photographed and interviewed, to
receive letters from women saying one made them
proud to be a woman and from men saying one had a
man's mind; to have taxi drivers, postal clerks, and sales-
ladies call one by name; even to provoke that hostile
comment which is in itself a confirmation of identity is
as seducing to the ever seductible ego as are knowing
hands upon the flesh. I will not say, however, that I
yielded completely. But had the seduction gone on
much longer than it did, the recess of my sense of proportion might not after all have remained intact.

I lived in those years on a diet of excitement, but an
excitement never unmixed with fear. Used as I had
become through my lecturing to the stricture of nerves,
the parched mouth, and the erratic pulse that I had to
master as I stepped up to the lectern and faced the dis-
maying cliff of time that yawned before each hour of
speaking, such tension paled by comparison with that of
my television task. On the platform, I was responsible
only for what I said myself and every word I uttered
had been prepared. On the screen, in unrehearsed discussion of books I had not been allowed to select and
between panelists—most of them of national repute—
in the selection of whom I had also been allowed no say,
I was responsible for them all, responsible for raising
the lid of Pandora's box and for making sure that nothing irretrievable popped out of it, responsible alike
for calumny, manners, and the content of the debate.
My comeuppance, when it came up, was perhaps over-
due. I had toyed with seduction, believing myself ultimately unseduceable. But I had a point of vanity of
which, like the rent in a skirt that everyone but the
wearer can see, I had been happily oblivious.

We were to discuss the autobiography of an influential liberal who had belonged for a few months in his student days to the Communist party. To defend him was an impassioned fellow liberal; to attack him, a conservative famous as a ruthless debater and sworn enemy of liberalism. On the day of the program I received my instructions. No matter what the provocation, I was not to defend the author. I was not even to introduce him with the usual flattering formula, but simply to announce his name. I protested. The voice at the other end of the telephone took on a razor edge. "We've been on the air ten years. Our survival depends on tonight. Has it ever occurred to you that you fancy your own intellectual integrity enough to put it ahead of the show?" The thrust went well and truly home. Indeed, I always had fancied, I did fancy, I fancied above all else what I believed to be my intellectual integrity. It was the ground I trod, the roof over my head, the hearth that kept me warm. Now the ground and the roof began to tremble, the hearth to grow cold. I did not remember, not that day at least, that I had a right to this house I had built for myself, and not only the right, but the duty to preserve it. Knowing myself bullied, resenting the bullying and the bully, I yet saw myself as ridiculous. It was only when the show was over that, too late, I knew that it was not before but during the program, not when I resented but when I obeyed my bully, that I had been a fool.

I wish I had back the hours I have since spent reliving that discussion, reliving the moment in the midst of the most contemptuous and lily-livered attack ever made on the air by gentleman upon gentleman when my conscience (not to speak of my upbringing) gave me the cue to leave my microphone and walk away and

I did not heed it. I wish I had back my ignorance of the fact that my house had been, after all, jerry-built. I would gladly also forget the post-mortem laughter at my discomfiture issuing from the same voice that had bullied me earlier in the day, and the apology, made to the author by word of mouth and by letter behind my back and in my name, for what was called my inexplicable failure to defend him. I wish that when, in shame and anger, I resigned, I had stayed resigned. I also wish I had not answered the challenge of a powerful friend by explaining what had actually happened, for then I would not have discovered that he was ready to use all his power to exploit the story at the risk, to me, since I had no written proof, of ruin. Indeed, I wish now that I had never let myself climb that high on the ladder, that I had never penetrated that far into the market place, for I have neither the head for the one nor the stomach for the other. And I wish, how much I wish, that I did not feel it incumbent upon me to admit that what bites most of all is having been, in the midst of moral defeat, a bargain.

Who am I then to cavil about money, who rue more my weight in money than in integrity? I fear I am everyman, or almost everyman, omitting but not forgetting the exceptions that redeem their kind. Money is not a god. Men do not worship it. But when they praise God for their blessings, it is not for the sun or the scenery, not for the health or the love they count purchasable, but for the money to purchase them that they give their thanks. This is their doxology of doxologies.

WHAT WAS YOUR PURPOSE, I HAVE ALWAYS WONDERED, IN writing, that second and last summer of our communal life at the Farm, the letter to my doctor which, if it startled him, yet did not cause him to question my sanity? Was it on an angry impulse or after due deliberation that you wrote it? Were you hoping to obtain his backing to back me further into dependence, or did you envision my being at least for a time, for an easily manoeuverable time, put out of what is so absurdly called harm's way—as though there were any way but that of one harm or another this side of the grave? You never knew how close you came, how close you had come each time you said it, to what was perhaps after all, if unconsciously, your aim. It was not others, but me, whom you almost persuaded that I was insane.

More exposed to my society than I had ever been before through the parties to which people still persisted in inviting my husband and me because even our thread-bare fortunes could not quite rob us of a certain panache, and more exposed to strangers than I had ever been before through the lunches and teas and receptions which, as a lecturer, I was expected to attend and which as long as I bore a title were always well attended, I felt more alone at the heart of this *brouhaha* than I had felt in the longest afternoons of my childhood or the most seemingly interminable days in Poland. Then, I had only to bridge the gap between dream and reality inside myself, while now, the dream spent, I had to build a bridge between reality and appearance, between the real and the apparent me. Apparently possessed of authentic information about a war from which I had run at the moment of its unleashing; apparently knowledgeable about a Europe in which I had not managed to find my place; apparently on the road to a success which had already eluded me; apparently the heroine of a romance which in fact I had murdered; apparently, but actually no longer, a wife; apparently deserving a respect which I had never been respectable enough to deserve; apparently unhappy because of outside circumstances in which I had had no say but in reality unhappy because of inside circumstances I had myself created—I could not be reconciled with my phantom nor could my phantom be reconciled with me. Only when I broke off relations with the phantom altogether was I able to effect between the real and the apparent a reconciliation.

Meanwhile there was one company in which, when I could keep it, I knew at that time at least (though as the stresses increased I was less sure) that I was not insane. It was the company of my children. Though in them too you tried to plant such seeds of doubt as might have taken root in their fresh soil, you failed, and for whatever doubts may since have flowered in them I alone, in my own irresponsibility, have been responsible. They do not know to this day, indeed how could they, that from their faces, the one so rosy, the other so pale, from the true pitch on which both spoke and which neither has lost in the deepening of their voices, from the trust still then implicit in their look, from their hands I so easily enfolded, from their very feet either scampering or trudging after me, I drew my sustenance. It was I, so tall above them, who leaned, and they, so exceedingly small, who were the leaned upon. Upon their dependence I depended. There have since been times when I wailed at their dependence as later at their independence that grew out of it. Often, I have felt not only that they were strangers to me but that I, unbeknownst to them, was a stranger. Indeed, the day was to come when I so forgot them as to believe that my life was no more theirs than their lives were mine. I had to learn again what I had once known but forgotten: that my life, being theirs, was not mine to take.

NO YEAR MADE ONE'S OWN FINALITIES LOOK SO INSIGNIFI-cant as the year you sold the Farm. No loss of home, no death of a friend, no going of one's husband to war again was an excuse for tears when history itself wept at man's violation of it. Bad news rode a foaming steed across the world, howled destruction from every roof-top, palsied the hand at its appointed task, made the pulse race with terror. Only at night, alone and un-observed, could one lift up one's woes and hold them before sleepless eyes for re-examination.

What was there so grievous after all about going for the last time down the back road of the Farm with the children for a look at the old gravel pit in which they had dug and slithered through sunny hours; about emp-tying the playhouse of its litter of parts of dolls and car wheels and crayoned drawings; about the hurried glance into drawers and closets for forgotten treasures; about seeing the children kneel on the seat of the limousine with their faces pressed to its back window as the house receded from view—when at that very mo-ment other children were seeing their houses burn, their parents stripped and shot? What was there to rend the heart in the news over the radio that the most alive friend one had ever had had been thrown to his death by his favorite horse, when over that same radio came the news from every part of the world of live men being thrown to their death by one another? What was there so hard to bear in seeing one's husband once more in uniform when the sight was the commonest to the world's wives? All the sorrow one could hold was but a raindrop on so deep-breasted an ocean of sorrow as had not yet been known. Yet this made sorrow no less sorrowful.

With America in the war, my husband had not rested till he was commissioned in the American army, nor had he looked so at peace with himself since the attack on Poland as on the morning he set out in khaki and shining boots on a road that was to take him from Washington to Africa to London to Normandy to Paris to the Bulge and to Berlin before bringing him back again, with new ribbons above his heart and new mysteries within it, to children who could not guess the cost of the ribbons and to a wife who knew all too well the cost of the mysteries.

Long before my husband left us, however, I had gone to work in a wartime agency where, if what I learned in this first experience of offices opened my eyes to the fact that an office is as much a battlefield as any place where blood is shed, what I learned about war itself brought me closer to my husband, at least in imagination, than at any time since before it had begun. Until then I had been so preoccupied with lectures and reviews and articles, and with (how I wish I need not mention it) my novel which a kind friend had not ineptly described in her review as "warmed-over rehash," that though the roll call of defeats on land and sea had drummed as incessantly on my ears as on the ears of all but those deafened by stony indifference, I had not visualized what those defeats meant to the peoples living in their aftermath. The cold, the hunger, and the fear that were the lot of my husband's fellow Europeans and which no comforts could have dispelled from his mind became real to me only when I was put to writing about them. The atrocities, never out of his consciousness, took on reality in mine only when I was put to assembling them as the *pièces de résistance* of American propaganda. However, though for a time then I may have lost more sleep over them than he, in the end pity and even memory were choked with custom of fell deed.

All the same, bound now by our equal preoccupation with the war (though for mine I was paid while for his he had done the paying), bound also by the loss of my home on top of the loss of his and by our common anxiety about the relative homelessness of our children who were living with you in a rented house just outside the city and over whom in my absence at work you were gaining a jurisdiction neither my husband nor I desired, we were being drawn together. Magnetized again by the same kind and degree of emotion, we might again have been well and truly met. But before it could happen, he was on his way back to the war from which not by so much as a heartbeat had he in fact been parted.

If there exists, even hypothetically, one setting better than another for the hour when a husband, a father, goes off to war, I cannot describe it. No more for Penelope surrounded by echoing palace chambers than for the woman in a crowded hovel can that hour be less than a little death. But the worst is not to have that hour to oneself. When my husband had been called up in Poland, his mother, two sisters, and all the household servants stood by at the door to bless and be blessed, with a resignation born as much of having lived through such hours before as of having long since learned to call men's most desperate acts God's will. That time, because they were his people and I was sure he would have had it the way it was, I did not allow even my thoughts to rebel. But when the hour came again, and you insisted not just upon sharing it but upon dominating it, you gave me what still seems to me the most senseless of the injustices in my collection.

All of us knew when he came for Christmas that within a week or two he would be gone. Had it not been in a house over which you presided, had it not been by your leave, so to speak, that we spent it together, that Christmas might have been our best. My husband, moved in his always secret self by the occasion, gave us the full gift of a gaiety than which there could be nothing gayer since it was distilled from pain. Unsolicitous as he most often was about family ailments, this time the fact that my son had a cold and fever made him more tender with the boy than ever before. Bored as he otherwise must have been by my daughter's red-faced intensity about Red Indians, he spent hours in her teepee in the cold back yard. With a small electric tool he painstakingly burned into a block of wood pictures of each of the four of us in embryonic, but recognizable poses. He helped to decorate the tree, gossiped with the governess, accompanied your uncertain voice in the carols you liked best. And to me, with a warmth in his voice for which I was no longer listening, he said when we went to bed that night: "I know it is hardest for the one who stays behind."

The next day was the last. You must have surmised that I wanted to spend that evening with him after the children had been put to bed. Yet no sooner had he said good night to them than you announced that you had several matters to consult him about and asked me to leave the room. When I protested, you cast yourself on the floor in a faint. Coolly, my husband bent over and picked you up. You seized your head then between your hands and turned on me that Shakespearean rhetoric about ingratitude which had been written specifically, you seemed always to suggest, with me in mind. If there is something sharper than a serpent's tooth, it is, I have cause to remember, a mother's fang. But if there were something sharper still, it would be a daughter's outrage. Had my feet been dragging me, as I returned from the station where I parted with my husband, to prison gates, I doubt if they could have been more leaden than when I turned them back to your door.

That parting was not, as for more than two years thereafter I prayed every night to God (on Whose existence I now found I had to bet) that it would not be, our last. Around the bend of the future lay one for which I can claim no solace since I chose it myself. But because our last wartime parting had been neither his choice nor mine, because it had been if not an Act of God then at least a *vis major*, it might have been the easiest to bear as also to remember. For the fact that it is not, I must either hold you responsible or parry thrust with like thrust now all these years later and too late and charge you in turn with having been insane.

TIME HAS ANOTHER DIMENSION BESIDES THAT OF MATHE-matical relativity. It has a psychological relativity accordion-pleated to fit not only the particular mind but the particular state of that mind, yet always beyond the reach of that mind to control. Just when the mind is most fixed on time, most eager to pace it, it adopts so stubborn a stance that neither wheedling nor lashing will budge it. But when the mind abandons time to its own devices and time takes over the reins, there is nothing the mind can do to catch up with it and halt it. Time, when considered outside the sphere of the sun, is so relative to its own relativity as to become quite irrelevant.

You, for one, did not attempt to control it. You lay like a dry leaf on the wind of time, waiting for it to lift and blow you where it listed. I, on the other hand, cannot even now altogether give up the attempt to master time, though I have not yet succeeded in hastening or detaining so much as a second of it. I have been far more concerned, however, with its hastening than with its detaining. So disproportionately many have been the hours I would have hastened that, looking back on them, I would gladly give those few that I longed to retain in exchange for a foreshortening in my memory of those that crept. If, in so saying, I seem to speak as though time were finished with me when clearly it is not, this is because I am finished struggling with its undetainability. I cannot imagine the hour I would still fight to detain. My concern now is only with its hastening. Let it bow my body and fold my face and snow my hair, if at the same time it fufills its implicit promise to even out my breathing and quiet down my heart. Only, please God, let it not ask of me ever again to be as patient as it asked of me at the peak of my impatiences. And please God even more, let it depart from me swiftly in its final victory. Let it be as generous, if I agree to wait it out, as it was on that day when I thought to give it the slip. Let me not have to cry time mercy.

How, I wonder, would you have handled the time I was compelled to handle, had it been yours? I cannot imagine, since your relationship to time passing was never the same, or at least not in the time I could observe you, as mine. You were afraid to use it, I to lose it. You wanted to fill it with dreams, I with reality. You chose to sit there on your chaise longue with time on your hands and contemplate it, whereas the very necessity of contemplating it instead of grasping it in both hands and squeezing the juices from it rent me asunder. You hoped less of it than I. It is because I could have loved it that I hated it. It was because you had no more desire to discipline it than to discipline yourself that you preferred drifting on it to battling with it. Though you found time, toward the end, heavier than so far I have ever found it, you did not rebel against it since you could see no uses to which to have put it. Time was the only dimension against which you did not rebel, while it was the dimension against which I rebelled the most.

I can see you now, on those still remembered long afternoons of my childhood, retreating from my too apparent loneliness (I was too old for a governess and too young to go forth alone) with a great air of preoccupation and taking refuge in your room where I knew all you would do was to lie down, as I also knew that to try to awaken your interest enough to keep you from lying down would end only in a scolding. No change in me or my circumstances was to change your afternoon ritual of escape. Not even when, with my stricken leg pinioning me to the house for so many months, I had all I could do, though by that time I was fully grown, to fill the hours between midday and evening, not even then did you think to invent me a distraction or lend me for a half hour a listening ear. And in those last years of yours, when the situation reversed itself and I, whose days were by then as overcrowded as once they had been undercrowded, paid you the diurnal call I knew to be your due, your eyes held the same preoccupation and your manner the same longing to escape, even though you betrayed your loneliness at eighty as plainly as I had betrayed mine at eight.

Supposing it had been you and not I whose husband had gone to war and who had undertaken to live in a small city apartment with children still too young, as I had once also been too young, to go out alone and from whom you would therefore have had no legitimate or even possible afternoon escape? Could you have gone on closing your door without questioning whose time your time was? Or would you have brought yourself to give time rather than to hoard it? Might you, in a drastically changed perspective, have expended that time of yours less grudgingly than I? Might you even, in my place, have showered the children with it, finding that time for which you had so little use was, when spent on them, well spent?

I feel as certain that you would not have minded what I minded as that you would have minded what I did not mind. You could not possibly not have minded, being you, walking in winter winds beside a tricycle along the gray river's edge or leaning, huddled within your coat, against some ramshackle car in the jalopy yard while keeping vigil over your small son lest, in his absorbed chauffeur's fantasy, he release the brake, any more than you could have not minded, when rain imprisoned you with the children, the disorder that was as essential a part as it was an inevitable consequence of whatever they wanted to do. Nor could you have not minded the dusting and cleaning, fetching and carrying, planning and not forgetting of which the daytimes were composed. Whereas for me, though I was seldom unaware of the tedium, that very tedium gave me the escape I needed from time itself.

But what I did mind, and mind to a pitch that made the rest of my minding inaudible, were the hours after the children had gone to bed and before I could hope to sleep. No longer then, at least in my own eyes, a mother; restored to myself so to speak as a woman, I had no one to look to for confirmation of my womanhood. All over the world wives and mistresses of men at war were prowling their confines with the same restlessness. Yet again I say that a common fate makes it no less uncommon to the fated. And besides, the comfort of knowing that the thread of longing to which one held so tightly was equally tautly held at the far end was not mine to derive. I thought I knew, and I thought and still think I knew as much as one can know of how safely one is ensconced in another's heart, that the far end of my thread was slack. And while I had had confirmation of my womanhood enough, and even aplenty, since leaving Poland, I had not had the only confirmation I wanted, the confirmation on which one can draw as well in sickness as in health, in poverty as in riches, the confirmation one promises and is promised until death and upon which, even when the promise fades from the memory, even when it is jeopardized, one never quite ceases to feel a claim. This was what I minded. Perhaps after all you would have minded it no less. But that is something neither you nor I could have guessed, since little as you yourself gave confirmation, you never appeared to lack for its perfect facsimile.

If, among the few friends I saw at the time, one of them may have noted this rust on my nerve, none said so. Yet it must have colored my voice and corroded the words I chose one day in a discussion over a radio network, for I received from a priest in a distant city a printed prayer in which he had underlined with red ink the phrase: "Grant that I may not so much seek to be loved as to love" and at the end of which he had neatly written: "I will pray for you." But when, in as veiled a manner as anyone so clumsy as I am with veils could manage, I wrote to ask my husband for his confirmation, he wrote back: "Marriage is an institution."

THAT FROM THE START I HAVE HAD A SPECIAL VULNERABIL-ity to words is hardly odd. My father, cautious with the spoken word and soft with it too, nevertheless wrote poem after poem in which the cadences seemed as germinal as the ideas implicit in them. Who can say, when he wrote "The sweetest flower that blows," whether form invited feeling or feeling form? Who can say whether it was the painted wild geese in flight across a piece of Chinese silk or the words themselves that prompted his poem about them? And was it not more than likely that the cartoonlike bathos of the line "The elephant packed his trunk one day" set him to elaborating a poem that, like the smile of the clown, concealed beneath its self-mockery a shy and anxious heart? Who dares call words mere sounding brass or tinkling cymbals when even before God's handiwork there was God's Word?

But it was not only my father who opened my ear to words. From the time I first remember my sister till she was full grown, she wrote verse as instinctively as other children skip rope or throw a ball. Almost as soon as I could be made to sit still and listen, those of her poems which she allowed you and my father to see you read aloud to me. And later, in the last flash of her poetic impulse as also of our confidences, she showed me, as she could not have shown either of you, the Swinburnian outpourings spilled from an imagination too voluptuous to bank.

Primarily, however, it was you after all who gave me my unassuagable, never-to-be-slaked thirst for the ichor of the word. Though what you yourself wrote was rather an educated echo than the cry itself, though none of your words were airborne as were the best of my father's and my sister's, the sound of words was equally important to you. You were as naked to their impress as the patient strapped down beneath the surgeon's knife. Words could not only offend and shock, but exalt and overjoy you. To whoever over the ages had mastered them you gave a veneration the more impressive for being withheld from others. The wrong word in any writing stuck like a bone in your throat. The right word, wherever and whenever you came upon it, cleared your brow of its frown and your eyes of their shadow. Often as your ear betrayed you in your own written choice of them, for the words of others your hearing was uncanny.

If therefore I had to settle upon a single word to describe that of which, from as far back as I remember, I have been the most sensible, it would be the word "word." Among all the sights and sounds so piled up now after half a century in my private storeroom that even to reach them, let alone to sort them out for this narrative, has required me to stretch higher and bend lower than I ever thought I could, by far the most pristine are words, words printed or written in a familiar hand, words sung, recited, or spoken by a voice known or unknown, loved or hated, that made them count.

Words need not be grand, though to the diapason of nobility I will not admit that I am unattuned. Like everyone else, I am accessible to their grandeur, whether tight-reined in the formula that follows upon "We hold these truths to be self-evident" or unleashed in the call of "I have nothing to offer but blood, toil, tears and sweat." No more perhaps, but surely no less than everyone else am I accessible to the sonorities of those who converse with eternity. But to small voices, I am more accessible than most. I catch their accent, I hear their underlying tone, I detect even when least hot upon detection their hidden tremor, rasp, or plea. Let no one write words for me who does not wish to be revealed in them. Let no one speak to me who does not wish me to guess in his voice the words he leaves unspoken. Let anyone who does not wish me to remember his spoken or written word forbear to speak or write it. Let anyone who wishes me to remember them rest assured that I will not forget. Whoever wishes to stab me, whoever wishes to revive me, the one or the other can be done by nothing more tangible than the word.

Yet of my own words, or at least of my own spoken words, I am as heedless as I am heedful of those of others. How ironic, how ridiculously ironic it is that, aware as I am of the power of the word, I have not yet learned to curb it. Though I often seek, more no doubt to avoid the repercussions on me than to avoid the percussive effects on those who hear them, to swallow instead of uttering the sharp jest, the jet of contumely, the acid reproach, and the jeremiads that leap so readily to my mouth, they are gone before I can take hold of them, and in the issuance of even the most ill-advised, unjust, and wounding of them, I experience almost a paroxysm of relief before the first sadness of their aftermath sets in. In this too, be it said, I am like you. Although through no fault of your own save the failure to make an opportunity, you did not win for your articulacy even such frostbitten laurels as I have won for mine, your sins of the tongue were equal. And you paid in your way as I still pay in mine a price for them that neither you nor I nor anyone could well afford.

Whether thought first gave birth to the word or the word to thought remains, and will remain, like the precedence of egg over chicken, forever debatable. But that the word can travel faster than the speed of light, can cause such fission as the bombardment of neutrons has not yet set off, there is no doubt. The greatest power we know is still the power of the word. The danger lies in its ambidexterity. But by ambidexterity I do not mean so much its equal use for good and evil as I mean that the word in itself can mean a thing and its opposite at one and the same time, depending upon who hears it. Right can be right and wrong, yes can be yes and no, love can be love and hate, God can be God and devil too. What it seems to come down to is that the power of the word is not inherent but separate from it, bestowed on it by pitcher and catcher alike, and can only achieve its maximum capacity when pitched and caught with the same intent. Thus if two nations bristling with arms both say what they seek is peace, each is apt to believe that to the other the word peace means war unless peace and war can each be made to mean the same to both. And thus also, to narrow my examples enough to fit my own accessibility, when you used the word insane it was what I meant by sane while what I meant by sane meant insane to you; and again, when my husband said "marriage is an institution," he meant that it is a public building no private person can remodel or tear down whereas to me it was institutional only as the home itself is an institution and could therefore be quite simply (I then believed) abandoned if it ceased to fit one's needs.

A whole science has been elaborated to explain the ambiguities of words, their personality changes, and the rifts between their conscious, subconscious, and unconscious behavior. Words have their genealogy, their history, their economy, their literature, their art and music, as too they have their weddings and divorces, their successes and defeats, their fevers, their undiagnosable ailments, their sudden deaths. They also have their moral and social distinctions. Among them are professional uplifters as also ne'er-do-wells doomed to disgrace and ignominy. Words can be divided and subdivided by their sociologists into upper-upper, upper-middle, lower-middle, and lower classes, but they also move with the rise and fall of their fortune from class to class. The intellectuals among them form a class apart, a class of technicians, speaking for the most part only for and to one another. And from among words there also occasionally arises—and more likely out of the common herd than the elite—a word endowed with that heaven-sent accident which is genius.

But today words are suffering from overpopulation. Moreover, their economy is not balanced. The haves are living well beyond their meanings, while the have-nots are seething with discontent at the despoilment of what they mean. Some have such a surplus of meanings that it constitutes a glut, while others must go poking for them in the dustbin. And between the soaring birth rate and the advances made in geriatrics, the time is not unforeseeable when words, which anyway so outnumber the ideas they feed on, may have to resort to organized warfare to determine the survival of their fittest.

Why have words split themselves into nationalities? How is it that the very letters of which they are composed, letters founded after all upon the capacity of tongue and lips and epiglottis to shape and voice them and therefore bound—one would think—by the same limitations, yet sound so different within the various enclaves of language? Is it a matter of prevailing winds, of distance from or above the sea, of geographic contour, of the way the rivers flow, or does it depend on the climate inside the head where the word is born? Why does the same word ring so otherwise in one head, in one ear, than in another, and even so otherwise in the head than in the ear that belongs to it? Why is it that one word rather than the other sends its clarion reverberations to the four corners of the earth? What makes some words concatenate as though each had been forged especially to link with the next, while others, as carefully matched, refuse to make a chain? How is it that certain words which, in themselves, are so tonic become toxic in juxtaposition? Why can some words be sung while with others no descant is possible? What arcane vitality keeps alive a cruel word but allows a kind word to die? Why must the word, to be authentic, have been suckled by the heart? And why should so insubstantial a substance as the word move mountains, roll back seas, traverse centuries, create or wipe out barriers between nation and nation, between friend and friend, between parent and child, and between lovers? Ambidextrous, ambivalent, ambiguous, the word is all the same a miracle. For however it may divide and estrange us, it is at the same time the mark of our species and our common denominator in time and space.

THE STATEMENT THAT "MARRIAGE IS AN INSTITUTION" IS, of course, unexceptionable. Indeed, the more exceptions one makes of it, the more clearly one sees that, revolutionary as marriage once was, it has long since passed, in a reversal of the usual procedure, from the order of men to the order of nature. If it began by being arbitrary, it is now instinctive. Nothing else could explain why the divorced, for instance, no sooner cancel one marriage license than they hasten to take out another. If this were true only of divorced women, one could suppose the explanation to be purely economic, but it is just as true of men, few of whom have anything to gain economically from marriage. Were marriage no more than a convenient screen for sexuality, some less cumbersome and costly protection must have been found by this time to replace it. One concludes therefore that people do not marry to cohabit; they cohabit to marry. They do not seek freedom to rut so much as they seek the rut of wedlock. Sexual freedom, like all freedoms, entails the necessity of choice and the assumption of responsibility, both of which are, it would seem, almost intolerable to the majority of mankind. Free, people have no one to commiserate with them (we all know the hunger for commiseration) and no one outside themselves to blame; married, they acquire someone from whom they have the right to demand commiseration and upon whom they have the right to cast the blame. Sharing their aches and disappointments, they can also find in each other's sins of omission and commission the best of excuses for their own. And whatever their mutual hostility, they will always find it easier to face the hostility of the outside world together than alone. Psychologically, at least, every marriage is a marriage of convenience.

To these conclusions of mine you would undoubtedly have said again, as twice you were justified in saying: "I knew no marriage with you could last." I could not expect you to have understood that in taking marriage at its bottom-most level, I am not denying the heights of tenderness and consideration it can reach, but merely supporting my theory that to marry is a need and that people will settle for no matter how bare or even how infested a room they can be sure of, rather than to have to look every night for another lodging. Those who leave that room, generally speaking, leave it only when they have found another and what they consider superior room.

Marriage is indeed an institution, bound to our needs as certainly as bench and court, police station and hospital, parliament and church. However often marriage is dissolved, it remains indissoluble. Real divorce, the divorce of heart and nerve and fiber, does not exist, since there is no divorce from memory. And no more than from one's memory can one be divorced from the father of one's children. But the phrase "marriage is an institution," written in answer to a wife who has asked her husband if he loves her, has a hollow, a forbidding sound. It is no incantation with which, by sedulous repetition through the day's dull tasks and on the night's hot, crumpled pillow, one can fend off even so poor a devil as self-pity, still less the fat, rich, succulent devil that is the body's but also the heart's lust.

I NEVER KNEW HOW SOON YOU KNEW, OR AT LEAST SUS-pected, that my solitude had come to an end. Had you even imagined, for that matter had I myself even imagined, how easy it would be to penetrate and disperse it, no less than you I would have been appalled. Frozen over with what I believed to be the thick ice of the most wintry isolation from my husband's love—an ice that had first formed itself, *nota bene*, long before the deep frosts of war's despair and was now, to my eyes at least, impenetrable—I would have supposed that it would take more than the sun of a casual smile, more than the fitful spring wind of awakening desire, more than the harbinger that is the first warm day, to melt me. But it did not.

The war by that time was over. Already, the almost unbearable constriction of the throat that follows upon all great tidings (and even upon any good news amidst the habitual preponderance of the bad) had eased. But the hope of my husband's immediate return, flaring so brilliantly with the cessation of danger, had guttered in the weeks that followed with no mention of it and, with the news that he would be staying on for some time in Berlin, had gone out. For the last weekend of the summer, during which my children had been away at camp, I was invited to fill in as an unattached woman at a seaside house party. Whether or not I would have accepted had I foreseen the consequence of my going, I cannot say. Consciously, though I knew my marriage for a failure, I had been willing it to last with just such tenacity as must have been carrying marriages since the beginning of marriage itself from failure into that compromise which is as good as, if not equal to, success. Unconsciously, however, it may well have been that my blinds were already raised and my windows and doors open to the chance guest of new experience. Perhaps this is why, when the guest appeared, I was, to my own surprise and I must suppose also to his, quite ready.

Capitulation even before a siege would seem logically enough to preclude not just the need for it but the impetus. Yet there are citadels within citadels and he is wise who knows that to have captured one of them is not to have the others fall to him automatically. There doubtless exist, even in our jerry-built times, women so staunch that however they may be crumbling within they still keep their ramparts standing. Clearly, I am not among these. Even if I had not come of age in a day when ramparts as a principle of defense were becoming outmoded, I would probably have neglected to hold mine intact. I had discovered when first they were breached that they were too far from the center of my being to justify grave concern, much less the sacrifice implied in defending them. It was therefore after what might have seemed, to a less distinguished veteran of such campaigns as was my captor, total capitulation, that he began, somewhat tentatively and with the reluctance proper to one inured to the spoils of victory, his siege.

You, who by then lived on the same city street as I and in the same block, could have seen from your window almost any evening and in any weather a tall figure leaning against the wall of the school that confronted both your building and mine, his face uplifted and motionless, his whole bearing one of too fixed an attention for even the most unobservant observer to have supposed him loitering. Indeed, had I been incarcerated high in some crenellated tower rather than peering from a third-story apartment house window, and had he been waiting for me to let down my long hair that he might climb up by it rather than for me to descend to him in an elevator, he could not have appeared more spellbound nor could I, transfixed by this most improbable of improbabilities, have felt dizzier. When, with dishes washed and children bathed, tucked into bed, prayed with, and finally silenced in sleep, I hastened out for a tryst with my gray-haired knight errant, the sooty pavements we trod, the delicatessens, funeral parlors, and bars we passed, and all the hurrying or lingering shadows with whom we shared the night might as well not have existed. I forgot, with that remarkable forgettability apparently accorded by the passions (by hate as well as by love) no less in middle age than in youth, that both he and I were absurd. And since, the moralists to the contrary notwithstanding, it is not the knowledge of sin so much as the knowledge of one's own absurdity that kills the illusion of happiness, I was happy. I was happy for once, and for a time.

I am not surprised, looking back on it, that somewhere beneath this recrudescence of fever, the fear of your guessing how high it had mounted was never entirely stilled, since as I have confessed before, you and my conscience, against both of whom I had spent so inordinate a number of hours rebelling, had not ceased to be one. Nor does it surprise me on the other hand, though according to every precept I was ever taught it should not only surprise but deeply shock me, that no feeling of guilt or anxiety then impinged upon my thoughts of my husband, the sight of whose handwriting on an envelope pushed under the front door lifted my heart as it always had, as now, these many years since I forced our parting, it still does, for it is not of a broken vow that love dies. But what I cannot understand is that I did not feel guilty toward my children. I, who had made it a principle not to lie to them, might and presumably should have felt compelled to cast down my eyes before their glance, knowing as they could not know that I was what is called living a lie. But the almost violent tenderness for them that was a concomitant of my reawakening contained not an ounce of shame. I can therefore only assume that my heart is not as other hearts (a deduction too hypothetical to warrant belief for though the rhythm of hearts can vary, their function is always the same) or that my heart was after all not living the duplicity of a lie but the duplicity of life itself.

How sophistical an argument this was and is, however, and how adept had been my heart (and I concede that it may be more adept than others) at sophistry, I was not many months in finding out. Early on a cold gray Saturday morning, when I answered the peremptory summons of the telephone, I heard for the first time in more than two years my husband's voice. Without preamble and on a note too quiet to be less than urgent, he said: "In about an hour I will be there."

"Papa! Papa!" In the children's cry there sounded, as though not a day, let alone a procession of slow-footed years, had passed since he had appeared in our hotel room in Genoa on the eve of our departure for America, the major chord they had sounded then, absolute and triumphant, in its joyful resolution. As with flushed faces and brightly expectant smiles they dressed themselves and set about the tidying of our three rooms with a sense of fitness and occasion I had not known they possessed, such a tremor seized me that my hands would not hold what I held in them and my feet would not move me from where I stood.

I had waited long for this moment, but not long enough. The river of hope, finding its banks too narrow and tortuous to contain such insistent waters, had cut itself another channel, had made itself another bed. What dam could now arrest so rapid a current? By what miracle could it be returned upon its former course? Hope does not flow, any more than any other river, back toward its watershed.

Suddenly, I knew what I had to do. Inventing an excuse for the children, I ran to the nearest telephone booth. Twice, I dialed the wrong number, and then, with icy fingers, the right one. "He's back," I said. "He's home."

It must have been the circumlocution, the terrible, the vulgar ambivalence of the "he" that first caught my breath and then drained all of it from my body in a kind of hemorrhage of shame. Only now can I realize in full how my future depended on that moment. Had the answer been anything but the blessing that it was I would not be, as I am now, under the same roof as he who gave it.

MY FAILURE HAD BEGUN, OF COURSE, AT MY BEGINNING. Every climax, or as in my case anticlimax, exists potentially from the start. It begins with the putting forward of that wrong foot. No sooner does the use of the wrong foot become automatic than the steps it takes multiply too fast to follow. One becomes a projectile, thrust forward by an internal rather than an external force, but continuing by one's own inertia to move in the wrong direction. One's course, voluntary at the start, becomes more and more involuntary until even the memory of the initial choice fades away, replaced by the conviction that it was not, that it could never have been oneself who made that decision, but chance, fate, providence (those pseudonyms by which the will's identity is so conveniently disguised)—or simply someone else.

There exist those who find in the wrong direction a peculiar stimulus, an air that is somehow native to them, and for such as they the wrong direction might as well be called the right. But these are few. Most of us who are caught in the trajectory of our errors find it too bumpy, too precipitous not to be tormented along the way. It is the degree to which that torment is supportable that determines whether we allow it to end itself or bring our own end to it.

I should make clear here that I speak, not of the comedy, but of the tragedy of errors. I know there are many to whom both error and its consequence are comic, many for whom the louder the error and its echo resound, the heartier their laughter. It may be that they will inherit the earth. If so, they are welcome to it. An earth preempted by those who can laugh at a Jew cleaning a sewer, an *auto-da-fé*, a Ku Klux Klan, a child being hectored by its fellows, a woman scorned, a smart chicanery, or a drowning cat, is an earth without shade or shelter for me. It is only because there are still those who weep and those past weeping who record others' tears that I call the earth my home. It is only because not all are yet engulfed by that positive thinking which is the negation of thinking itself, by that peace of mind which so passeth understanding that it passes even the wish to understand, by that love of self which delivers us not only from hearing the answers but from asking the questions; it is only because in every generation there are still those whose hair stands on end and whose voices stick in their throats at sight of the abyss between what we are and what we might be, what we practice and what we dream, our ends and the means we use to achieve them, our reach and our grasp, that I do not despair at being human. I can find no laughter in me for the tragic sense of life. All other sense, to me, is nonsense.

It is with unceasing wonder at the lengths to which irony can go that I consider how disturbed you would have been to read these words. You, yourself so mournful-eyed, so rooted in your conviction of unhappiness, so constantly alluding to escape in death from what you considered an intolerable life, shrank nonetheless, and for all your melancholy, from any bitterness save your own, and most especially from mine. "That child always had a poor constitution," you would have said, and did say, apropos of my fellow feeling for tragedy. You would not have understood, you did not understand that the degree of one's vulnerability does not stem from the accident of a *petite nature* but from the accident of one's vision. The only safeguard against the tragic sense is not a splendid physique but myopia.

But in the progression of errors, what enables one to accept its rude buffetings while driving another into that death which is the only escape from the consequences of one's own acts, is the purely individual, the wholly incalculable matter of stress tolerance. The prisons of the world bulge with criminals not one of whom seems to hesitate to choose the protracted agony of a life sentence over a swift and one would think infinitely kinder release in death. It must be presumed that theirs is a stress tolerance only less than that of the martyrs themselves. On the other hand there are those who, whether out of real or false pride (if anyone is to determine which is which), suffer so much, if not from error itself then from its consequences, that even by errors generally admitted to be weaknesses rather than crimes and even by consequences known only to their secret selves, their integument is fatally corroded. In these it must be presumed that the stress tolerance is so low as to be close to non-existent.

History spills over with testimonials to those who have accomplished a Herculean lifework despite lifelong physical distress, to those who have endured the rack in silence, to those who have died willingly for friend, idea, or God; and for every such recorded triumph uncounted triumphs over blood and tissue, nerve and fiber, have gone unsung. Indeed the graves of our time alone —graves with and graves without the cold comfort of a headstone—contain more brave bones, charred and mutilated not by God but by fellow men, than the graves of any other age since graves were first dug. But who is to measure stress tolerance? Who is to say whether the woman who rips the air with her screams as the child rips her flesh to be delivered suffers more, or suffers less, than the fallen soldier who mutely holds together his gaping belly? Who is to say, between the man crying out in the death throe, "My God! Is this the end?" and the man whose exsanguine lips frame a last smile, which has the greater pain? Who is to say of the peasant woman I once saw who had walked six miles to the doctor with her womb hanging down from her body that she was in greater distress than were you when, lying on that chaise longue of yours, you palped your abdomen with fingers trembling lest they discover the lump that was not there? Who is to say that a man who throws himself from his office window to escape the aftermath of ruin is flayed by a sharper pain than the woman who cuts her veins in the bathtub for the sake of a telephone call she knows will never come? Who is to say why some can repair themselves after irreparable loss and others not? Who is to say, when a load has long been carried, why a straw should break the camel's back? Who is even to say which among all the straws on the wind was the straw that broke it? Of the straws on mine at the time I speak of, I would be hard put, even now in the afterglow of retrospect, to say which did the actual breaking.

I have said, and said while fully aware of the arrogance of saying it, that your endurance of stress was puny, the implication being of course that it did not brook comparison with mine. I have pointed out how relatively safe you were from the Acts of God which afflict most lives (why, I wonder, do we count as God's Acts only the disasters He visits on us, while such joys as we garner we attribute to acts of our own?). I have also pointed out how safe you were from the grinding anxiety over bed and board that is the prevailing human condition. You looked at the world, when you chose to look at it at all, from the balcony of privilege, flanked through the heat of your day by that bodyguard of bodyguards, my father, and supported in the cool of your evening as much by what he had been as by the provision he had made for you. But it occurs to me now as it did not occur to me in the years when I saw myself borne into the open sea by an imperious, one-way current, that in fact you were cheated by such benevolent circumstance from discovering and revealing what powers of endurance you had. You were not asked, and therefore had not to ask of yourself, to act well and quickly in war, to outwit outwitters on the market place, to meet public admiration and animosity alike with sangfroid, to protect your children singlehandedly not just from the world but from your own distempers, to take ups and downs of recognition and cordiality without loss of footing. You were not asked either to expose or to grapple with your limitations. On the contrary, you were asked, and therefore had to ask yourself, to accept the small though unending disappointments of any keeper of a household, of any wife, of any mother. And being what I now see that latently you were—driving, ambitious, imaginative, articulate, and intensely (though always angrily) alive—I will hazard, now that all hazarding is too late, that you were asked too little. Such a hiatus between reach and grasp could have been enough to cripple you, could have been enough to explain your tragedy. And in the same sense, for all that I was asked what seemed to me so much more of me than were you of you, a relative hiatus between my reach and my grasp may also, at least in part, explain my defeat.

Who can say that by having invariably put forward the right foot the circumstances of life would have been better? None can say who has not tried it. Different, however, different for certain, they would have been. But by the time my husband had returned from the wars to follow again, presumably, a common road with me, if not so much for our own sake then for the sake of the children, my wrong foot had so accustomed itself to leading, had developed a musculature so much more resilient and dependable than the right one, that to step out first with it had become almost—though not quite—instinctive. If I still felt as I lifted it and before I put it down a fractional hesitation, a twinge from the *tic douleureux* of my conscience, I was ready with the unfailing anesthetic of self-excuse. What I wanted was not to understand him but to be understood.

How was it that, after having been dominated or perhaps I might better say preempted for more than twenty years by the image I had of him, I still had not attempted to put myself in his place? Why is it anyway that for me to put myself in another's place has always represented so unimaginable a gymnastic feat? After all, it is not as though, to do so, one had to make some anthropomorphic leap across the divide between human and non- or supra-human. From inside one's own skin to inside the skin of another is such a relatively tiny trans-

mutation, demands such a relatively slight adjustment.
There is no question of having to remain there for more
than a flash of time, no need to make more than the most
fleeting inquiry. An instant suffices to recognize that the
prickle of that other skin is the prickle of one's own,
the pain of another's nerve ganglia one's own pain too,
the fear that lifts the hackles and shivers into gooseflesh
as also the joy that can peal through the heart like Christmas bells are the same for both. It is strange that imagination, ready to bridge eternity to envision God, bog-
gles before the effort of making a bridge to its neighbor.
It is strange too that although it has always been known
that to put oneself in another's place is indubitably the
swiftest, the most discreet, and the most efficacious
technique for communication and although it has been
preached in every age and tongue, of all such techniques it is the least practiced. And stranger still is the
fact that it is easier to put oneself in the place of a stranger with whom one is destined to pass no more than an
hour than in the place of those with whom one is destined to live out one's life.

ON THAT RAW DAY WHEN MY HUSBAND REJOINED US IN
the three rooms into which four of us would now be
packed to the exclusion of any possible seclusion, I no
more thought of entering his skin than I had ever
thought of entering yours. He was returning with a
kaleidoscope behind his eyes of battlefields and bombed
cities and broken bodies, himself deeply wounded by the
certitude that the repayment for all Poland's sacrifices
was another and more certain enslavement, and cold
with the knowledge that the exile he must have dared
hope was temporary was now to be for good. He

could hardly have returned wholehearted, since his heart would not again be whole. But all this made no difference in my expectations. I knew he would not be dithyrambic. But I expected him to be glad of a safe country. I expected him to be approving of the children and of what I had done with them. I expected him to be sorry for the burden I had carried alone. I expected him to be moved, wooing, anxious to reach me. I expected him to be all that he had not been before and could not possibly be expected to be now. And he was not.

Yet of all people I should have been the first to understand him, not because I was his wife (who will gainsay that a wife is quicker to understand her husband's sensitivity to draughts than to griefs, more apt at gauging his capacity to digest venison than pain?), but because I too had been an exile and had suffered, though my exile was voluntary, as much from the unease of displacement as though I had not sought it. Having chosen Europe as he had not and would never have chosen America, and having spent nearly seven years looking not at what Europe had that America had not but at what Europe had not that America had, I should have been the last to fail to understand that a man forced to abandon both what he had that was part of Europe and what Europe had that was part of him would inevitably weigh his loss against his gain, and no matter how objective, brave, and mature, would find the gain outweighed. Moreover, coming back to that America which I had inflated with my longing as long as I was in Poland, I had discovered not only that it, but that I, had changed. After the first bemusement that mists the gaze of the returning native, I had seen it, if not quite through his eyes, then through a perspective insensibly shifted from dream to fact. I had seen its brassy smile, had heard its tinny voice, had felt its metallic texture beneath the surface pliability. I had discovered, for the first time in that last of my home-comings, that of America quite as much as of Europe, though for other reasons, one could be afraid. Therefore when my husband faced the necessity of rerooting himself in so alien a soil, I and I alone was in a position to have understood his resistance to transplantation. But I did not.

The time came, though by that time it was too late, when I could not help but understand. As so often for me—perhaps for everyone—it was from strangers that I learned what I had been unable to learn for myself or from a friend. My son having been sent away to school and my daughter being by then sufficiently grown to fend for herself in streets and buses, I had gone to work, first for the publishing house where I learned how mutually exclusive are disinterest and trade no matter what is traded, and then for a non-profit political agency designed to meet the needs and maintain the hopes of the exiles from Soviet-dominated countries. It was here that at last I saw exile for what it is.

The symptoms of the malady never vary except in intensity. The patient's posture, manner and mannerisms, timbre of voice and quality of glance, his very utterance, to speak only of visible signs, point to his soul's exacerbation. Like the children's game in which, when a whistle blows, one must stand frozen in whatever position one finds oneself, so when the whistle of exile blows, the exiled are transfixed in the awkwardness of self-defense. Even had I not had this attitude bred into my bones, I would have come to recognize it, once I saw its unnatural shape repeated again and again in such varying personalities as were assembled, through the happenstance of their landing on our shores, in the rows of partially glassed-off offices it was my duty to visit every day. Symptomatic, too, was the similarity, indeed the seeming interchangeability of their opinions about the American way of life (a phrase one and all of them despised and in which none saw the truth that hides beneath it). For American culture, or American foreign policy, they had a controlled or uncontrolled but always present contempt, as instinctive as the mistrust with which they viewed each other's nationalities. Unhorsed, disarmed, prostrate before an America which they could not admit as a friend because to accept charity from a friend is so much greater a humiliation than to accept it from an enemy, they took the favor of our patronage since they had to, but kept their eyes down to conceal an unmistakable hostility.

Yet if exile is an illness, it is not mental. There is nothing schizophrenic about it. The exiled are not, however much they may appear to be, walled off from our reality and hence from communication with us. To them, as not to the mentally ill, there exists an access. They can be reached, they can be touched. Since the plight is not ours, however, but theirs, it is up to us to find the key, the lock, the door that opens to them. And that key is not kindness, that lock is not tolerance, that door is not charity. It will not do to speak louder and more plainly to them as though what divided them from us were merely another language; it will not do to force our will upon them with the professional smile and the ubiquitous slap on the back; it will not do to exhort them to concerted effort in the parlance of a baseball or football game they have never even seen played; it will not do to offer them slogans instead of deeds, any more than it did to offer another people burning with injustice cake instead of bread. Nothing less than to go home again could cure them, since to go home, however little that home now needs or wants them and however much by now that home has changed, is the only antibiotic that can destroy the bacteria of homelessness. That America cannot give them back to their homes they understand and accept. What they cannot accept is our lack of understanding. The way to reach and touch the exiled is to put ourselves, just for the moment of recognition, into their exiled skins. But this the American executives in the agency where I was working failed to attempt to do. It may be that our American skin is too thick, too tightly stretched across our self-esteem, for us to slip out of it. Perhaps, for all our manoeuvering and manipulation of one another, we lack imagination. Perhaps this is not just my flaw, but a flaw that is characteristic of Americans.

Unlikely, far-fetched, arbitrary as it may sound to say so, I do not believe that the fact that my days were being spent among the exiled, at the time when I precipitated the crisis which was to divide my past from my future as much as the past can ever be divided from the future, was purely incidental. I am not saying that I would not in any case have reached the impasse I reached and chosen the means I chose to step aside from it, since by then both the way back and the way ahead seemed to me equally and unalterably blocked. But that I was enjoined as much in that office as at home to carry on a relentless, a passionate argument, aloud and also in my conscience, not only between America and Europe, but between the America I had thought I knew and the America I was discovering, was as surely as a high wind to a tight-rope walker an added peril. When each morning I closed the door upon the home which I was still trying to make home for the children though it was never to be more than the night's shelter for my husband and was no longer home to me (since he whom I had decided to trust neither could nor would cross its threshold), I could not banish for the day that particular argument. No sooner did I reach my cubicle than I had to take sides again, for or against some freshly embittered European, for or against some freshly outraged and impatient American. But while at home I stood foursquare for America since in defending American schools, American manners, American social customs, American food, and even American immoralities, I seemed to be defending myself, at the office, despite all the stubbornness and even the occasional venom of the European staff, I found the opacity, the superciliousness, and the indifference of many of their American counterparts, and therefore myself too as an American, indefensible.

Since that time not only I but most Americans have changed. They have changed, if not much in their fundamental mistrust of Europeans, then much at least in their attitude toward themselves. Overnight, as it were, their characteristic chest-thumping has turned into an uncharacteristic, un-American breast-beating. The more they hear themselves accused of sheeplike imbecility, piggish acquisitiveness, wolfish predatory habits, the more they wallow in these accusations. Let someone but find the rhetoric to describe their depravity and he will become rich and honored among them. Let someone but heap new coals of contempt upon their heads and he will enthrone himself in their hearts, providing, of course, that he is no foreigner but one of them. From the conviction of inevitable progress and triumph they have swung in an irrational arc to the conviction of inevitable decline and defeat. They have forgotten (except for a few of their politicians who still find it useful to remember) that their experiment was noble; worse still, they have forgotten that it was and still is an experiment, and hence never fixed, never immobilized, always subject to the modifications, mitigations, and qualifications that accompany a test of truth.

If I have other and private reasons—my children, my last marriage, my final home, the secret excitement that has been the welling up of so much that was unbidden into this narrative, and (let me not pretend to ignore it) the purely physiological but perhaps after all paramount reason of being able to see the sun and feel it on my face and back—for being grateful that I did not die when I thought the reasons for living had ceased, I have also one reason that you would have commended and understood. I have come to see an America in which, all evidence to the contrary, I can and do believe, in which I can see the stars above and beyond the neon lights, in which if I cannot condone or overlook the self-interest (what an ironic rationalization is the phrase "enlightened self-interest"!) I can at least put it back into the American context, in which despite all that is regrettably said and done, there is, as there always has been, a heart of unassailability.

FOR THE LECTURING THAT HAS TAKEN ME UP AND DOWN and across this country, in and out of forty of our fifty states, I have been paid and repaid extravagantly. But let there be no mistake: it is not of money that I speak. I speak rather of that most intangible of payments which is the stretching of a parochial vision and the forcing of a reluctant understanding—a payment which, gratis, thrown in for good measure, has been the unexpected and unsought concomitant of my one-night-stand journeys through my native land. I do not speak, however, of purple mountain majesties and amber waves of grain, nor of the loonlike cry of a train crossing night-clad prairies, nor of the clustered brilliance of cities seen from a swooping and descending plane. I speak of people, of Americans who—overdressed and undereducated, harassed by triviality and oblivious of tragedy, awestruck by prospering flesh and indifferent to the soul's hungers, drenched in the siren music of success and ill-attuned to the stark tonalities of endeavor for its own sake—nevertheless, as I have seen them, transcend any pettiness anyone can bring up against them in their inherited, inbred, innate, transcendent good will.

For every man I have seen at my lectures, I have seen a thousand women. Audiences—at least for such lecturers as I—are seldom, and to no surprise of mine only grudgingly, composed of men. Yet I can hardly be gainsaid the right to generalize about a people from its women (if in general to generalize is my right), since it is after all the women who make the men. And anyway, lest I appear to boast of what is still only a newborn, tentative grasp, I will admit here and now that it has always been women rather than men (and at my age I am not likely to develop new adventitious buds of understanding) whom I have understood. I will not at this point warm up the platitude—too little substantiated in any case to deserve so solid a designation—that American women run America. They do not, though if they did, who is to say that America might not be better run? But it can hardly be argued that by its women, not less than by its men, America can be judged.

Paradoxically enough, in view of the fact that you, all woman if ever woman was such, were of all women the one I least understood, it was from you that I learned, so thoroughly that it became instinctive, my pride in

women and in being one of them. My sister, trusting you
no more and indeed still less than I (despite the greater
hope you manifestly invested in her), grew up with a
profound mistrust of women while I, despite finding
both you and her untrustable, grew up to trust them.
I have been hated by women—by you, by her, by my
best friend, by three mothers-in-law who for reasons
good and bad have viewed me with the enthusiasm they
might have been expected to feel for a daughter-in-law
culled from the streets—as I have never, to my knowledge, at least, been hated by men. Yet if, in some test of
mental associations such as are given to plumb the subconscious, I were asked to give my immediate response
to the word "woman," the word that would spring unhesitatingly to my lips is "friend." And it was you nonetheless, you who were not my friend for as far back as I
can remember, who taught me not only not to laugh at
women with that easy, vulgar laugh reserved especially
for women by most men and by those among women
themselves who boast of being "a man's woman" (what
woman is not, at least potentially, at least in her dreams,
some man's?), but also taught me to see how beneath
any bluster and behind any intellectual fireworks
women are petrified, have always been petrified body
and soul, in the posture of self-defense. From you I
learned to see that if theirs is not the courage of fearless-
ness, it is that other, less dazzling but surely no less cou-
rageous courage of mastered fear. From you I learned to
measure their triumphs in terms of the initial defeat out
of which these triumphs had to be forged. From you I
learned that what is human, not to say humanitarian in
humanity, and hence what has been more truly civilizing
in history than even history's greatest monuments and
masterpieces, derives from women. Frail as you were of

body and nerve, cruel as you were of mind and heart, unsatisfied and unsatisfying, you were woman's champion. And of the good that somehow emanated from you as good somehow emanates from all but the truly lost among us, this was the best.

For once, therefore, you would have felt precisely as I felt on an occasion I have not been able to forget when, finding myself in an antechamber together with several other speakers before a vast women's luncheon, I turned to the beflowered, preening actress who so outshone the rest of us and asked if she were not afraid. "Me? Afraid?" she gave me an indescribably amused look. "Don't you know they're all God damn fools?"

That we are all—men and women alike—God damn fools at one time or another and from time to time, I would hardly care to deny, having been and being nothing less myself, and chronically. But that there could be two thousand damn fools assembled at the same hour in the same room I can and do deny, since it would be too bitterly preposterous a coincidence, though in a larger sense which I allow myself to doubt that the star speaker intended, everyone of the billions of beings on this planet is God's fool, as much those who deny as those who attempt to explain His existence and His intentions.

When an American woman calls American women fools she implies, as it is perhaps needless for me to imply, that she is the exception who proves the rule. But I take total exception to the rule itself (as I take exception to all windy and sweeping generalities save my own). I take total exception, moreover, to all classifications, all categorizing and lumping together of the sexes, the nationalities, and the races, there being no label one can pin on them that someone else cannot unpin, any more than there is one label—despite all the drawers full of new

labels prepared by psychologists—that will completely
fit and cover any single individual. Like the steam aris-
ing from a pot, part of our substance escapes in un-
recapturable vapors from whoever would confine us
beneath an arbitrary lid. Yet there can be found in the
residue, of course, some elements of truth. Why therefore should I, any more than any other self-constituted
generalizer, forswear that almost sensual delight which
is generalization?

If I were to generalize from what I have myself seen
of America and Americans and describe what, because
of my limited experience as also because of the limitations of my capacity for experience, I have not seen, I
would say that, for all our pride of region, we Americans are not regional but national, and would be, given
the same income which means the same status, trans-
plantable from any part of the country to any other,
neither losing nor changing the ambitions, hopes, interests, and dreams with which we started out. To the accusation that we are primarily and essentially materialistic, I would answer an affirmative to be sure, since the
haves are always at least as jealous of their having as the
have-nots are resentful of their not-having, but I would
so qualify my affirmation as to change the whole intent
of the word "materialistic," for where else among posses-
sors could one find such concern as Americans dem-
onstrate again and again for the unpossessing and the
dispossessed? But as to whether we are tolerant or intoler-
ant of each other's race, creed, and color, I would have
to conclude ours to be an intolerance far deeper than our
denial of it, since we adhere, and adhere with an obsti-
nacy as remarkable as it is foolhardy, to the myth that
the American reality is Anglo-Saxon, Protestant, and
white, and that whosoever differs here in America is un-

American and hence inferior in proportion to the degree of difference, while also adhering to the myth that whosoever outside America in the rest of the world does not strive to be more nearly American is beyond the pale. Moreover, while in the case of color, at least a minority of white Americans dedicates itself unremittingly to the pursuit of more equal opportunity for black Americans, in the case of race, few Anglo-Saxon Protestants devote themselves to abolishing the myth of their superiority to, say, Jewish Americans. Even among the self-styled Christians, the supposedly educated among us, we who committed ourselves to a war against the enemies of the Jews, continue to perpetuate the historic calumny that no Christians but all Jews are grasping, cannibalistic opportunists, quick to climb up the backs of the weak and the simple, and masterly at an outwitmanship Christians pretend with shameless pretension to be above (and here I would add that I can speak without extrapolation, and can stress, if such distinctions are to be made, that I have had more Christians than Jews tread on me when I was down, as I have had more Jews than Christians hold out a hand to help me up, more Jews than Christians participate with their hearts in what I said on the platform, more Jews than Christians open and enrich and furnish my mind). Dedicated as we Americans are to treasuring, as no other people has ever dared to treasure, the individual, we still fear to live by the principle that it is only caliber that counts.

Yet, to tack once more into the wind of my generalities about America and Americans, I would say, whatever may be said to the contrary, that ours comes nearer than any other to being a classless society. I am not sure that the ideal society is classless. I am not even sure that classlessness is not a compromise forced upon an elite which has—classically enough—lost its sense of responsibility and thereby its right to privilege. But I am certain —or at least as certain as one can be when engaged in grappling with ideas too large to be handled by any but those trained in the handling of the *largesses* of generality—that, notwithstanding our exact, acute, and quite painfully self-conscious consciousness of class, notwithstanding the class tabulations of our real and our pseudo sociologists (which latter now proliferate so alarmingly as to have become a clear and present danger), we are yet mobile enough within our classes to be, for most intents and purposes, classless. If it is hardly true, as we boast, that anyone can become President, it is still true that anyone theoretically can strive for it, anyone theoretically can hope for it. Perhaps it is by our extension, in theory, of the plausibility of hope to the point where hope itself has become more nearly the common heritage of Americans than of any other people on earth that we have achieved our classlessness. We often call our mobility "elbow room." So high it is, and so wide, that I would admire to call it "imagination room." The pity is, of course, how much more we use it for elbowing than for the exercise of imagination.

IN ATTEMPTING AGAIN AS I HAVE SO OFTEN ATTEMPTED IN this narrative to put myself in that place of yours which, though apparently empty now, will still be filled with your fierce little presence as long as my consciousness survives, I know for sure that, while you would have found my emotions as unacceptable in my remembering of them now in tranquillity as you found them at their fevered pitch, you would have actually enjoyed and even approved of my generalities about America and Americans.

Indeed I have always thought it the most ironic of the ironies that lay between us that, though you did not trust me as daughter, friend, or woman, you trusted and even took pride (pride which, of course, you sedulously hid from me) in my public utterance. Whatever I was against or for in private, whether it concerned child or husband or myself, you took by instinct a contrary stand. But whatever I was against or for in public— against the dropping of the atom bomb, against the persecution of anyone in the name of loyalty and patriotism, for freedom in personal conduct, for the right to dissent —you took my side. Where you mistrusted *ad absurdum* the least of the decisions I made in my own life (you had grounds, I concede, for reasonable doubt, but not, I insist, for the unreasonable doubt you manifested), you trusted, more than I myself ever quite managed to trust, the opinions I expressed in reviews, articles, debates, and speeches.

It was I, and not you, who trembled when speaking in public for the irreproachable posture I strove to keep, knowing as both you and I knew how easily in private that posture could be reproached. Indeed, when once a member of my audience came up and said, as she took my hot hand in her cool ones, "What a good person you must be!," the blood drained so rapidly from my head that it was all I could do to phrase the protest that I knew was incumbent on me in the face of her trust. "But if that is what you would like to be," she said then, "it is enough," and from that answer I have been drawing solace ever since.

Yet she, and you, and I, and all of us in America allow ourselves to be hypnotized into believing that it is enough for words to be free to make them true. Required as we are to obtain a license to shoot bullets, we pride ourselves on not requiring more than a stump or a cracker barrel, a podium or a microphone, from which to fire words. For this casual arrogance—or is it gallantry?—in the face of nameless danger, we have formulated, being the self-justifiers and self-explainers that we have been since that beginning which exacted of our forebears so much explanation and justification, a rationale. We say that in the very fecundity of our words, in their mathematically as also philosophically incalculable multiplicity, in the fact that they represent as many views as there are people, lies their safety. Up to now, this irrational rationale (irrational, because why should a hundred million bullets prove safer than one?) has appeared to be rational. Trigger happy, we shoot our words at foe and friend with a singular, an astounding impunity, delighting—whether they overreach, fall short of, or achieve their aim—in the intoxication of our freedom to shoot them.

Surely, it was this hypnosis which made you, who refused till your last breath to grant me my share of power in your home and even battled against my having power in mine, nonetheless took for granted the inordinate power that arrogates to me in those hours behind the lectern when I not only can but must—if I am to come up to paid expectations—command a hearing. In part, perhaps, you accepted the *persona* I had to create for myself because it was a compromise fulfillment of your own unfulfilled drive to power. But in greater part, I am tempted to believe, you accepted my public self as, being a genuinely American American, you accepted the right of even the least of us to be heard by anyone whom we can compel to listen, the right of each or any of us to adapt the air of freedom to our tongues. You might have accused me, without having your judgment impugned, of megalomania. The irony is that you did not. Nor would you have questioned, had you read these extrapolations from the small, the narrow, the circumscribed particular of my own experience to the formidable generality that is America, my right to make them. No *ex cathedra* pronunciation, no matter how falsely whited the *cathedra*; no bombast, however bombastic; no oratory, however escapingly gaseous—providing of course that it was grammatical—seemed to frighten you. What did frighten you, what did antagonize you, were the simple, immediate, crying needs of the heart. And in this, too, I fear I must say that you were unmistakably American.

HOW AWARE YOU WERE OF MY HEART'S NEEDS AT THE time I am now come to I can estimate only by your unawareness of them throughout the years that led, and led ineluctably, up to it. Perhaps you bled for me in secret, but if so the secret was kept. Or perhaps you felt that, since I had failed to learn from you (I failed less than you knew, though what I learned was not always what you set out to teach), I must be left to attend life's lessons by myself and prepare whatever homework life exacted unassisted. Often enough across the past you had liked to quote, with the little air of resignation that so became you, whichever poet it was whose muse betrayed him into writing "Cast the bantling on the rocks." Bantling, to be sure, I no longer was by the time I speak of (except that vis-à-vis life only a few, and not I among them, reach full fledge). Moreover, I had long since forestalled the moment of your casting me forth

by casting myself upon those rocks which could not, I
had supposed, be less grateful, less welcome, than my always and inexplicably nettled home. But once fledged, I
had not known how either to adapt myself to the jagged
terrain or it to my purpose. By now my beak, my wings,
my very instincts were battle weary. I hated alike the
immeasurable seascape and the immeasurable sky of
freedom.

The heart, so puny, so queasy an organ to look at, so
vast, demanding and omnipotent in the mind's eye, cannot perform without ceaseless refueling its double function which is to maintain both life and the will to live.
The needs of the heart, of every heart, are always immediate and crying, but mine, in the hour of decision about
which I now at last must speak, were more immediate
than they had ever been before. They were crying a cry
so shrill that the sound embarrassed my inability to
muffle it yet at the same time the fact that no one else
appeared to overhear it caused me continual, shocked
surprise. But that the needs of my heart were not after
all so simple as I then believed them to be I find myself
compelled, in the name of the honesty I claim in my narrative, to recognize and concede. If the heart has not
only reasons but inalienable rights (which to say the
least is moot), they are not those I then asked for in the
name of mine.

Almost five years had gone by since the morning my
husband had returned, divided in feeling though not
in principle, to a wife divided in principle though not in
feeling. When I hear people say of the darkest period in
their lives how time dragged, I am amazed that it is thus
they remember it, for to me pain of any kind—pain of
giving birth, pain of filling a blank page, pain of waiting
and incertitude, pain of effort, of crisis, of loss, even pain

of monotony—escapes the control of time altogether and plays such havoc with it that old time, with its fussy, spinsterish precision, becomes unaccountable, a moment being stretched so interminably that one has time to die the proverbial thousand deaths before it passes and a year being so compressed, so tightly screwed in by the vise of anxiety, that one has not had time to reckon a single day of it. Such is my reckoning of those almost five years.

Yet by forcing my memory, always reluctant at careful computation, to compute the milestones with which those years were marked as everyone's years are marked by milestones of varying size and hence significance, I see that I cannot write them off as being all one darkling plain. I see now that their countryside was actually rolling, with hills often so thickly wooded that one was not aware when one had reached the crest, but occasionally with hills bare enough at the summit to bathe one in sudden light. But it is the long, troughlike and overshadowed interstices between the hills and the inescapable toiling through their thorny underbrush that stick in my memory, since from the fatigue which then settled on me I still do not, nor do I expect to, quite recover.

As always with me, experience is not really experience until it has been formulated, encapsulated, crystallized in words. As with pain, so too this is true with comfort. And therefore the comfort I remember from that uncomfortable, not to say comfortless period, came in a letter from my husband who had gone back again to Europe for a few months and who wrote, in one of his rare instances of self-revelation: "How good that the day ends." I have read and heard spoken phrases, intended for me, which should undoubtedly have been more memorable if only because they were sweetly intended, yet among them this is the sweetest to me. It became my private, my secret, my unfailing incantation. It took for me the place of a prayer.

Of all life's goods—its sunlight, its colors and textures, its accolades of friendship, the almost intolerable sweetness of its breath in one's children and of its breathlessness in one's act of union with a lover, its breath-taking panoramas and horizons and unpremeditated plenitudes —the best, all the same, is sleep. For sleep, once achieved, is utterly, is wholly dependable. Sun can be clouded over, color can fade and texture wear away; friendship can shipwreck, children turn hostile, love die even of such slight ailing as embarrassment; panoramas can vanish and horizons close down in the mind's fog, and plenitudes can suddenly empty. But sleep, for as long as one is cradled in it, has the tidelessness, the warmth, the unthinking vigilance of the maternal waters. There is no room in sleep for the intruder. Sleep is the only room one can call one's own.

Would you now have reminded me, contentious as always, of the intrusion of dreams? I will answer at once and unhesitatingly that no dream, however nightmarish, can so disturb the sleeper as reality disturbs him who is awake. While from a nightmare one wakens to relief, to a real, a positive upsurge of joy in the fact that the dream is not a fact, from the nightmare of reality one wakes only to the realization that it is no dream but fact. Dreaming or dreamless, therefore, sleep is the bath, sleep is the balm of God's mercy.

Always less often, however, in the years I now seek to recapitulate, could I count, though my days came to an end as do the days of all creatures save the nocturnal, on the spontaneous, uninvited guest in my bed of sleep. Though I had the sure means to entice and snare sleep, I seldom made use of it.

Long before the time I speak of, even before I had precipitated myself into the dilemma of being married yet not truly married to one man and truly married yet not married to another and thus been exposed to the erosions of ambiguity; well before my husband had returned from war, I had consulted a doctor, not of the mind but of the nerves that determine the mind's equipoise, and had besought him to teach me how to manage my unmanageable self, no more for my own sake than for the sake of my children whose eyes I saw darken often before my successive bursts of temper and shame. I had hoped with a hope as irrational as my tempers that he would give me some simple key to self-mastery. And indeed, he had proffered me a key. Lying on his couch, I had followed as faithfully as it was in me to follow them his commands to release toe by toe, finger by finger, gut by gut, the tension that gripped me. On the day when I felt certain of having mastered it, he had tested, standing over me, every muscle from my feet up and only when his hand had reached my jaw had he found it as immovably contracted as in *rigor mortis*. It was thereupon, and with rather a hollow laugh, that he had given me the prescription for yellow pills which were to become more precious to me than gems. But the prescription, more rightly than he knew, was parsimonious, and could not be renewed without his say. Automatically, therefore, and at first I believe quite unconsciously, I had begun to make myself endure a few nights of wakefulness between each night of sleep, to spare the pills, to hoard them—though as yet I did not tell myself why I, a habitual spendthrift, had turned into a miser. It was only later, much later, deep into the fifth year of my dilemma, that I fell to counting deliberately, to sifting through my bemused fingers, these little premiums of death insurance which would mature when I had saved enough.

NOW THAT I STAND AT MY VESSEL'S PROW, IF NOT EN-tirely self-poised then at least with what is still lacking in self-poise well enough hid to defy all but the gimlet eyes of foes or, as in the case of him with whom I now live, the hypersensitive eye of affection; now that I no longer pine with noting the fever of my own or some differing soul—I am, I admit it, aghast at how lightly, how easily I once let go the helm. Comparison of my particular storm with the storms through which others have sailed intrepidly, with no more than a passing thought, if a thought at all, of abandoning their ships, is too humbling even for such as I who believe, in theory at least, that one cannot be, if humility is not merely an extra garment, too humble. Nor do I have to search the files of the great defilements of our times in order to suffer the humiliation that any comparison of my story with such stories as they contain would of necessity impose. I need only glance in the direction of my acquaintance—at the woman who watched her daughter dying and the daughter who had to watch herself die; the widow left to bring up children without hope of companionship or funds; the man forced to commit his wife, and the parents forced to commit their child, to an institution; the girl who waited till the time of her withering for a lover who would not and could not marry her, and that other girl who, having waited and at long last been wed, woke up to find her husband dead beside her; and all those I have known who have so tortured each other in their common living that it would have been better for one or both to be dead. There is no need, in seeking comparisons, to draw in my imagination upon the joblessness, homelessness, hunger, and pestilence that I have not seen for myself. I need only look at the ill-fortune and tragedy among the cushioned lives for which I can speak, to place such stress as proved too great for my own tolerance in true perspective. Yet was my perspective at the time so false? I can only say that, unjustified and unjustifiable; inexplicable and—I must suppose—unexplained; undefinable, yet demanding definition, that stress was too much.

How much of this too much was you and how unhesitantly you would have denied to the end your share in it, my narrative by now has made, I believe, more than clear. That, ultimately, it is not you but me, me alone whom I hold responsible, I hope I have made clear enough. I have sustained the breath I took at the start far longer than I dared imagine I could sustain it, even with the sudden expansion of my capacity to breathe that was your unexpected legacy. I have only a little longer now to hold it, only a little longer before at last I can exhale. Since the beginning, I have known what I must say at the end. But to know the inevitable does not mean not to quail before it, not to balk at it, not to turn and twist and writhe in its presence; not to seek, with the conscious, unconscious, and subconscious for once united in a single aim, the evasion of that inevitability.

Frankly, I have not minded, as you could not have failed to note, the exposure of myself that my exposure to you has thus necessitated. If I have been sorry for my limitations and ashamed of my weaknesses, I have not —as by now you could hardly have doubted—been sorry and ashamed enough to cloak them from either of us. Had what I have had to tell you up to now been all I need tell, my sorrow and shame would not have ex-

ceeded that minimum without which one would be in-
human. But the narrative is not ended. It is the ending
that I dread. For that, I must strip to the bone.

IN THE FIFTH WINTER OF WHAT IT WOULD BE A QUIXOTIC
understatement to call my discontent, my husband, back
once again from Europe, and my daughter and I were
still living in the three rooms that forced on us a prox-
imity which, at best never fitting, became more and
more Procrustean as we two adults grew further and
further apart and yet strove, for the sake of the now
flowering daughter we both loved, to hide our separate-
ness. Our son, over whom I had trembled with what I
have since learned to see as a far less damaging solicitude
than the professional and amateur sages had made me
believe, was in the boarding school for which my best
friend had volunteered to pay and where no one and
nothing could mitigate his feeling of not belonging and
of having been cast out from home. He could not know,
of course, and how good it was that for the time being at
least he was spared the knowledge, that we who had
given him life felt no less outcast in our respective ways
than he.

Of the grindstones that ground upon our nerves day
in and out, the most obvious was money. While my pay,
which no man of like capacity would have considered
adequate, was better than the pay of many women in
more responsible positions, it could not encompass what
we saw as our needs. My husband, who had borrowed
a small capital to start a business in which he had made it
a point of honor to employ unemployed and perhaps
unemployable fellow exiles, felt in these circumstances
that their pay came first and that he could not take for

himself, though he worked as long and relentless hours as a man can work, a living wage. From you, though you were not ungenerous with your limited substance, I could scarcely endure to take extra help since the strings attached to each check you gave were not less cutting for being invisible. Out of this merely material, purely calculable impasse there existed, needless perhaps to underscore, a way other than the one I took. We could have downgraded our needs by moving into some quarter in or out of the city where people expected no more of daily life than its subsistence level. I could, as my best friend had once suggested, have taken in others' wash. But that I should be doing so did not occur to me. What I did take, at first with a suffusion of shame, an awareness of betrayal such, strangely enough, as nothing else I had done or was doing had brought me, but as the months went by with an ever more slumberous conscience, was help from him whose help I had no more right to than to the love that enveloped it. If I was returning love for love, I was also returning it for money. And all morality to the contrary, to do so, once the first hurdle of shamed reluctance has been taken, is by no means as bitter or indeed as unnatural as anyone ingrained with distaste for such apparent debasement might expect to think.

Nevertheless, I am aware of how this would have shocked you for whom a like temptation could not, in the very nature of your experience, arise. But by what I must now tell you, you would have been, I believe, less shocked than I. You would have been certain that you knew why he, who offered me such succor and solace, who never so to speak left my side, did not want me for his wife. You would have said, had I somehow in a moment of aberration so trusted you as to bare this

wound, that no man in his senses would undertake marriage with a penniless, middle-aged woman with two
half-grown children, and especially, you would doubtless have added, when that woman was such a woman
as I. You might even have hinted, though to be sure
more delicately than the friend of his whom I once consulted in desperation and whose advice—"If you want
him, don't give him what he wants"—was like a blow on
my face, that a lady who drops the armor of her *noli me
tangere* does not deserve to be wed.

But in thus generalizing from a particular, you could
not have known that so vulgar an oversimplifying did
not apply to this equation which was neither vulgar (no
matter how wrong) nor simple (no matter how commonplace). You would have failed to equate the reality
with the truth. For about him, if there was nothing
vulgar, there was still less that was simple. I had seen
with what reluctance he had abandoned not only private
grief over the death of the wife he had buried long
before our coming together but even the public demonstration of a black tie with which he had continued
to remind me of his bereavement when I was already
inside his world. I had detected too, despite all his efforts
to conceal it, the extraordinary weight of his mother's
opinion that still lay upon him after more than fifty
years. To be sure, he was free. Yet I knew, Catholic as
he was, and also, as an intellectual more innately versed
in the poetics and more consciously bound to the great
tromperie mutuelle of Catholicism than was my Catholic
husband, that he was just as convinced that God's institution of marriage was indissoluble. All too well, I
knew his reasons. I could not bring myself to yield to
them.

But what under heaven could you, could my husband

have said, had either you or he surmised that in this siege I was not the besieged but the besieger? What else could either you or he have said save that I was, and was proving beyond the peradventure of doubt that I was, insane? To myself, as to whoever bothered to look at me in those dark months, I looked ridiculous, suspended between a marriage and a love affair apparently and equally without future. Nor did it make me less ridiculous in my own eyes to know that it was not I with either of them, but they with each other who, not having exchanged a word, yet saw eye to eye. Between me and each of them there was disaccord, but the accord between them was perfect. One night, in an effort to show me the enormity to him of my wanting a divorce and remarriage which, though legally possible, would place me (not to speak of him I wanted to marry) forever outside the Church, my husband had said: "To live with him is to borrow a thousand from eternity; to marry him would be borrowing a million." These words were still roaring in my ears when I repeated them to him who was most concerned. And to a formula which seemed to me not so much unworldly or otherworldly as plain immoral, he answered only: "Your husband is right."

I might have gone on indefinitely swinging, like some unarrestable and seemingly indestructible pendulum, without recourse to the hoard of pills at the back of my bureau drawer, since the impetus of motion is as integral to the heart as to the earth itself. But if to put one's own end to motion is unnatural, a *perpetuum mobile* as hectic, as dicrotic as was mine by that time is unnatural too. And anyway, who is to say, since the best of man's story consists precisely in his effort, generation after generation, to so bend and master nature as to make the unnatural natural, at what point this good becomes no longer good but bad? Who except God can determine it? And if one has not the ear for His high frequencies, one can but listen to the frail, easily sickened, quickly atrophied voice of conscience.

"IF IT WERE DONE WHEN 'TIS DONE, THEN 'TWERE WELL IT were done quickly" fits any murder whether of another or of the self. But there are murderers and murderers. Some are born to murder, others have murder thrust upon them, and there are those who advance toward it blindly, insensibly, cutting off one retreat after another without seeming to know that the moment will come when they have no recourse left, or at least when they are convinced that no recourse remains to them except to strike. The dogma that we are all potential murderers I refuse to accept unless within this generality potential self-murderers are included. But if to take one's own life constitutes a murder (and I now incline to concede that it does since, in contradistinction to the rest of one's paraphernalia, one's life seems not to be one's own), I will subscribe to the theory that we are born implanted with a seed of murder which, when fertilized, may well come to bloom. There have breathed few mortals on this earth, I would suggest, who never once in the whole course of their lives said to themselves: "I wish I were dead." And from saying it to meaning it, to bringing it about is only a matter of progressive intensity of intention from a limitable to an illimitable nth degree. One has only to wish to die to achieve the first step in the formula that leads to dying. However, long before reaching this advanced postulate of fatality, one must of course be versed in the simple arithmetic of desperation. I was.

One morning late in that raw winter I received from my son's boarding school a letter written by the head-master. "Your boy," he wrote, "does not seem to want to go outdoors this year. He prefers to remain in his room. We do not know how to handle it." With this communication in my pocket, I spent my office day bank-ing the fury it enkindled. Not my hundreds of dollars, to be sure, but the hundreds of dollars of my best friend were being spent purportedly for the health and de-velopment, not to say for the whole future, of my son. That evening I called her to explain that I would with-draw him from the school at the term's end and to thank her for a generosity I would no longer need. There was a silence when I had finished. Then she spoke. "I can find better ways to spend it," she said. This was indubitable, and I acknowledged it. But, I reminded her, it had been she, and not I, who wanted the boy to go to that school. "All the same," she answered, "you have not been honest with me." I was speechless. Now, sud-denly, the little hints and reticences, the occasional barbed thrusts I had rejected as figments of my too quickly offended imagination, fell into place. What she had seemed to give freely I should not have felt free to take. But, to the fact that she had not honored the shared years enough to say so, I had no answer. Dazed, mortified, eyes stinging with tears, I hung up. I hung up on thirty years of what had been a trust only less prized, only less rooted in my being than were my children. In hanging up on that best of my past which, together with the memories of my father, had seemed to counter-balance the woe you and I had occasioned one another, I hung up on friendship itself.

Must I say, after all the high flying I have risked in

these pages, that money, merely money, counted most in my determination to anticipate my natural end? Must I say that out of all that had been said and done, all that had been learned, endured and felt, all that had been lived, there was nothing to hold or not hold the balance in my life but the money that was not enough? I cannot quite concede it. Yet, resolved as I have been, however dizzied by rhetoric, to keep my eye if not riveted then at least fixed on reality and not to let the sheer multiplicity nor yet the effectiveness (at least on me) of words in themselves becloud the truth, I will have to say at this point that, had I possessed money, I likely would not have done what I did. Money, then, was the whip. The money you gave me you were using as means to a power over me which, had you but known it, you needed no money to keep. The money given me by him who was not my husband I could only imagine repaying in a marriage he did not want. The money given me by my best friend for my son's schooling had purchased, not his welfare, but her enmity. And lastly, and this, ironically enough, appears to have been the straw upon my back, the money that I discovered my husband had to raise for the survival of his business happened to tally, and tally exactly, with the sum for which I was insured.

So it was because of money, though in those last hours of my planning the word "money" did not so much as stir from the bottom of my consciousness to which I had firmly relegated it, that, after announcing one afternoon in my office that I was unwell, I went home to give myself what I believed would be my final order. But if it was because of money, why then, as I turned down the bed I had never before so gratefully contemplated; as I removed the clothing from a body for which—even at the times when it had most hurt me—I had never had less use; and as I prepared, most carefully prepared, not knowing whether to expect a slow or sudden loss of consciousness, to leave no sign of how unnaturally the death I was resolved to make appear natural had come about; why then, if this chain of reaction had been set off only by mathematics, was I never so far as that moment from counting its cost?

Often in your last years, how often I could not attempt to say, you were to speak to me, in anger, in desperation, or just in impatience with the tedium of petering out that is old age, of the relief that awaited you in death, of how gratefully you would welcome it, of the legitimacy and, too, the desirability of putting your own end to awaiting it. But as often as an overwhelmingly affirmative yea rose to my lips, I did not utter it. I could have told you, having felt it in every fiber of my being, how much sweeter is that last moment of life, even and perhaps especially when self-imposed—presupposing of course that it is not a moment of violence —than any other. I could have told you that the fall from consciousness is as light and lovely as the fall of a leaf. I could have told you that the relief of knowing oneself at last inaccessible to the demand upon nerve and tissue made as much by joy as by sorrow brings such ease as, until one begins the drift into oblivion, it is impossible to conceive. I could have told you, who by instinct suspected it, how good, how very good it is when the day ends. But I did not. I withheld this only comfort I might ever have given you, not because I begrudged you comfort nor because I was not as certain of it as I am certain that I am still alive, not even because I did not want you to know what I had done and had so carefully hid from you afterward with an elaborate pretense, but because to have told you would have laid on my conscience another murder. It had been after I murdered myself that I came to believe that it were better with self-murder as with any other that it were never done.

Let me not seem, however, in extolling death's sweetness, to be saying that it was altogether sweetly that I died. Indeed, had it been so, I would not now be alive. It was because there is in my nature no sweetness that is not bitter that, having swallowed my full hoard of pills and established myself against my pillows with a report for the office and a red editorial pencil on my lap, I knew suddenly that even in this final argument I must have the last word. Quickly therefore, and with sure fingers, I put in the call to him who was then—unbelievable as I now see it to have been for a wife to so forget her husband, a mother her children—uppermost in my mind. "You needn't worry any more," I said. "I have done what I should have done long since." "I am coming," he answered. "There has been enough scandal," I said. "There must be no more." But almost as soon as I had laid down the receiver, the telephone rang. "Tell me your husband's number," came the voice, peremptory as I had never heard it. I told him. Why not? I was certain that, with whatever haste my husband crossed the city from where he worked to this home of his which he had never looked upon as home, he would find me gone. Why should I care, I thought as I lay back with as warm, liquid, and sensationless a sensation as I cannot have had since the day you expelled me from the primordial ease which had been my birthright until birth and was now to be my death right until death, who first tells whom that I am dead? I will no longer be there to hear even unspoken recrimination.

* * *

IF AS THEY SAY WHO CLAIM TO HAVE PENETRATED BEYOND the limits of consciousness and even beyond the known limits of the existence of consciousness, birth itself is a conscious experience, how closely, I wonder, would they say that the experience of rebirth resembles it? Physically, it is not, or anyway in my case it was not, much less bloody and painful, though this time the blood and the pain were not yours but mine.

Some twelve hours had gone by, I was later informed, when I opened my eyes to find myself on my back beneath a machine. I tried to sit up. I found then that I was strapped down. Tubes were sticking out from every aperture of my body. I saw I was spattered with blood. But I was not afraid. There was no place for fear on the top of the world where, transcendent, I seemed to be standing. From this eminence all that was fearful had vanished. It was light. The almost intolerable blaze of light that I thought I was bathed in had banished not fear alone but mystery. How obvious, how magnificently obvious, now that at last they were so illumined, had become the mysteries!

"I understand!" I called into the silence. A face, a face I did not know, swam into my field of vision. I tried to say what I was seeing. I wanted to share the pristine knowledge. But when I reached out toward the face, I felt my hands firmly grasped, and all at once, with a horrid certainty, I recognized in its closed, passionless efficiency, the face of a hospital nurse.

If there was an all that I might have learned from my caffeine-inspired vision, that all was gone as swiftly as is the day behind the curtain of the night. But of what I had to learn in the shaming, I would even say the agonizing aftermath of that transient affair with death, though much has since been conveniently glossed over by my glossary of self-excuses, there remains all the same a saving remnant.

As I lay on the mortuary slab I had prepared for myself and performed the post-mortem I had to perform when I discovered that I must prepare to reinhabit my life, I came to the conclusion that the disease I had died of had been after all, and quite simply, operable. I need not die of it again. I saw my exposed viscera for what they were: cramped, spastic, knotted, so intertwined indeed that the heart, for all its pumping, had not been able to infuse them with enough blood to function. I resolved then (when the devil is sick, how saintly his resolutions!) that, too late as it was to redeem the past I had killed, I need not forfeit the future. Henceforward and never again would I fail to stomach what till then my stomach had rejected, nor allow my brimming gall to expel its poison. Henceforward and forevermore I would so expand my lungs as to inhale the air of others, so flex my muscles as to render them pliable enough to master, so tune my sympathetic nervous system as to attune it at last to sympathy. For the rest of my life, since there was to be a rest of it, I would be humble, I would be grateful, I would remember that I might possibly be—even when most convinced that I am not—mistaken, I would consider no good news good save that of some noble trait of character, I would spend more time in the skins of others than in my own, I would step forward only and always with my best foot, and I would not again forget that my life belongs not to me but to whatever lives it has touched and touches and above all to those lives for which I am answerable in having given them life.

It was a good resolution. It went, *vanitas vanitatum*, the way of all good resolutions. But when, oh, very occasionally, I make my imagination leap and find my-self—*presto*—in another's skin, I discover at the instant of transmutation that, understanding, I no longer need to be understood.

I WAS NOT TO BE THERE WHEN NINE LONG YEARS LATER, the morning came for you to make your *salto mortale*. I could not tell from your proud, cold face, when I looked upon it, whether in your going out you had such a burst of illumination as I in my coming in again. The day before, in that uncontrolled and perhaps uncontrollable exacerbation which had so increased as you decreased toward the end, you had said again: "I always knew you were insane." Was it, or was it not, the same play of chance that was to make these your last words to me as that which kept me from being present, despite all the hours I had spent at your bedside, in the hour of your death? I will never know. I choose, therefore, to call your saddest of valedictories an accident, as I choose to call valedictorian all these pages you will never have read and for which, had you read them, I would not have received your imprimatur. I know they are no benedic-tion. I know they are not ample enough to house your elusive spirit. I have not built you a cenotaph. These are no more than the tears I did not shed.

Rideau Lake, 1959

Sasqua Hills Road-Oenoke Ridge, 1960

VIRGILIA PETERSON

For most of her adult life, Virgilia Peterson, who was born in New York City and attended Vassar College and the University of Grenoble, has been a reviewer of books. Over the past decade, she has given book talks in forty out of the fifty states. She is the author of Polish Profile, *an account of her experience as the wife of a Polish landowner before the Second World War, and of the novel* Beyond This Shore. *She has also translated from the French Alexis Carrel's* Voyage to Lourdes, *Lucie Marchal's* The Mesh, *R. L. Bruckberger's* Golden Goat, *and, in collaboration with her husband, Gouverneur Paulding, Bruckberger's* Image of America. *For more than two years, Miss Peterson moderated the network television program* "The Author Meets the Critics," *and in 1956 received the Peabody Award for her program* "Books in Profile," *which was until recently a weekly broadcast over New York City's Station WNYC. Her husband is senior editor of* The Reporter. *She lives in New York and has a grown daughter and son.*